SYMBOLIC LOSS

SYMBOLIC LOSS

THE AMBIGUITY OF
MOURNING AND MEMORY
AT CENTURY'S END

EDITED BY
PETER HOMANS

UNIVERSITY PRESS OF VIRGINIA
CHARLOTTESVILLE AND LONDON

Grateful acknowledgment is made for permission to reprint
"Song of the Son," from *Cane,* by Jean Toomer. Copyright 1923 by
Boni & Liveright, renewed 1951 by Jean Toomer. Reprinted by
permission of Liveright Publishing Corporation.

THE UNIVERSITY PRESS OF VIRGINIA
© 2000 by the Rector and Visitors
of the University of Virginia
Printed in the United States of America

First Published in 2000

♾ The paper used in this publication meets the minimum
requirements of the American National Standard for Information
Sciences—Permanence of Paper for Printed Library Materials,
ANSI Z39.48-1984.

Library of Congress Cataloging-in-Publication Data
Symbolic loss: the ambiguity of mourning and memory at century's
end / edited by Peter Homans.
    p. cm. — (Studies in religion and culture)
    Includes bibliographical references and index.
    ISBN 0-8139-1985-1 (cloth : alk. paper) — ISBN 0-8139-1986-X
(pbk. : alk. paper)
    1. Mourning customs. 2. Funeral rites and ceremonies.
    3. Bereavement. I. Homans, Peter. II. Series.
GT3390 .S85 2000
393'.9—dc21   00-036649

This book is dedicated to Paul Ricoeur, in gratitude for his work. It was he who first called attention to the importance of mourning for Freud's work as a whole, as well as for the understanding of cultures.

Mourning is regularly the reaction to the loss of a loved person, or to the loss of some abstraction . . . such as liberty, an ideal, and so on.

—SIGMUND FREUD

Mourning is, for most people, a difficult and dangerous period.

—MELANIE KLEIN

In this terrible battle for meaning . . . nothing and no one comes out unscathed. The "timid" hope must cross the desert of the path of mourning.

—PAUL RICOEUR

CONTENTS

PART III. HISTORY

PART IV. PSYCHOLOGY

PREFACE

IN THE past, most of the world's cultures have linked together three disparate phenomena: the painful experience of collective loss; mourning, or the healing response to the pain of that loss; and the building of monuments or the construction of cultural symbols to re-present the loss over time and render it memorable, meaningful, and thereby bearable. For the past fifty years or so, scholars and writers have pointed out that this ancient emotion and its assorted rites have gradually lost their given-ness, such that it is their absence rather than their presence that has merited scrutiny.

Since the end of the Second World War, and especially in the last twenty years or so, a growing number of scholars in the humanities and the human sciences have engaged in the task of "coming to terms with the past." Many of these scholars have become interested in (1) theories of loss and mourning found in contemporary psychology, especially in both classical and revisionist psychoanalysis; (2) the ways in which experiences of loss are expressed or represented in the symbols of cultures; and (3) the function of both traditional monuments and today's abstract memorials and countermonuments. It is no accident to find modern and postmodern scholars focusing upon one or more of these linked phenomena, for we are repeatedly told today that ancient ways are no longer ours. The triad of ancient answers has become a new set of questions for us.

The purpose of this book is to render this emerging work on mourning appealing, cogent, and accessible to a variety of scholars in the humanities and the human sciences who wish to orient themselves to it. It should serve as an introduction to the uses of mourning in the study and understanding of contemporary cultures. As far as I know, no book-length study exists that is given over entirely to the experience of mourning, understood as a lens for clarifying a variety of different cultural processes.

To achieve this goal, this book offers an introductory essay and ten research essays. The introduction begins with a short sketch of the cultural universals in mourning and of the decline of mourning practices in the West, moves on to a discussion of major themes or topics in contemporary work on mourning, as these appear in several representative studies and in the papers, and closes with brief summaries of each paper.

The scope of these essays is broad, and their style is nontechnical. The topics represent four areas of study that have generated important work on mourning: literature, history, architecture (chiefly monuments), and psychology. However, all also are highly interdisciplinary. Despite this wide range, all the essays are closely held together by the volume's central research question: How do the processes of mourning, ordinarily thought of as a response to the death of a loved other, also have validity for our understandings of culture, history, groups, and symbols?

The essays published here were written exclusively for this volume. The authors shared and discussed their penultimate drafts with one another at a closed, three-day meeting at the University of Chicago.

ACKNOWLEDGMENTS

MOST OF all, I wish to thank Clark Gilpin, Dean of the Divinity School of the University of Chicago, who funded the three-day meeting of all participants, which made it possible for us to discuss our work and interests with each other.

A number of other people provided valuable assistance in the preparation of this book. During the early stages of planning, Dominick LaCapra, Henry Rousso, Eric Santner, and Anthony Vidler gave generously of their time. Patrick Hutton was constantly available, encouraging, and patient: he read an earlier draft of my introductory essay and provided much valuable advice as preparation progressed. As a research assistant, Dana Venator was skillful and reliable and helped in every phase of preparation.

In this design, the great weight of memory at Majdanek stands on a proportionally undersized base, which creates a sense of top-heaviness, even danger, for those standing beneath it. The sculptor has intended this effect, he says, not only as a symbolic reference to past danger, but also as a literal gesture to the hazards in memory itself, which can jeopardize our current sense of well-being. In fact, Polish officials were so concerned with the safety of rememberers that they proposed a railing along the outline of the sculpture's overhanging rock to keep people from standing beneath it. Pleased with this anxious response, Tolkin assured authorities that the memorial only looked dangerous: no fence was necessary.

—JAMES E. YOUNG, *The Texture of Memory:*
Holocaust Monuments and Meaning

At a distance of half a mile, the memorial appears conventional, or recognizable, in its shapes and materials. Coming closer, this familiarity gradually changes to a sense of strangeness. And close up one realizes the stone mass is disorganized, full of holes, and there is no overall pattern or coherence. The legs are too short and too thin. The memorial is not what it at first appeared to be. It is ugly and repels. By engaging the way visual perception cues emotion, the artist has given us not only a perception of Jewish memory but a relationship to it as well.

—PETER HOMANS

Holocaust Memorial at Majdanek, Lublin, Poland.
(Wiktor Tolkin; dedicated 1969. Photo by Peter Homans)

PETER HOMANS

INTRODUCTION

The Decline of Mourning Practices in Modern
Western Societies: A Short Sketch

THE BASIC features of mourning and its historical developments
form the background for today's thinking about mourning. That
background consists of three perceptions: (1) mourning practices
have been fairly stable throughout the history of cultures but have
recently declined, primarily in modern western societies, especially in the United States and Great Britain; (2) this decline is due
to the erosion and fragmentation of community caused by the
processes of modernization; and (3) mourning today is no longer a
concern of society as a whole but has become a personal and family affair. This essay reviews the origins and development of these
three assumptions and then explores a fourth, still in the making,
that mourning today occurs not only "in" individuals but in the
workings of culture as well.

When something as essential to human living and self-understanding as mourning undergoes change, and we ask how and
why, we can assume that no one discipline or field will have the
answers. Rather, we need to consult a combination of disciplines
and establish connections between them. These connections can
create a cumulative sense of cogency and plausibility. In sum, we
want to know if universal patterns in mourning exist across cultures; what mourning has been in Western culture; what has led
to the decline of these mourning practices; and what is the relation between this decline and mourning today.

BACKGROUND: GRIEF AND MOURNING
IN ANTHROPOLOGY

We begin with the view from anthropology because it provides
stable definitions of grief, mourning, and mourning practices. If

we judge from the wealth of research on the subject, it is clear that many anthropologists consider mourning to be virtually universal across all studied human cultures. Death is the primary reality, grief and mourning the universal human response to it.[1] This view has its roots in anthropology, evolutionary theory, and biology. The anthropological dimension describes the social-symbolic context of loss, whereas evolutionary and biological findings describe the biological contexts. The anthropological findings came first.

In 1909, the French investigator Arnold van Gennep published *The Rites of Passage,* which identified a class of rituals characterized by "separation from one status, then an intermediate period, followed by reincorporation into a new status."[2] Two years earlier, Robert Hertz (also French and also an anthropologist) had set forth a similar understanding in which he also included mourning.[3] Much later, the social anthropologist Victor Turner expanded upon the work of both with his concept of "liminality," which refers to a transitional period between two well-established roles. The liminal stage characterizes the mourners and mourning. The mourners are "between" roles (or van Gennep's "statuses"). We may call this the anthropological component in an emerging view of mourning. It accommodates the biological and evolutionary view nicely.

Hertz's observations can be helpful here. Hertz spoke of the relations between the deceased, the mourners, and mourning. Both deceased and mourners pass from attachment to society to a liminal or transitional state (not attached to society) and from this transitional state back to society. The deceased dies, thereby leaving society, enters the liminal state, and then passes to the "land of the dead," the society appropriate for the dead. The mourners also leave society and enter the liminal stage (they are "in mourning" and segregated from society); when the deceased has been finally laid to rest (reaches the land of the dead), the mourners return to society, and "the mourning is over." Together, the deceased and the mourners undertake parallel journeys. This framework also organizes several important distinctions between grief and mourning.

Although many thoughtful people use the terms *grief* and *mourning* interchangeably, strictly speaking they are not the same. On one hand, grief refers to "the feelings of sorrow, anger, guilt, and confusion which occur when one experiences the loss of an attachment figure."[4] On the other hand, mourning refers to "the culturally constructed social response to the loss of an individual."[5] Grief is a painful emotion that is, so to speak, looking for a "cure." Mourning is a ritual that, so to speak, "heals" the pain of grief.

This distinction between grief and mourning is grounded in adaptive and evolutionary criteria, as well as observation. These criteria have established that the grief humans experience is also experienced by some nonhuman primates such as monkeys and apes. On the other hand, these same nonhuman primates do not mourn. That is because of the different levels of complexity in expression: "mourning rests in a social and symbolic context which is not available to primates. Humans exist as both physical and social personae. The ritual, religious and theoretical under-standing of the meaning of death which gives order and shape to the human expression of loss, and allows the laying to rest of the social person, is beyond the level of primate social responses."[6]

This difference in biological and evolutionary endowment is closely related to another kind of distinction, that of individual and group behavior. In the event of the loss of an attachment fig-ure, young nonhuman primates are less able to reattach them-selves to an attachment figure than are young human children. That is because nonhuman primates respond to loss on an indi-vidual rather than a cultural level. Many investigators think that grief is a product of evolution. For example, primates live in groups and depend for survival on social relations with others. Therefore grief provides an adaptive advantage. On the other hand, mourning assists the human in the face of nonattachment circumstances. Mourning, it seems, enhances the capacity to "let go" of the lost object and to be alone. Rituals of mourning heal human grief, but nonhuman primates who grieve must turn to others to assuage their pain.

In a nutshell, grief is an emotion, mourning a grief-infused symbolic action. Both are a response to the loss of an attachment. This virtually universal but also very minimalist understanding of mourning can be schematized as follows:

attachment → loss → grieving → mourning → reattachment

This is the schema or pattern that, as already noted, specific cultures have clothed with their own particular needs, habits, and customs.

THE TAME DEATH: MOURNING
PRACTICES IN THE WEST

What did those practices foundational for the West look like? To reply, we move from anthropology to history and to the history of mourning practices in the West, as described by Philippe Ariès in his sweeping study of Western treatments of death.[7] Ariès is a reliable guide for several reasons. As a historian, he is extremely interested in the problems addressed by this essay, especially the decline of mourning practices. He is also interested in mourning-related phenomena such as memory. His work is well regarded by many in the historical field (but not by all, of course). He achieved recognition early in his career as an important figure in the *Annales* school, which emphasized the study of attitudes common to collectivities.[8]

Ariès begins his survey of mourning practices with what he calls "the tame death" as it is found in the early European Middle Ages. He also refers to the tame death as "the traditional attitude" and thinks that it arose much earlier in time. The tame death "is the unchronicled death throughout the long ages of the most ancient history, and perhaps of pre-history. . . . It goes back to the dawn of history and is only now dying out before our eyes."[9] The tame death is "ordinary" in the sense that the dying man knows full well that he is dying. Death has been fully expected since birth because it was, and has always been, an essential part of life. Therefore the dying man is the center of a group of family, clergy, and friends. That is to say, the dying man is "in charge," and everyone present knows this. There are tears, prayers, and the sacrament, and grief is openly expressed and shared.

Most important of all, the tame death is primarily "public" rather than private: no man dies alone. By "public," Ariès means that mourning is for the most part communitywide. It is the community that bears the burden of the loss, not the family, and least of all the dying person. In particular, it is the affective burden of the loss—its emotional pain—that is born by the community and, within that, by the rite. The ritual in effect "contains" (in the sense of "is a container for") the loss. It succeeds in doing so by "re-presenting" death to all concerned, even to time itself, for the dying man will be buried in the churchyard and represented by a stone.

Ariès uses the word *tame* to describe this view of death and these mourning practices because they help carry out the central task of every culture. According to Ariès, all cultures perform the same functions but do so in different ways. The task of every culture is to protect its members from "the ravages of nature," which consist of both internal (or intrapsychic) and external forces and phenomena. Internal forces consist primarily of the ecstasy of

love and the agony of death; external forces refer to nature's in-
temperate seasons and sudden accidents. The tame death tames,
in the sense of "consoles," the dying person, making not only
bearable but even meaningful what might otherwise have been
chaotic and intolerable agony. Notice the likeness to Freud's theory
of the instincts and their vicissitudes at the hands of culture.

This description of the tame death does not differ, in all its essentials, from the anthropological understanding described above.
The same elements that make up the mourning process in the
first are for the most part present in the second: attachment to
culture and its members, loss (through death), mourning (plus
grieving), and eventual reattachment to culture. These, however,
were grounded in the pervasive presence and authority of the
Christian faith.

These mourning practices were utterly taken for granted by
large numbers of people over many centuries. The tame death became the ideal-typical form of mourning in the West. It is what
people have in mind today when they speak of the view of death
"that my grandfather and grandmother had" or the mourning
practices "that 'they' used to have." It is often referred to as "the
traditional view" of death. These mourning practices have declined
over the last two hundred years. What brought about the decline
of the tame death? How did the tame death become "the invisible
death" of today?[10]

MODERNIZATION AND THE DECLINE OF
MOURNING PRACTICES IN THE WEST

The decline of mourning practices refers to the weakening and
gradual disintegration of the tame death over a period of several
centuries. It is but one specific aspect of a far more general phenomenon—usually referred to as modernization, or development,
or secularization. In the context of this essay, modernization refers to the massive social change produced by the political (demo-
cratic) and scientific (industrial and technological) revolutions of
the West. These upheavals fragmented and gradually dissolved
the traditional sources of authority, guidance, and consolation
that had been in place for centuries and that had in turn created
a cohesive society grounded in a widely shared common culture.
As Robert Nisbet pointed out some time ago, this fragmentation
or waning of community and of its ancient traditions was the central insight of the founders of "the sociological tradition": Marx,

Durkheim, Weber, and many lesser lights as well had their own word for it, as do their respective followers today.[11] And so the question is: In what sense did the sweeping sociohistorical process of modernization and the consequent waning of community bring about the decline of mourning practices?

Let us go back for a moment and look closely at the tame death and especially at its supporting social and historical context. All the actors in this "scene" were able to mourn as they did because they were attached to and surrounded by an effective community of guidance and support, itself grounded in and attached to a tradition and a past. This community provided the foundation for what Ariès calls a "public" understanding of mourning and death. "Public" meant that the surrounding, commonly shared community took upon itself, in the form of its rituals, much of the burden of mourning that would otherwise have been overwhelming. But without the support of this community, mourning practices gradually weakened and then disappeared.

Let us consider the consequences of the modernization process for the individual. This is an instance of the social construction of psychological understanding. The erosion of tradition-informed institutions forced more and more responsibility for living upon individuals. Answers to moral questions once taken for granted now required more self-awareness and more reliance upon one's own resourcefulness. A cultivation of the inner life began. Sociologists and historians have created a host of different terms for this complex change. Most relevant for understanding changes in mourning practices are *privatization, individualization,* and *psychologization.*

Privatization is the splitting of shared social experience into public and private dimensions of experience. It removed mourning practices from the public sector. Individualization is the conscious and intentional personalization of choices and attitudes. Gradually, the burden of mourning became the responsibility of the individual. These changes required a psychological understanding of the social world. Psychologization also forced mourning theory and practices to migrate out of the churches and into the consulting rooms of psychologists and psychiatrists. As massive social-structural change reorganized the social contexts within which mourning could be experienced, understood, and practiced, the ideas of Darwin and Freud became increasingly relevant—even necessary.

THE MODERNIZATION OF MOURNING:
DARWIN AND FREUD

Darwin's discovery that humans share the emotion of grief with nonhuman primates and the fact that he, a naturalist, wrote about grief and other emotions opened the way for others—for example, zoologists and comparative psychologists—to anchor the study of grief in a scientific context.[12] Henceforth, we would know that grief was an emotion and that, as such, it was a mental process with biological and physiological dimensions. This in turn enabled others—for example, anthropologists—to formulate a more precise understanding of mourning as well. Henceforth, mourning could be thought of as a preeminently social phenomenon and related to grief as ritual is related to emotion. But Darwin's observations were incorporated into anthropology in this way only many years after he had made them.

Few think of Darwin as a "modernizer" of mourning practices —that is, one whose work contributed in a major way to the decline of mourning practices. However, Darwin did just this. Or rather, Darwin's discoveries enabled others to do just this. Darwin located—or, relocated—grief "in" the body of the individual, demonstrating that it could be studied scientifically. He thereby removed it from the control of the traditional sites of mourning practices, that is, from the influence of the clergy and their churches. Mourning gradually came to be recognized as an internal, and principally psychological, activity. And so the need emerged to understand it as such.

It is difficult to find a contemporary discussion of mourning that does not make use of Freud's now famous description of it in "Mourning and Melancholia."[13] At first glance, this is puzzling, for Freud himself did not think that mourning, however understood, was a significant moral or social issue, nor did he further develop this view of mourning from his essay in the course of his own work. Furthermore, he considered his paper to be primarily on melancholia or depression and only introduced mourning into it as an analogy, in the hope that it would clarify a bit further the analysis of melancholia he was proposing. Still, Freud's understanding of mourning has played a crucial role in the decline of mourning practices, albeit inadvertently. He refashioned the human response to loss in a way that took into account and addressed the changing cognitive, social, and subjective-internal possibilities and limits of his time and culture.[14]

The Freudian view of mourning differs in several important ways from the traditional or tame death, and it is these differences that make it modern. First, mourning refers to one person's inner experience of the loss of a loved other through death. It is without public (that is, communitywide) significance, and mourning practices are not mentioned. The burden of loss, once supported by the community, is now carried by the individual alone. Second, the tame death assumed that all affects accompanying loss were conscious and accessible to voluntary recall, and that the pain of loss undergoes a gradual and seemingly automatic attenuation over time. On the other hand, Freud considered such attenuation the end point of a complex internal process resembling "psychical working out," in which painful memories of the deceased are repeatedly recalled and relived, until the energies of attachment (called the "libido"), and the attachment itself (called "object-love") are gradually neutralized and relinquished. The key phrase is "working out" or "working-through," which refers to the expenditure of quantities of psychological energy and implies mental struggle and labor.[15] And third, in juxtaposing mourning and melancholia, Freud in effect introduced "the inability to mourn" and linked it to depression. However, those who lived in the time of the tame death could expect loss and mourning to occur again and again, as it always did. There was no reason for it to turn into its opposite—indeed, there was no way for it to do so. Finally, Freud also thought that one could mourn the loss of an idea or an ideal, not only the loss of a person, and he illustrated this point briefly in a short and moving essay, "On Transience."[16] As if prescient, Freud prepared moderns in the West for a century full of losses, for his psychology of the loss of an ideal is, in effect, a psychology of disillusionment.

One more point is ordinarily not mentioned in reviews or summaries of Freud's work on mourning. The term *mourning* is of course associated with death, grief, and bereavement, and this is both its commonsense and its dictionary definition. However, Freud's actual description of mourning in his essay is also a statement of his basic psychology of object-loss and object-love, and there is nothing intrinsically funerary about this theory. As such, this basic psychology refers to the fundamental structure of the inevitable developmental losses that all of us undergo—for example, adolescence is very much the final separation from and "loss of" the nurture of childhood. Freud's essay on mourning supplements and is supplemented by another essay written at about the same time, "Repetition, Recollection and Working-Through," and the two are sometimes taught together. This point is take up in more detail in part 2 of this book.

In sum, both Darwin and Freud, each in his own way, rendered the traditional view of mourning private and "natural"—that is, as natural as any other psychological process. However, theirs was mourning without mourning practices. (We cannot here explore the possibly critical point that the process of "working-through" of grief or the work of mourning is itself a ritual.)

MOURNING BECOMES A PROBLEM:
GORER, FUSSELL, AND ARIÈS

It is a short step from Freud's modern view to the complexity and flux of the experimental views of today, where the work of this book begins. However, between the two lie three important studies that together make this transition. The first is Geoffrey Gorer's *Death, Grief, and Mourning* (1965).[17]

Gorer was a gifted British social anthropologist who also wrote on political and historical subjects. His book was one of the first studies to openly recognize the decline of mourning practices and an "inability to mourn." He also understood that the roots of these were complex and cultural and resisted easy explanation. And he was one of the first to link these failures historically to the devastation of the Great War. His book continues to be cited in many of today's discussions, and with good reason: it is as sophisticated and well informed as some studies published much later.

Gorer was born in 1905 and died in 1965. He wrote his book late in life. It opens with a long autobiographical introduction that centers upon mourning in his own life. As a boy and a young man, he recalled, everyday life in Britain simply took for granted the sincere, deliberate, public ritualizing of grief: mourning dress for men and women, deferential behavior toward the bereaved in public by the public, family customs and ceremonies, and the like. Later, in midlife, Gorer noticed that these customs had gradually disappeared. By that time he had undergone a number of personal losses, none of which he considered unusual in either nature or number. However, he did very much miss having these customs, for their absence made bearing his losses more painful. His pain turned into anger, and from there into outrage and contempt. Then he wrote his book, which is very much a deliberate gesture of violent indignation.

Gorer's study was based on 1,600 structured interviews with a statistically representative sample of people in England, Scotland, and Wales, supplemented by 212 in-depth interviews. Major topics of inquiry were the death in the family, religion, the funeral, grief and mourning (public, physiology of, dreams), styles of mourning (denial of mourning, absence of mourning, hiding grief, unlimited mourning, despair), and types of bereavement (death of a father, of a mother, of a child, etc.). His main conclusion: the historical emergence within the course of his own life of "the social denial and individual repudiation of death, grief, and mourning." An appendix contains an article—"The Pornography of Death"—written in 1955 for *Encounter*, reprinted a number of times in Great Britain and the United States, and translated into several European languages.

Despite its novelty at the time, the book was also strangely narrow and parochial. Gorer made virtually no mention of World War II, postwar travail, or the Holocaust. The writings of Freud and also of Melanie Klein and John Bowlby are mentioned, but Klein's and Bowlby's innovations are scarcely noted. It is as if events and ideas beyond Britain during its interwar years did not exist. Yet, only two years later, the Mitscherlichs' *The Inability to Mourn* was published in Germany and Wolf Lepenies's *Melancholy and Society* appeared just two years after that.[18] Gorer simply could not fathom how thoroughgoing the disintegration of the traditional view was: it was already upon him.

Paul Fussell's *The Great War and Modern Memory*, published in 1975, took the discussion in a very different direction.[19] He demonstrated the extensive and intimate relations that existed between the experiences of the war and literary tradition. Literature was the way the war was remembered—it was the only way in which it could be remembered. By using the word *memory*, Fussell moved "history" closer to the experiential bases of culture. He brought to literature—what the men who fought the war wrote and what they read—a capacity to become interior to their inner subjective worlds, which were filled with suffering. Although Fussell did not use the words *loss* or *mourning*, the presence of loss and its ironies pervades his writing. I think of his book, which is a great book, as an elegy.

Finally, in the hands of Ariès, the principal elements of death are denial and resignation: death as it is today, especially in the United States, is "the invisible death," a biological transition without significance, pain, suffering, or fear.[20]

In sum, if we simply link together Gorer on the decline of mourning practices, Fussell on literature and memory as experience and its meanings, and Ariès on resignation and the denial of death, we can sense the reaching out of western societies for the kinds of discussions that are now taking place.

Mourning Becomes a Problem: Themes in Contemporary Studies of Mourning and Culture

Current explorations of loss and mourning ask in one way or another, Does the process of mourning, usually thought to be an individual, psychological process, also have validity and usefulness in the understanding of cultures—of history, groups, and symbols? Today's discussions carry forward this question by addressing four themes or issues. These can also be called "tensions" because in some cases traditional and modern practices are both present. Most studies contain more than one, or all, of these tensions, although one often stands out more than the others. These four are not intended to be exhaustive.

To illustrate these themes or tensions, I have chosen four studies that address collective mourning, the most prominent of the four issues, while illustrating the other themes as well. In the case of each theme, I first use these studies to illustrate the theme and then turn to additional materials that further clarify the exposition, when this seems necessary. When pertinent, I allude back to the short sketch and also forward to the paper or papers in this volume that illustrate or highlight the theme under discussion.

INDIVIDUAL AND COLLECTIVE MOURNING

Perhaps the best known and certainly one of the earliest studies of collective mourning is Alexander and Marguerite Mitscherlich's *The Inability to Mourn: Principles of Collective Behavior.* Published in Germany in 1967, it was widely read and discussed there, and an English translation appeared in the United States in 1975. The senior author, Alexander Mitscherlich, a German psychoanalyst, spent the Second World War under house arrest and after the war became a member of the German Medical Commission to the American Military Tribunal at Nuremberg.

The Inability to Mourn focuses on postwar Germany and what quickly came to be called the "German economic miracle." The

Mitscherlichs asked, How and why, so very soon after their defeat
and all that it entailed, could the Germans industriously and ener-
getically pull themselves together and achieve such remarkable
economic and industrial success? Why no exhaustion? Why no
depression? Why no disarray? But above all else, Why no thinking
about, and attempting to come to terms with, the past?

That was because, the Mitscherlichs explain, Germans idealized
and loved their leaders, especially Hitler, because these leaders had
promised economic and moral revitalization—the reader should
note that such revitalization includes enhanced self-esteem. Only
at the end of the war did the German people realize and confront
Hitler's crimes, their own complicity in these crimes, and their
own complex and shifting feelings about these offenses. The ensu-
ing disillusionment and the acute sense of loss were so great, so
sudden, and so rapid that it was experienced by most as simply
unbearable. Therefore, Germans responded to this pain with "the
manic defense," the "first line of defense," so to speak, against the
more primary psychological reality, a pressing sense of loss and
injunction, or invitation, to mourn or come to terms with that
loss.

This term, the manic defense, is often used in psychoanalytic
theory and practice today. It evolved from the work of Melanie
Klein and her interest in depression and was later used by D. W.
Winnicott not only clinically but also culturally.[21] This defense
begins with a loss and the refusal to become introspective toward
oneself in the face of that loss. Denial of the loss ensues. Then,
denial shifts into an interest in depersonalized aspects of the external environment, such as technology, and one develops endless
energy, always directed outward, for the pursuit of such tasks.
Successful closure is accompanied by an enormous sense of relief,
and the final state of affairs is rightly described as "the inability to
mourn," to which we in effect add "the inability to be depressed"
as well. The rapidity and thoroughness of the German postwar
recovery was widely remarked upon and admired at the time.

The Mitscherlichs' study has become a milestone for several
reasons. It engaged German accountability directly and forcefully
but not moralistically—that is, it appealed to readers' imagination
as much as to their will. It utilized a set of explanatory principles
(the discourse of psychoanalysis) that had become widely credible
in advanced western societies, especially in the middle classes of
those societies. And it did not criminalize or pathologize German

accountability. It was advanced by Germans and not by their con-
quering enemies. Finally, it simply had a ring of truth about it for
many.

On the other hand, the Mitscherlichs' thesis was from the start
vulnerable to a criticism already made of virtually any psychoanalytic study of society: it was bereft of sociohistorical methods
and data. Such studies, many say, simply repeat Freud's strategy
in all his cultural writings, claiming only "an analogy"—which
he did not define—between individual and social behavior and
then going on to draw sociological conclusions from dynamic and
metapsychological insights derived from working with individuals. For this reason it is crucial to note Dominick LaCapra's more
recent observation that in Freud's work the intrapsychic and the
social, the personal and the cultural, are continuous.[22] Still, the
Mitscherlich study remains one of the first to pose the question of
collective loss and mourning with psychodynamic depth and precision and to advance it rigorously and cogently in relation to a
catastrophic event.

Only two years after *The Inability to Mourn*, Wolf Lepenies, an
intellectual historian with strong sociological interests, published
Melancholy and Society. An English translation appeared in 1992.
Lepenies's book differs from the Mitscherlichs' in its subject, its
orientation, its methods, and its conclusions—but it too is about
collective loss. Lepenies is interested in the kinds of social and
historical circumstances that compel whole groups of people—
principally elites and classes—into melancholia. These are well-
defined and easily identifiable collectivities that have lost their
public significance. Historical and political change has cast them
aside and rendered them useless. They know it, and they believe
—correctly or incorrectly—that there is nothing they can do about
it. They are not ill—they are not, for example, depressed—and they
do not mourn. They are bored. They suffer from ennui or "the
blues." But it can also be said that they suffer from "the inability
to mourn."

Such was the fate of the German bourgeoisie in the eighteenth
century, who were deprived of political power and dignity, and the
Russian aristocracy in the late nineteenth and early twentieth
centuries. The Paris salons were a haven for such persons, and the
intellectual as a social type is especially vulnerable to this form of
melancholia. Literary works are a primary source for understanding such persons. The plays of Chekhov are a case in point. An

example familiar to many is *Uncle Vanya*, or Louis Malle's film adaptation of it, *Vanya on Forty-second Street* (1994), depicting Russian elites.

Lepenies's study is important here precisely because it asks, in a very different way, the same questions that occupy this present volume, and at critical points the author thinks along similar lines. Lepenies in effect introduces issues of collective attachment and the loss of such attachments in a new and compelling way. His approach provides fresh access to such familiar sociological concepts as "class," "anomie," "alienation," and the like, as well as issues in biography and especially in the history of ideas and of culture.

Among Lepenies's subjects are some people who, in times of social change and its stresses, undergo loss and alienation but then respond to it by generating fresh and convincing sets of cultural symbols. I call such persons "culture makers." Freud and his followers are familiar examples, as are leaders of revitalization movements. The sociological displacement of a cohort or generation can provoke a range of responses, and melancholia is but one. In addition to melancholia and creativity, persecutory anger is also a possible response. In short, Lepenies's work is an important resource for those interested in the way processes of mourning, whether successful or unsuccessful, shape and are shaped by culture.

Henry Rousso's *The Vichy Syndrome: History and Meaning in France since 1944* (1991) examines postwar France and the conflict about the parts played by the resistance and by the Vichy government during the German occupation.[23] In 1945, France was virtually of one mind in thinking of itself as having been resolutely opposed to the Nazis and their policies throughout the occupation and supportive of the resistance. The presence of the resistance movement seemed to prove this. Then, more and more evidence gradually appeared supporting the view that France was far more collaborationist and less resistantialist than had been thought. Subsequently, a bitter struggle polarized the nation over a long period of time, and Rousso's book charts its many events. At the outset, he explains that the word *mourning* is only a metaphor for him: France was not and is not "really" or "literally" mourning or unable to mourn. Still, Rousso's argument depends entirely upon the psychoanalytic concept of mourning.

Rousso traces French collective memory through a series of well-described historical periods. These periods correspond to the stages of the mourning process: the onset of the Vichy syndrome is the initial phase of conflict and a time of unfinished mourning (1944–54); that is followed by a period in which the resistance seemed more prominent than was thought (repressions, 1954–71); then, evidence that the predominance of the resistance was a myth is discovered (the broken mirror, 1971–74); this information generates a period of endless and unresolved arguments (obsession, 1974–present). The conclusion is clear: the syndrome has not healed.

Each of these periods contains an array of cultural symbols. Among the most prominent are monuments and memorials, films, television (especially documentaries), speeches, and autobiographies and biographies. Rousso describes, contextualizes, and interprets each period in the light of those sets of symbols that are the most prominent. For example, he often creates mini-biographies of specific symbols—when the film came out, how the two contesting sides interpreted it, how it was interpreted later in a different period, and so on. Then he draws together different symbols into coherent clusters organized around periods and links them up to the organizing principle, the Vichy syndrome.

The focus of mourning in the work of the Mitscherlichs is the human, individual person, and the collective is simply a very large person. The authors also provide specific case studies drawn from psychotherapy practice and research with individuals. In sharp contrast to this, there simply are no people in Rousso's book. The focus of mourning in his study is not upon persons or a people and their emotions; rather, it is upon memory, the collective memory of the French past generated by the French people. This memory is a structure created by a historian. If we judge Rousso's book in the light of this point, his study as a whole takes on cogency. His approach is also convincing from a very different point of view, that of collective psychology, at least at one point. Although this view will not appeal to everyone, it deserves mention.

A common observation of group psychology is that individuals in a group will often ascribe to the group as a whole attitudes, values, and emotions that they themselves, as individuals, do not share with the group. However, in such instances, observation sometimes demonstrates that in fact those same individual members do in fact very much share the attitudes of the group as a whole. To put the same point in a different way, an individual's deepest desires and fears sometimes can achieve representation only in a collectively shared memory, and not even there unless they are registered in highly symbolic form. For this reason, collective memory and an individual's conscious memory of the same event may contradict each other, but this need not always mean that one is right and the other wrong.

Jay Winter's *Sites of Memory, Sites of Mourning: The Great War in European Cultural History* is the most recently published of these four books (1995), is the only one about the Great War, and, unlike the books by the Mitscherlichs and Rousso, studies and compares all combatants.[24] Its narrative weaves together the lives of soldiers, their families and homes, their villages and larger communities, the frightful events of the war, and the creation of monuments after the war. It then turns to cultural reflections on the war represented by interwar artistic experimentations and movements in literature, the arts, and popular religiosity. The process of collective or mass mourning is the single thread linking these clusters. Winter's focus is how mourning and cultural symbols come together—how a people can create ceremonies, religious beliefs, monuments, and art in response to their shared loss, and how the workings of the culture they have created can represent and to some extent heal the wounds of loss and the sufferings it causes.

Winter's study provides a helpful contrast to the work of the Mitscherlichs, Rousso, and Lepenies. He convincingly shows, for example, that the English people mourned "as one" the losses of the Great War, as seen in their many traditional memorials and monuments. England mourned its war dead successfully—that is, in the same ways it had done many times before, thanks to its capacity to mobilize its heritage of traditional monuments and mourning customs. And, of course, much the same is said of the other combatants.

In sum, this review suggests that there are different kinds of collective loss and mourning. During and after the Great War, mourning was very much as Freud, writing at that time, described it. Individual and collective mourning were identical, as Winter's study demonstrates. However, in order to explore collective loss and mourning, these studies have found it necessary to speak as well of the "inability to mourn." The melancholia of Lepenies's socially marginalized elites is one example. Their "collective melancholia" also resembled, structurally, Freud's descriptions.

However, in the case of post–World War II Germany and France, the collective response to shared loss was more complex, and so, too, was the nature of the loss. These two studies focus not only on collective mourning but also on various manifestations of the failure or the inability to mourn: denial (the Mitscherlichs) and a good deal of interactive persecutory anger (Rousso). The following essays further clarify this second form that mourning sometimes takes in the workings of culture.

Among the essays that follow, those by Doris Bergen and Paul Anderson address collective mourning. Bergen carries forward LaCapra's viewpoint noted above and further develops the Mitscherlichs' thesis by using her own extensive historical research on ethnic Germans. Anderson explores the usefulness of psychoanalytic concepts of mourning in his discussion of African American spirituals as a folk inheritance.

THE ABILITY AND THE INABILITY TO MOURN

The inability to mourn appears to be a modern aspect of mourning —it is not part of the tame death but is more an inversion of it. We have come to know it through the writings of Freud, Melanie Klein, and D. W. Winnicott. To clarify its dynamics and the shapes it takes, I trace this inability through these three sources and into the four representative studies just reviewed, where it exists alongside collective mourning.

Freud did not speak of "the ability and the inability to mourn," but rather of mourning and melancholia. He based his distinction between them on the difference between two types of object-relation between mourner and lost other, object-love and narcissistic identification. In the case of mourning, the giving up of the lost object proceeds gradually through repeated rememberings of it, each contradicted by reality. This can occur because the mourner is psychologically separate from the lost object. Each was an independent center of initiative and emotion in relation to the other. In the case of melancholia, however, the subject cannot tolerate the loss and attempts to overcome it by identifying narcissistically with the object. That is to say, the would-be mourner makes the lost person into part of his or her self. The two are no longer psychologically separate from each other, if they ever were. As a result, the subject unconsciously comes under the influence of the lost person, does not even have a memory of an experience of loss, cannot for that reason work through the loss—as is possible in mourning—and becomes melancholic (depressed). This was Freud's view toward the end of the Great War, when he first published it.

A few years later, Melanie Klein began her work in London. Over time, she altered Freud's views decisively by transposing loss and mourning into the very center of the life course. Klein believed that all psychological growth and development was an inner struggle with different kinds of loss during different times in the course of life. In early childhood, the infant struggles with strong impulses and emotions and is intensely dependent on its mother for help with these, because it has little sense of itself as physically and emotionally separate from its mother. At the time of five years or so, the infant enters "the depressive position." In this crucial period, the child recognizes its mother as a whole object, a separate person with wishes and emotions of her own. This allows the child to see himself or herself as also having feelings and wishes separate from those of the mother. The depressive position brings with it pain, guilt, and feelings of loss. The pain is due to the mourning of the lost infantile gratifications and care. It is also the pain of letting go of the mother and her nurturing functions and "moving on." Much the same occurs at adolescence and then again at midlife—and at sundry other times as well.

The concept of the depressive position also clarifies Klein's understanding of the manic defense (a concept that originated with her) and persecutory anxiety. Winnicott adopted both of these to his own thinking. The two terms are closely related. Both refer to an inability to become introspective and to tolerate feelings of sadness and pining, and to imagine loss. Winnicott spoke of the capacity to be depressed as a form of mental health. It is the opposite of a denial of inner, psychological reality. Klein also spoke of "persecutory anxiety," where one feels that others are persecuting him or her, or that one is being punished in some way or other. Developmentally, the manic defense is thought to derive from the inability to experience the feelings associated with the depressive position.

Klein's view of loss and mourning helps us understand what the Mitscherlichs mean by the manic defense and an inability to mourn. Their definition is virtually identical to hers. As noted, the Germans' economic miracle was dependent upon their ability to concentrate entirely on the "outer" world. They did not allow themselves to think about anything that might remind them of an "inner" world of introspection with its feelings of doubt, fear, sadness, and so forth. In the case of Rousso's France, his observation that clashing memories became an "obsession" during the final period of the Vichy syndrome suggests that the two dominant factions, representing Vichy and the resistance, saw in the other an essentially persecutory force, one to be opposed and fought. This stance assured that neither group would ever experience feelings and thoughts of sadness, regret, and the like. Both sides preferred repetition over recollection.

Despite what he himself may or may not say, the inability to mourn also appears to be very much a part of Lepenies's study of marginalized elites. When we read the literary works that describe them, such as Chekhov's *Uncle Vanya*, we repeatedly find streams of quarrelsome banter. These keep everyone's self-awareness occupied with shallow, inconsequential ideas and events. It is unlikely that such persons could possibly speak about or even think about how and why his or her attachment to the center of society became broken. Such thinking and the sharing of it might allow them to move from melancholy to mourning, perhaps even to change their situation. On the other hand, it would appear that some of the loss Chekhov describes is symbolic loss (discussed below) rather than the inability to mourn.

Even Winter's study, which describes so many different forms and occasions of traditional mourning, has a place for its reverse, if only by anticipation. As he moves into the interwar years, when the deepest awareness of the catastrophe gradually set in, Winter points out that Europe began to undergo its final secularization (noted in more detail below). This loss was one that many could not work through, but instead had to live through or live out, in resignation, as best one could. Secularization is also a form of symbolic loss and is discussed below.

The inability to mourn is a prominent theme in four of the essays that follow: Mitchell Breitwieser's study of Fitzgerald and Kerouac, Julia Stern's look at the narratives of an African American slave girl, Paul Anderson's examination of the spirituals as an African American folk inheritance, and Peter Shabad's psychodynamic analysis of trauma and mourning and their relation to witnessing.

PERSONAL LOSS AND SYMBOLIC LOSS

Mourning the loss of a person is one of the oldest and most widely recognized forms of mourning; however, one can also lose and mourn one's attachment to an abstraction, such as an idea or an ideal. Freud was the first to recognize this form of loss and mourning, and he offered several examples. In "Mourning and Melancholia" he referred to the loss of such abstractions as "liberty" and "one's country." And in "On Transcience," his charming four-page essay written as an afterthought to his major effort, he spoke of a friend's inability to accept the passing of beauty in the realms of nature, art, and other forms of culture—even in the full knowledge that spring would follow winter and that civilizations can and will create new forms of culture. This, too, was for Freud an instance of the inability to mourn. It is a suggestive thought. It would seem to follow that even regret over the passage of time itself—we could call it "raw diachrony"—is, if taken too far, also an instance of the inability to mourn.

However, Freud did not develop this idea, nor have any of his followers—nor have any others, as far as I know. Nonetheless, I find it not only original and perceptive but also suggestive and highly significant for understanding the kinds of losses that scholars today are exploring in their work on mourning and culture. Although they themselves do not use the term *symbolic loss,* the processes it describes and explains can be found in much of their work. To understand symbolic loss, however, is to depart somewhat from Freud's view of loss and mourning.

Typically, symbolic loss refers to the loss of an attachment to a political ideology or religious creed, or to some aspect or fragment of one, and to the inner work of coming to terms with this kind of loss. In this sense it resembles mourning. However, in the case of symbolic loss the object that is lost is, ordinarily, sociohistorical, cognitive, and collective. The lost object is a symbol or rather a system of symbols and not a person. And the inner work of coming to terms with the loss of such symbols is by no means always followed by generative or creative repair or recovery, but as often by disillusionment, or disappointment, or despair. Some sort of combination of "resignation," along with some mourning, is the best way to describe the most common form of this kind of "coming to terms with the past."

The four historical studies under discussion in this collection each contain elements of what is here called "symbolic loss." These exist alongside and in connection with the other kinds of loss, as noted. When Hitler's crimes became widely known at the end of the war, the Mitscherlichs' Germans were unable to separate the end-of-the-war reality of Hitler and his crimes from their memories of his prewar promises of "a better Germany." Instead, they continued to love, value, and idealize these memories; they could not endure the pain of de-idealization. But Hitler's promises were also cognitive-symbolic: he also resacralized—in the Durkheimian sense of the sacred—German memory by embedding his promises and person in a frame of symbolic meanings. Clothed as well in his charismatic self-presentations, Hitler's promises inspired conviction. But end-of-the-war realities destroyed these symbolic structures and the meanings they represented—it broke the Germans' attachments to them.

Rousso's French people faced similar circumstances: de Gaulle appealed to the French people's self-esteem by embodying and promising the ideals of *patrie* and *gloire,* which had been embedded for centuries in shared, collective memories of a national past. Attachment to the symbols of that past formed a portion of the self of many French citizens. As these symbols were gradually unearthed, recontextualized, reinterpreted, and then subsequently in important ways discredited, symbolic loss loomed large. In Rousso's eyes, the French people's attachment to these symbols could not be given up—that is, they could not be mourned.

As already noted, Winter's book is a study of collective mourning in the traditional sense. That was because Europe in the early twentieth century was still a common culture. Elements of the religious faith and the social organization supported by this common culture were still present. However, Winter's conclusion also explains that the Great War accelerated secularization, especially in the case of the combatants. After the monuments and the mourning, a time of disillusionment and disenchantment with the Christianity of the past set in. This was an extended period of symbolic loss, the dynamics of which have yet to be understood.[25]

Although Lepenies's study is in many ways a case apart from the other three, his marginalized aristocrats and bourgeoisie in the seventeenth, eighteenth, and nineteenth centuries were also struggling with symbolic loss, albeit of a kind very different from the above. This may be one reason why he chose to label their plight as "melancholia," that is, as wholly irreversible. What these men and their families had undergone was not the death of a loved other, but a loss of social status and esteem, an attachment that can only be conferred by society as a whole. They no longer belonged to society. And, equally important, they lacked a language through which they could represent their plight to themselves, to each other, and to others. Their loss was symbolic, and as such it was resistant to simple mourning. But symbolic loss can include some mourning, and vice versa.

Among the essays that follow, Patrick Hutton discusses Ariès's gradual loss of his Roman Catholic faith and Vovelle's loss of his Marxist credo. Marie-Claire Lavabre analyses the difficulties that the disclosure of Stalin's crimes in 1956 created for leaders and activists in the French Communist Party. And Peter Homans proposes that Max Weber's concept of disenchantment is a form of symbolic loss and searches for its origins in Weber's life and thought.

MOUNUMENTS AND THE COUNTERMONUMENT

Monuments are probably as old and as ubiquitous as the experience of mourning, which may explain why the two are routinely associated with each other. Traditionally, the monument has been the material structure around which both personal and collective mourning have taken place, and it has facilitated that mourning through a process of return and release. The monument "re-presents" a past event and serves as a carrier of memory back through time to that event. After the event has been recollected and reflected upon, memory is released, and one comes back, so to speak, to the present. Through this process, memory of an earlier experience of loss is assuaged and rendered, or rerendered, less stressful.

Recently, critics, scholars, and writers have called into question the efficacy and appropriateness of the traditional monument. Some have observed that many people today generally ignore monuments, even when directly confronted with them. Others have called attention to the privileged role given to the traditional monument in Western culture, while still others have challenged the idea and ideal of monumentality itself. Further, some suggest that other cultural symbols or symbolic processes now perform the functions once performed by monuments. Finally, some have advanced a still more radical critique of traditional mourning and the traditional monument by proposing the "countermonument." After describing and illustrating the countermonument, I reflect on several other recent attempts to move beyond the traditional monument.

Some of the most interesting work on countermonuments has been done by James E. Young. According to Young, the term *countermonument* (*Gegen-Denkmal*) originated with two artists, Jochen and Esther Gerz, who together designed a "Monument against Fascism" for the city of Hamburg, Germany, which was unveiled in 1986. It is a twelve-meter (thirty-nine-foot) high aluminum pillar plated with a thick layer of soft dark lead and a steel-pointed stylus for visitors' memorial graffiti. Young explains how the countermonument works to oppose the traditional monument: "As one-and-a-half-meter sections are covered with memorial graffiti, the monument is lowered into the ground, into a chamber as deep as the column is high. . . . After several lowerings over the course of four or five years, nothing will be left but the top surface. . . . the vanishing monument will have returned the burden of memory to visitors. . . . [thus] the vanishing monument challenges the idea of monumentality and its implied corollary, permanence."[26]

Unlike the traditional monument, the countermonument does not console or reassure—it does not heal. On the contrary, it "torments" its neighbors. As those living in its vicinity repeatedly look at it, as they must, they form memories of the events it re-presents, or else they imagine these events, if they have not experienced them personally. These accumulate in viewers' minds, but also "on the monument," so to speak. By this I mean that the monument is a bearer or carrier of viewers' memories, imaginings, and fantasies about the events it represents. But when it has disappeared into the ground, viewers are left alone with their imaginings and memories. They can no longer assign responsibility to the monument for supporting and carrying their memories. The absence of the monument forces viewers to take upon themselves the burden of remembering, that is, the burden of their own memories and imaginings. Young summarizes: only within this kind of frame can a nation remember its complicity and "commemorate its misdeeds." He concludes that "even resentment is a form of memory."[27]

The countermonument compels one to think beyond traditional views of mourning and monuments. For example, How might a countermonument affect the process of mourning itself? Young himself does not address this question. So let us speculate. The countermonument could lead to a reexamination of the concept of "countermemory," either in Foucault's use of the term, or possibly in some quite different sense. On the other hand, the countermonument might require the positing of a new concept, "countermourning." What might such an experience look like? This concept would ask mourning to move against itself. That would eventuate in a very different kind of response, a principled, deliberate, and self-conscious refusal to mourn. Such countermourning in effect counsels attitudes such as "acceptance" and "resignation." Or is "countermourning" simply a psychological impossibility?

At the very least, the countermonument is a much-needed stimulus to fresh thinking about mourning and memory and the

representation of both in material form. It is a long overdue critique of the academicism in the study and understanding of monuments that has dominated thinking about them by privileging
aesthetic values and "expertness" about these. This has discour-
aged and often excluded the exploration of the complex emotional
and symbolic processes that take place in the minds of today's visitors and beholders. These processes have now become the subject
matter of other disciplines, and this is one reason why studies of
monuments have become interdisciplinary. Below I mention two
such explorations and track them into the four representative
studies.

If we understand the countermonument in the above minimalist sense, as the strongest existing critique of the traditional monument, then we can speak of a continuum with the traditional
monument on one end and the countermonument on the other. In
between lie numerous ways in which people devise material objects of one sort or another in order to remember and memorialize
the past. Modern, abstract memorials are experiments with new
forms of the monument, and we can also point out the ways in
which cultural forms other than the traditional monument—such
as film—can serve as a "functional equivalent" of a monument.
The studies of Winter and Rousso engage directly and in detail the
issue of the monument, whereas the work of Lepenies and the
Mitscherlichs, which do not even mention monuments, engage it
indirectly.

The first part of Winter's study centered upon the loss, mourning, and monuments of the Great War. The second part turns to
the interwar period. He links together films, the graphic arts, and
popular piety and discusses the interplay between these and the
traditional mourning of the first part. This second part of the book
contains a wealth of instances in which film, art, and religion are
shown to have been in constant and supportive interplay with the
traditional forms of mourning and monuments of that historical
period. In this sense we may speak of film, art, and piety as functional equivalents of mourning. At other times, as Winter points
out, film or art resisted the war and traditional mourning and
monuments, and thereby moved in the direction of the countermonument or its functional equivalent. And, as already noted, the
interwar period was also a time of secularization and therefore of
sweeping symbolic loss. By the time of the Second World War, the
general sense of desperation and despair had increased, eventually

forcing the creation of the countermonument as a distinct genre in its own right.

Many of the cultural symbols that Rousso stitches together to create the fabric of French postwar collective memory are either monuments or the functional equivalent of them. For example, a prominent political symbol of the collaboration-versus-resistance conflict was the burial of persons who had been major players during the occupation. During the early period of the Vichy syndrome (repression of all thoughts that France collaborated with the Vichy government during the German occupation) it was decided to move the body of Jean Moulin, leader of the resistance during the occupation, from its first burial site to the Pantheon, thereby confirming *in French memory* that France, as a nation, was always resistant to the Nazis. On the other hand, one of the major events disconfirming this memory was the showing of the film *The Sorrow and the Pity*. The ashes of Jean Moulin were perceived as a traditional monument, but the film had several meanings, one of which was to remember and memorialize "the crimes," as it were, of collaboration. In this sense the film functioned as a kind of countermonument.

Certain forms of literature sometimes serve largely as functional equivalents of monuments, and this bears directly on the work of Lepenies. We have noted his view that many of Chekhov's plays describe Russian elites who lost their status when displaced by new emerging social classes. They lost their attachments to the center of society. The plays represented this loss to society at large in the forms of theater and literature, one kind of cultural symbol. However, the plays also represent to us and remind us that such elites once existed and underwent this loss. As we read, they draw our imagination and along with it the potential for memory back into the past, engage it, and then release it into the present. In all this, these plays function or "work" in a manner quite similar to traditional monuments.

The Mitscherlichs centered principally upon the complexities of motivation in individuals and groups. As long as Germans were under the sway of the manic defense, denial, and disavowal, the need to represent the Nazi past in material forms of one sort or another could never occur. On the other hand, the very intensity of their resistance to remembering the Nazi past, which the Mitscherlichs so clearly present, was so great that one might well think that only a countermonument could match or stand up to this resistance. In this way, the Mitscherlichs implicitly validate the principles that authorized the countermonument.

Three essays in this volume directly address the significance of the monument. Levi Smith's essay on the social history of the Vietnam Veterans Memorial explains the ways in which its design has evoked different aspects of the mourning process at different times in its creation. James Young's essay discusses the new Jewish Museum Berlin as a countermonument and the importance of Freud's theory of the uncanny for understanding its disturbing effects. And Peter Shabad introduces his original and provocative notion that symptoms function to memorialize the suffering of trauma.

Additional Resources: Four Mourning-Related Trends or Clusters of Thought

In addition to specific studies of mourning, there are others that are related to mourning but that may be overlooked. These studies are too recent or too interdisciplinary to be as yet established, but they are substantial enough to be visible. They add much to our understanding of mourning while challenging some of its major tenets. In some cases, their contribution to the understanding of mourning is direct; in others, the questions they ask are as important as any answers they may offer. I briefly call attention to four of these, note one or two of their actual or potential contributions to the study of mourning, and suggest one or two representative texts.

MOURNING AND TRAUMA STUDIES

Trauma is an injury, mental or physical or both, that the organism experiences as overwhelming. For this reason it cannot mobilize internal self-healing mechanisms and cannot respond to external efforts to heal by intervention. In its physical forms, trauma is a well-established reality in the history of medicine. Interest in mental trauma is much more recent, and the discussions of trauma in interdisciplinary studies more recent yet. Only with these most recent studies do we find mourning and trauma discussed together, but how that evolved is also part of the picture.

Modern psychiatry first spoke of mental trauma in conjunction with the hysteria diagnosis, using terms like *traumatic neurosis,* in the work of Janet, Charcot, and later Freud. Train accidents produced "railway spine"; the Great War, "shell-shock"; World War II, "war trauma"; and the Holocaust, the "concentration camp survivor." But not until the Vietnam War and the publication of the DSM series *(Diagnostic and Statistical Manual of Mental Disorders)* by the American Psychiatric Association did the term *trauma* become fully legitimated, in the specific form of PTSD (post-traumatic stress disorder).

More recently, interest in trauma has become interdisciplinary, to include an exchange of ideas and perspectives between the humanities and the biological sciences. In the humanities, some scholars in cultural studies have begun to read and write about psychiatric problems and their literatures, and some physicians, psychiatrists, and psychologists now read what the literary scholars are saying. Teachers of literature have been reading the dynamic and especially the psychoanalytic psychologies ever since their emergence. But this early effort at exchange was quite one-way and focused primarily on motivation rather than trauma. The current dialogue is so recent that only now has the stage been set for a discussion of the process of mourning in relation to trauma.[28]

Both trauma and mourning are responses to stressful and potentially overwhelming experiences of loss. Such losses are difficult for the victim to remember and describe. Two points in the study of trauma greatly enhance our understanding of mourning. The first is clinical, the second sociological.

Clinically, the ability to mourn is a response to a loss that can be remembered and worked through in memory over time. On the other hand, a loss that is traumatic does not permit this work of mourning to take place; rather, all such efforts only take the form of repetition. As clinician Donald Kalshed explains: "The inability to mourn is the single most telling symptom of a patient's early trauma. Normal mourning requires an idealized self-object with whom the young child merges and around whom the child's omnipotence can first be experienced." If this empathically attuned self-object is never experienced, he concludes, the emotion of grief can never be experienced. In mourning, existing structures are activated; in trauma, those structures do not exist and must be brought into existence by a different kind of work.[29]

In a very different vein, the work of Kai Erikson on disasters and collective trauma clarifies the relationship between this clinical observation about individuals and trauma in groups. This can also illumine further similarities and differences between individual and collective mourning. Erikson is a sociologist, and his subjects are communities that have undergone human-made (i.e., techno-logically induced) disasters. To illustrate, two such communities are a group of homeowners in Colorado threatened by vapors from silent pools of gasoline that had gathered in the ground below and an Ojibwa Indian reserve in Canada plagued by contamination of the waterways along which members of the band had lived for centuries.[30]

Erikson makes a valuable distinction between individual and collective trauma. First, he makes a fundamental distinction be-tween the individual and the collective, beginning with a generali-zation: "one can speak of traumatized communities as something distinct from assemblies of traumatized persons. Sometimes the tissues of community can be damaged in much the same way as the tissues of mind and body . . . but even when that does not hap-pen, traumatic wounds inflicted on individuals can combine to create a mood, an ethos—a group culture, almost—that is different from (and more than) the sum of the private wounds that make it up. Trauma, that is, has a social dimension."[31] Next he defines individual trauma: "By *individual trauma* I mean a blow to the psyche that breaks through one's defenses so suddenly and with such brutal force that one cannot react to it effectively. . . . [One suffers] deep shock as a result of . . . exposure to death and to dev-astation . . . [people] withdraw into themselves, feeling numbed, afraid, vulnerable, and very alone." Then Erikson defines collec-tive trauma:

> By *collective trauma* . . . I mean a blow to the basic tissues of social life that damages the bonds attaching people together and impairs the prevailing sense of communality. The collective trauma works its way slowly and even insidiously into the awareness of those who suffer from it, so it does not have the quality of suddenness normally associated with "trauma." But it is a form of shock all the same, a gradual realization that the community no longer exists as an effective support and that an important part of the self has disap-peared. . . . "I" continue to exist, though damaged and maybe even permanently changed. "You" continue to exist, though distant and hard to relate to. But "we" no longer exist as a connected pair or as linked cells in a larger communal body.[32]

Under circumstances such as these, Erikson concludes, people become especially vulnerable. Then, if the disaster they experience "is thought to have been brought about by other human beings" (that is, it is not natural), and if it is motivated and mean-minded, collective trauma easily becomes irreversible. People begin to think that the world is ruled by "a kind of natural malice that lurks everywhere," and this in turn hardens into a new view of the world. As one informant said to Erikson: "This disaster that happened to us, I believe it opened up a lot of people's eyes. . . . I believe there will be wars, and there will be a bomblike thing that will just destroy this place to pieces. . . . it'll happen."[33]

In the case of individual mourning, the ability to mourn requires a certain amount of psychological structure or integration. If that is missing, then the individual is unable to mourn, and the condition is that of trauma. In the case of collective mourning, the same is true, but in a group sense. Collective mourning requires a certain amount of group integration. What Erikson calls "the basic tissues of social life" cannot be too badly damaged. If this network of bonds is destroyed, then the condition is traumatic. In both the individual and the group examples, the identifying feature of trauma is the absence of, or great destruction of, psychological structure (the social bond).

One further speculation is in order. Currently, studies of collective mourning tend to examine large group formations such as the nation-state, the church, and the like, while using evidence drawn largely from close studies of individuals. I think more attention should be given to what I would call "intermediate social structures" or "social structures of the middle range"—for example, movements, generations, cohorts, and political parties. These are social structures that take shape and exist "between" individuals and institutions, and in them individual and collective factors, and especially the interplay between them, are more observable. Kai Erikson's study cited above illustrates this point.

MOURNING AND MEMORY STUDIES

Although common sense tells us that memory and mourning are closely related, ordinarily the two are not studied together. However, as we have seen, the study of memory is of great importance for the understanding of mourning. Patrick Hutton has pointed out that historical studies of memory today have been largely inspired by French scholarship.[34] The foundation for this work began with Maurice Halbwachs's study of collective memory.[35] Halbwachs was a student of Emile Durkheim's, and he followed his teacher closely, transposing the problem of memory into the Durkheimian structuralist framework. Halbwachs perished in a Holocaust death camp, but his work was rediscovered some years later. He proposed that those living in the present see and regularly interpret— that is, remember—the past in ways that serve their needs in the present, although they claim "objectivity" for their interpretations. On the other hand, history and historians do indeed distinguish between the needs of the present, however pressing, and the "facts" of the past. History is empirical, memory is not. In such fashion did Halbwachs frame the task that confronts every age, period, or generation: how to come to terms with the past.

More than any other single author, Halbwachs distinguished between the facts of history and the needs of memory in the present and thus set the stage for what has come to be called the "history-memory problem." More recently, the writings of Michel Foucault and, after him, Pierre Nora have developed this discussion further. Foucault evolved the crucial term "counter-memory" to signify undercurrents of resistance to the dominant modes of discourse in the present.[36] These legitimate their claims by pointing to the ways the authority of the past supports them. Nora pressed this development of the history-memory problem still further by then claiming that historians can study only memories that are inscribed into material form—a typical instance of which is, of course, the monument. Nora's work constitutes the most advanced version of the history-memory problem.[37]

More recently, a second cluster of authors has emerged, also writing about memory but for quite different reasons and in quite different ways. These scholars have concentrated largely on memory and the Holocaust. Although they represent a number of different disciplines, some trained and worked earlier in their careers in literary studies. Especially well known are Saul Friedländer, Geoffrey Hartman, William Langer, and James E. Young. The central questions of the Holocaust writers are: As survivors and witnesses of the Holocaust age and die, how can and how will later generations remember the Holocaust? How does one understand and write about an event one has not witnessed firsthand? Under such circumstances, what forms will memory take?[38]

Neither of these two groups of scholars addresses mourning in a sustained way, and neither do writers on mourning speak of memory in a sustained way, as we have already seen. But that is not important here, because those investigating and writing about mourning have much to learn about memory from the work of both of these groups.

For example, both the French tradition and the Holocaust writers prefer the use of the word *memory* to the term *history*, for a variety of reasons. In doing so, they have brought the study of history into closer proximity to mourning. Memory is closer to mourning than is history and closer as well to psychology and anthropology, the two disciplines most accessible to mourning. Memory is much closer to immediate experience than is history. In short, memory is "experience-near," whereas history is "experience-distant." This proximity provides an opportunity for those interested in drawing psychoanalytic perceptions into the contexts provided by historical phenomena without making the mistakes of the ill-fated psychohistory and psychobiography movements.

Second, both the French historians and the Holocaust writers center their interests on both memory and loss, although in different ways and for different reasons. Like mourning, memory is deeply implicated in loss. Freud's theory of mourning is principally a theory of loss, and both are implicated in memory. Furthermore, in the case of both sets of writers loss is the loss of the past. The French historians say they have come to realize that French memory has "lost" the Revolution as the unquestioned national heritage in which to anchor collective memory. In like fashion, writers on Holocaust memory are writing about "the loss" that historic communities have undergone.

Finally, many—but not all—of the writers on memory and the Holocaust have made generous, complex, and powerful use of a wide range of psychoanalytic thought and practice, quite apart from its theory of mourning. In this they challenge those interested in mourning to do the same. Interestingly, the French historical tradition has not done so.

MOURNING AND PSYCHOANALYTIC STUDIES

Since its inception, psychoanalysis has consistently addressed not only clinical issues but theoretical and cultural problems as well. For example, all three receive substantive discussions as early in Freud's career as *The Interpretation of Dreams*. However, most of the work to date on mourning has been generated by the clinical situation, and those who wish to work on theoretical or cultural questions about mourning have had to defer again and again to

clinical work. So it is important to know that clinical understandings of mourning have evolved and changed greatly as psychoanalysis has developed, and what these views are. These developments
in turn raise a second but quite different question: Why has the
psychoanalytic theory of mourning captured the minds of so many
of those who want to write about loss?

Three figures stand out in any discussion of clinical psychoanalytic understandings of mourning: Freud, Klein, and Bowlby.[39]
Together they serve as a kind of spine or backbone for the subject.
The views of Freud and Klein were discussed above. In significant
ways, Bowlby's innovations have become even more important
than the views of Freud and Klein. First, Bowlby made "attachment behavior," along with issues associated with it—such as loss,
grief, and mourning, as well as dependence and affection—the central human reality of the life course. The human and social "bond"
or lack thereof became the unit of analysis in psychoanalysis—
not drive or instinct, not ego, not self, but object-relation.

Second, Bowlby did an impressive amount of empirical observation and research in which he grounded attachment behavior
and linked it to ethology, thereby giving attachment theory two
empirically based sources of information. This gave psychoanalysis a method of observation that was much more precise and disci-
plined than the conventional case study. Third, Bowlby shifted
the focus of thinking about attachment away from the individual
and in the direction of the group. The loss of an attachment is the
loss of a social bond. That means that loss is first and foremost
loss in the realms of sociality or community. And that in turn suggests that loss and mourning (and, by implication, memory as
well) are—also first and foremost—about loss and gain in sociality
and community.

One of the strongest reasons why psychoanalytic thinking appeals
to a great many humanists interested in writing about loss lies in
the tremendous amount of attention it gives to the experience of
loss. As we have just seen, Bowlby's work has moved psychoanalysis in this direction. It has also been argued that psychoanalysis
is, virtually, a complex and elaborate theory of loss and its vicissitudes.[40] Freud's theory of mourning actually supports this view.
The word *mourning* often evokes images of things funerary, such
as wailing walls, graves, and so forth, and this can distract one
from its meaning in Freud's actual discussion of mourning. That
discussion has nothing to do with funerary objects or practices. It
is worth repeating that this paper of Freud's is simply a very pre-

cise and introspectively sensitive description of the way he thinks the mind, and also memory, work when faced with loss. As such, the content of the famous paper on mourning is very much on the same subject as an equally admired essay, "Repetition, Recollection and Working-Through."[41]

MOURNING AND DEATH AND
BEREAVEMENT STUDIES

"Death and bereavement studies" simply refer to a large cluster of work that has a firmly defined and shared focus and that is, I think, an essential resource for those interested in mourning and the workings of culture. These are established health professionals— clergy, nurses, physicians, psychologists, social workers, and others —who center their attention on understanding and helping their patients, clients, and parishioners who are bereaved. More than any of the other trends discussed in this essay, these persons come together around a shared orientation to a specific practice. Practice is crucial, and research and theory serve it. Some work in institutional contexts, others are in one or another form of private practice. Many also have academic appointments.[42] This cluster is not a movement, or "school of thought," or an emerging trend.

The work of Colin Murray Parkes is perhaps the most widely known.[43] During the 1970s and 1980s Bowlby and Parkes worked together on attachment behavior, conducting research and publishing their findings. After Bowlby's death in 1990, Parkes has continued to teach, carry out research, and publish on bereavement and other related subjects. What is distinctive about his own approach to attachment behavior is in part conveyed by the opening pages of his most recent publication, *Bereavement: Studies of Grief in Adult Life.*[44]

To introduce his subject and point of view, Parkes rediscusses the famous case referred to as Anna O., thought by many to be the first psychoanalytic patient.[45] Anna O. developed severe hysterical symptoms while nursing her dying father at his bedside late at night. Freud claimed that he could trace her symptoms and their onset to developmentally earlier sexual conflicts. But Parkes points out that loss, separation, and grief (after all, her father was dying) were probably at the root of her emotional struggles in this particular instance. Parkes goes on to add that anxiety states as well are disguised attempts to cope with loss and separation. In other words, Parkes thinks that issues of loss and separation are far more prominent in the full range of human mental suffering than Freud ever imagined. Parkes's point of view has more in common with Bowlby's theory of attachment behavior than it does with Freud's psychoanalysis.

Parkes's work on loss and grief, and work like it, are essential for those studying mourning in collective, historical, and biographical contexts, for such findings are grounded in empirical and sometimes even experimental observation. We also know that grief, which precedes mourning, has a physiological and biological dimension and that it occurs not only in humans but in some nonhuman primates. These methods and their findings provide a measure of epistemological stability lacking in historical, philosophical, and literary studies of loss, grief, mourning, and monuments.

The Essays: Mourning and the
Workings of Culture

Loss and mourning in the workings of culture is the theme that brings together the essays in this collection. With that in mind, I have arranged the essays into four broad groups: cultural studies (as found in this case in literature and music), architecture, history, and psychology. Each essay reflects all the tensions or themes just discussed, even as it may settle in on one or two in particular. Below I note the subject of each essay, its relations to the several tensions, and, when relevant, its relations to the decline of mourning practices as well.

Mitchell Breitwieser uses the concept of mourning to understand the writings of Fitzgerald and Kerouac. Both were convinced, he thinks, that mourning lay "at the heart of consciousness" but that neither could articulate it. His study leads him beyond their writings to their lives and from there to speculations about the culture they lived in and wrote about. Here Breitwieser in effect uses the concept of mourning to identify a theme in American culture. In so doing, he continues his work on the specifically cultural uses of mourning begun in his *American Puritanism and the Defense of Mourning*.[46] Here Breitwieser writes about "the inability to mourn" and expands this formulation to include the inability to mourn a system of symbols.

Julia Stern makes it clear at the outset of her essay that the work of Mitchell Breitwieser has inspired her own work. She indicates that she has found in Breitwieser's work "a representational history of emotion." Stern concentrates on three fragments drawn from the autobiographical account of Harriet Jacobs, a slave girl, published in 1861. Stern first points out that slavery is "natal alienation," or the obliteration of organic family ties, and "social death," or the disenfranchisement from and actual erasure of any place in the free community. She then uses Freud's concepts of loss, mourning, and melancholia to link Jacobs's fragments to this social condition and to formulate the meaning Jacobs's narrative had for her life. Stern reads the narrative's emotional symbols politically. Her essay is also a study of the inability to mourn.

Paul A. Anderson explores African American slave spirituals and the controversy they generated in the Harlem Renaissance of the 1920s, in light of collective memory and the ability to mourn. First, he likens bell hooks's depiction of "the very easy death" among the black diaspora to the tame death described by Philippe Ariès and contrasts these deaths with Freud's secular and individualized description of mourning. Historically, the spirituals assisted in the ability to mourn, based on collective ties. But as modernization progressed, these ties weakened. Anderson tracks this development into the thought of W. E. B. Du Bois and of several intellectuals of the Harlem Renaissance, describing the different and conflicting ways the significance of the spirituals was debated. He concludes that the spirituals are at once a folk inheritance, a form of collective memory, and a resource for the ability to mourn. In Anderson's hands, they also become important sites on which the interplay between memory and mourning takes place.

Despite their many differences, the papers by Levi Smith and James E. Young ask a similar question: How does design or structure evoke the memory of loss? In the case of the Vietnam Veterans Memorial, Smith's analysis centers on its polished black surface, which can be perceived as either a window or a mirror. Drawn by the names, some look "through" the surface into time-past and their memories of the war; others see the same surface as a mirror that directs them to time-present by reflecting the immediate surroundings of the memorial. Smith relates these two forms of memory to the social and political struggles over the creation of the memorial and goes on to show how these two forms of memory resemble two stages in the mourning process, the first remembering and grieving, then a gradual distancing from the past, and finally a return to the demands of the present. Smith's interpretations challenge us—and also equip us—to think more deeply about the ways traditional and modern memorials and monuments actually affect us, both as individuals and as a people. His essay is a study of the memorial and collective memory in the light of mourning processes.

In the preceding part of this essay I discussed James E. Young's studies of the countermonument in his book *The Texture of Memory: Holocaust Memorials and Meaning* and in particular the "Monument against Fascism" designed by Jochen and Esther Gerz. Young's essay for this volume is a continuation of his work on countermonuments and the principle that a monument against fascism is a monument against itself—and against the traditional view of monuments in Western history. Here Young discusses the recently opened and already widely visited Jewish Museum in Berlin, designed by Daniel Libeskind. But unlike his previous work, Young makes use of Freud's theory of the uncanny, especially as the art historian Anthony Vidler has developed it in his concept of "the architectural uncanny." The uncanny accounts for the arresting and disturbing effects of the museum's design upon the attention and memory of the beholders and visitors. In this it contrasts sharply with the reconciling and consoling impressions that traditional monuments often evoke.

Patrick H. Hutton's essay compares the place of death, loss, and mourning in the writings and the lives of Philippe Ariès and Michel Vovelle, two major figures who engaged in and shaped the continuing debate about memory in French historical writing. To carry out his task, Hutton explores shifting ideologies, intellectual interests, writing projects, political contexts, and personal circumstances as these occurred in the lives and works of Ariès and Vovelle. In so doing, Hutton puts to the test Freud's claim that loss and mourning occur in relation to cherished ideas and ideals as well as in relation to other persons. By transforming Freud's concepts of loss and mourning into historical tools, Hutton shows how these can illumine the many different kinds of attachments and losses that beset not only the lives but also the values, ideals, and commitments of scholars, intellectuals, and writers.

Doris L. Bergen examines ethnic Germans (*Volksdeutschen*), people who identified culturally with Germany and Germans, but who lived in eastern Europe and many Balkan countries in the 1930s and 1940s. When World War II began, the Nazis declared that the ethnic Germans were "racially pure." Some became perpetrators, others bystanders, still others victims. All in their social surround hated them. Under such circumstances, Bergen asks, did ethnic Germans come to terms with their past? Were they able to mourn their many losses? To explore her question, Bergen turns to the theories of Alexander and Marguerite Mitscherlich but adds to them Dominick LaCapra's important point, that there is nothing intrinsically individual about such Freudian concepts as repression or mourning. Using her own extensive historical research on ethnic Germans, Bergen documents the psychological defenses against mourning that the Mitscherlichs enumerate, and she demonstrates in detail the consequences of these defenses for second- and third-generation ethnic Germans.

In his clinical essay, the psychoanalyst Peter Shabad introduces a fresh and original understanding of trauma into discussions about loss, mourning, and monuments. Trauma's distinguishing mark is the time delay between the injury and talking about it. Delay has the effect of generating doubt: Did this happen to me, or did I invent it? The more time passes, the more doubt creates the necessity to bear suffering alone. Then, symptoms emerge. Shabad's unique contribution to this well-known sequence of events is his claim that symptoms have the function of "witnessing" the traumatic event. Symptoms serve to memorialize the traumatized person's lonely suffering. They are a monument to it. Often, however, the psychotherapist is in a position to serve as a convincing witness. When this happens, trauma can give way to mourning, and healing can occur. Shabad points out that terms like *monument* and *memorial*, ordinarily used in design and architecture, also clarify the workings of loss and mourning. Perhaps a relationship —perhaps an internal or homologous relationship—exists between the way trauma, memory, and mourning do and do not work in the individual's inner life and the interplay between them that occurs in society as well. Shabad's essay is an intensive study of the ability and the inability to mourn.

Marie-Claire Lavabre's essay studies collective memory, mourning, and the inability to mourn in the French Communist Party at the time of Stalin's death (1953) and Khrushchev's revelation and denunciation of his crimes (1956). These events are examples of the two kinds of loss to which Freud applied the work of mourning: death of a loved person and death of an ideal. Lavabre studies party leaders, their binding principles, and their ritualized activities, as well as individual party activists. She uses in-depth interviews, widely publicized and recognized photographs (as projective techniques), biographies, memoirs, autobiographies, and the like. In so doing, Lavabre brings a dimension of empirical precision to the study and understanding of collective memory and collective mourning.

Peter Homans thinks that not all experiences of loss demonstrate the recuperative processes that characterize successful mourning or the repetitiousness of traumatic loss. Homans thinks that Max Weber's well-known "nervous breakdown" was one such experience, and that his concept of disenchantment was the result of a creative action through which he came to terms with a double loss—his personal past (his "breakdown") and also the collective past of his family and of his generation (the waning of Christianity). Generalizing from his analysis of the latter, Homans proposes that disenchantment is the loss not of a person but of a set of symbols that gave meaning to one's experiences of life and the world, and that this loss was not worked through (mourned) but rather was reworked by being made into an object of study. For these reasons it is more accurately described as "symbolic loss."

Notes

1. D. G. Mandelbaum, "Social Uses of Funeral Rites," in *Death and Identity*, ed. R. Fulton (Bowie MD: Charles Press, 1976), 344–63.
2. Peter Metcalf and Richard Huntington, *Celebrations of Death* (New York: Cambridge University Press, 1991), 30.
3. Robert Hertz, *Death and the Right Hand*, trans. Rodney and Claudia Needham (Aberdeen: University Press, 1960).
4. David R. Counts and Dorothy A. Counts, *Coping with the Final Tragedy: Cultural Variation in Dying and Grieving* (Amityville NY: Baywood, 1991), 284.
5. Ibid., 7.
6. Ibid., 7.
7. Philippe Ariès, *The Hour of Our Death*, trans. Helen Weaver (New York: Oxford University Press, 1977).
8. For further reading on Ariès, consult the chapter by Patrick Hutton in this volume.
9. Ariès, *Hour of Our Death*, 5. In the original, "the tame death" is *la mort apprivoisée*. The adjective translates as "tame (animals), made tractable, won over (people)" in *Cassell's French Dictionary* (New York: Macmillan, 1962).
10. The phrase "the invisible death" is the term Ariès uses for today's highly medicalized understanding of death. See Ariès, *Hour of Our Death*, 559–601.
11. Robert A. Nisbet, *The Sociological Tradition* (New York: Basic Books, 1966).
12. Charles Darwin, *The Expression of the Emotions in Man and Animals* (Chicago: University of Chicago Press, 1965), chap. 7.
13. Sigmund Freud, "Mourning and Melancholia," in *The Standard Edition of the Complete Psychological Works of Sigmund Freud*, ed. James Strachey (London: Hogarth Press, 1957), 14:243–60.
14. Strachey points out that in German, *trauern* means both "to mourn" and "to grieve" (ibid., 14:243). However, he does not mention the distinction made above that grief is grounded in biological-physiological processes, whereas mourning is a cultural-symbolic action.
15. See the entry entitled "Work of Mourning" in J. Laplanche and J.-B. Pontalis, *The Language of Psycho-Analysis*, trans. Donald Nicholson-Smith (New

York: W. W. Norton, 1973). Note that Laplanche and Pontalis state that Freud's psychopathological data have been "brought into conjunction with the findings of cultural anthropology on mourning." As evidence, they cite Robert Hertz's essay, "The Pre-Eminence of the Right Hand: A Study in Religious Polarity," in Hertz, *Death and the Right Hand.*

16. Sigmund Freud, "On Transience," in *Standard Edition,* 14:305–7.

17. Geoffrey Gorer, *Death, Grief, and Mourning* (Garden City NY: Doubleday, 1965).

18. Alexander Mitscherlich and Marguerite Mitscherlich, *The Inability to Mourn: Principles of Collective Behavior* (New York: Grove Press, 1975); Wolf Lepenies, *Melancholy and Society,* trans. Jeremy Gaines and Doris Jones (Cambridge: Harvard University Press, 1992).

19. Paul Fussell, *The Great War and Modern Memory* (New York: Oxford University Press, 1975).

20. Ariès, *Hour of Our Death,* chap. 12.

21. See, for example, Melanie Klein, "Mourning and Its Relation to Manic-Depressive States," in *The Writings of Melanie Klein,* vol. 1, *Love, Guilt and Reparation and Other Works, 1921–1945* (New York: Free Press, 1975), 344–69, and D. W. Winnicott, "The Manic Defence," in *Through Pediatrics to Psychoanalysis* (New York: Basic Books, 1975).

22. See Dominick LaCapra's essay "Is Everyone a *Mentalité* Case? Transference and the 'Culture' Concept," in *History and Criticism* (Ithaca: Cornell University Press, 1985), 71–94.

23. Henry Rousso, *The Vichy Syndrome: History and Memory in France since 1944,* trans. Arthur Goldhammer (Cambridge: Harvard University Press, 1991).

24. Jay Winter, *Sites of Memory, Sites of Mourning: The Great War in European Cultural History* (New York: Cambridge University Press, 1995).

25. Winter likens this period of disillusionment to a phrase used by Julia Kristeva, "symbolic collapse." However, while the phrase is suggestive, it makes no dimension of loss. Winter, *Sites of Memory,* 112.

26. James Young, *The Texture of Memory: Holocaust Memorials and Meaning* (New Haven: Yale University Press, 1993), 30–31.

27. Ibid., 30–34.

28. For example, see Cathy Caruth, *Trauma: Explorations in Memory* (Baltimore: Johns Hopkins University Press, 1995), and Bessel A. Kolk, Alexander C. McFarlane, and Lars Weisaeth, *Traumatic Stress: The Effects of Overwhelming Experience on Mind, Body, and Society* (New York: Guilford Press, 1996).

29. Donald Kalshed, *The Inner World of Trauma* (London: Routledge, 1996), 27–28.

30. Kai Erikson, *A New Species of Trouble: The Human Experience of Modern Disasters* (New York: W. W. Norton, 1994), 11.

31. Ibid., 231.

32. Ibid., 233.

33. Ibid., 237–41.

34. See Patrick H. Hutton, *History as an Art of Memory* (Hanover VT: University Press of New England, 1993). Hutton also provides reliable discussions of the work of Halbwachs, Foucault, and Nora.

35. See Maurice Halbwachs, *On Collective Memory,* trans. Lewis Coser (Chicago: University of Chicago Press, 1992).

36. In Michel Foucault, *Language, Counter-Memory, Practice: Selected Essays and Interviews,* ed. Donald F. Bouchard (Ithaca: Cornell University Press, 1977), especially pp. 139–64.

37. One of several convenient sources for this important essay is Pierre Nora, "Between Memory and History: Les Lieux de Memoire," in *Representations* 26 (spring 1989): 7–25.

38. For an example of the work of these writers, see James E. Young, *Writing and Rewriting the Holocaust: Narrative and the Consequences of Interpretation* (Bloomington: Indiana University Press, 1998), and Young, *Texture of Memory.*

39. Freud, "Mourning and Melancholia"; Klein, "Mourning and Its Relation to Manic-Depressive States"; John Bowlby, *Attachment and Loss,* vol. 1, *Attachment,* 2d ed. (New York, Basic Books, 1989); vol. 2, *Separation: Anxiety and Anger* (New York: Basic Books, 1975); and vol. 3, *Loss: Sadness and Depression* (New York: Basic Books, 1980).

40. Two studies advancing this point of view, in very different ways, are Fred Weinstein and Gerald M. Platt, *The Wish to Be Free: Society, Psyche and Value Change* (Berkeley: University of California Press, 1969), especially chap. 5, "The Introspective Revolution," and Peter Homans, *The Ability to Mourn: Disillusionment and the Social Origins of Psychoanalysis* (Chicago: University of Chicago Press, 1989), especially chap. 6, "Framing the Argument: Why Think Sociologically about Psychoanalysis."

41. Sigmund Freud, "Remembering, Repeating and Working-Through," in *Standard Edition,* 12:145–56.

42. For a general overview of this group of professionals and the writings representative of it, see Dennis Klass, Phyllis R. Silverman, and Steven L. Nickman, eds., *Continuing Bonds: New Understandings of Grief* (Washington: Taylor and Francis, 1996).

43. See, for example, Colin Murray Parkes, *Bereavement: Studies of Grief in Adult Life,* 3d ed. (Madison CT: International Universities Press, 1998), and Colin Murray Parkes and Robert S. Weiss, *Recovery from Bereavement* (New York: Basic Books, 1983).

44. See especially chap. 1 of Parkes, *Bereavement.*

45. Sigmund Freud, "Lecture 1," in *Five Lectures on Psycho-Analysis,* in *Standard Edition,* 11:9–20.

46. Mitchell R. Breitwieser, *American Puritanism and the Defense of Mourning: Religion, Grief, and Ethnology in Mary White Rowlandson's Captivity Narrative* (Madison: University of Wisconsin Press, 1990).

I

CULTURAL STUDIES

MITCHELL BREITWIESER

FITZGERALD, KEROUAC, AND THE PUZZLE OF INHERITED MOURNING

GOING BACK to a writer's beginning is difficult: perhaps the greatest frustration in consulting literary biographies is the fact that the time of life that most powerfully determines personal destiny, childhood, is the most skimpily documented. Though one's own memory assures one of the existence of enormously important events during the first five years, biographies typically discuss that period cursorily, say on ten or fifteen out of a couple hundred pages. The writer is usually going to college by the end of the first chapter. It could not be otherwise, of course, because so little is perceived as significant enough to be recorded: the account of childhood, in its brevity, emblematizes the mystery of early consciousness, and the biographer's frugality represents a principled attempt not to crowd out the reader's speculations. The aim of psychoanalysis is in part to fill in this generic hiatus in biography, recovering by complex and ingenious means the reactions to events that set the self in play. Think, for instance, of Hitchcock movies such as *Marnie* or *Spellbound*, in which the successful recollection of a childhood experience renders intelligible a well-documented but puzzling adulthood.

But what if the determining event happened to someone other than the subject it came to determine? In a 1937 sketch entitled "Author's House," F. Scott Fitzgerald takes an unnamed companion on a tour through his consciousness and memory, allegorically represented as the several areas of a house. In the "dark damp unmodernized cellar" where the tour begins, Fitzgerald seeks to explain the origin of his career: "The intangibles are down here. Why I chose this God awful metier of sedentary days and sleepless nights and endless dissatisfaction. Why I would choose it again. All that's down here and I'm just as glad I can't look at it too closely."[1] Premier among these things down in the cellar are the deaths of two sisters: "three months before I was born my mother lost her other two children and I think that came first of all though I don't know how it worked exactly. I think I started then to be a writer."[2] Notice the ambiguous phrasing: "I think *that* came first of all." To what previous noun does the word *that* refer? None, directly, but to the two sisters' deaths, presumably. Actually, not really to the sisters' deaths, but rather to the mother's loss of the two sisters: "three months before I was born my mother lost her other two children and I think that came first of all." The mother's loss, three months before the son was born, of two daughters he never knew determined the course of his life, "all though I don't know how *it* worked exactly." To what does the word *it* refer? It should refer to the same thing as *that*, to the mother's unnamed sorrow, but it means somewhat more, the process whereby the mother's grief developed into the life the son led. Though he is unaware, or unwilling to be aware, of the steps of transmutation between the experience of one and the profoundest identity of another, Fitzgerald is convinced that his career begins in mourning, but not his own. Revisiting in memory the sites of his own losses will not dissolve the spell of trauma because the spell was cast three months before his power to lose began.

How does one receive the transmission of another's grief? What is the mechanism or procedure whereby the subjective configuration of one becomes the identity of another? From the first, critics of Fitzgerald's fiction have faulted him for failing to sustain fully imagined separate characters: Dick Diver, for example, the protagonist of *Tender Is the Night*, begins as a fictional re-creation of Fitzgerald's elegant friend Gerald Murphy but quickly subsides into a fictionalized F. Scott Fitzgerald. But if in his writing the blurred boundary between oneself and another seems to have resulted in little but self, in his life as he understood it Fitzgerald found a self that was little but the other.

A year before writing "Author's House," Fitzgerald wrote two essays together entitled *The Crack-Up* in which he concentrates on the dangers that identification poses to identity. Announcing that, in reaction to a breakdown, he had retreated from society, Fitzgerald explains he was seeking "absolute quiet to think out why I had developed a sad attitude toward sadness, a melancholy attitude toward melancholy and a tragic attitude toward tragedy."[3]

Notice that he is not seeking the source of his own sadness, melancholy, or tragedy, but rather the source of his emotions toward those emotions.

The next phrase clarifies somewhat the origins of these second-order feelings: "to think out why . . . *I had become identical with the objects of my horror or compassion.*" He has a sad attitude toward *another's* sadness, a melancholy attitude toward melancholy, a tragic attitude toward tragedy. He becomes the other's feeling: "identification such as this spells the death of accomplishment. It is something like this that keeps insane people from working." Because he is under the influence, he fails to achieve the temporally sustained egoic poise required to experience himself as a distinct agent acting within and upon the world—working "So there was not an 'I' any more—not a basis on which I could organize my self-respect—save my limitless capacity for toil that it seemed I possessed no more. It was strange to have no self—to be like a little boy left alone in a big house, who knew that now he could do anything he wanted to do, but found that there was nothing he wanted to do."[4]

His self-isolation, then, was not a reflective interlude but rather a panicked flight from the awful drowning power that identification had over his ability to believe in his own distinctive existence: "But I had a strong sudden instinct that I must be alone. I didn't want to see any people at all. I had seen so many people all my life—I was an average mixer, but more than average in my tendency to identify myself, my ideas, my destiny, with those of all classes that I came in contact with. I was always saving or being saved—in a single morning I would go through all the emotions ascribable to Wellington at Waterloo. I lived in a world of inscrutable hostiles and inalienable friends and supporters."[5] The trace of paranoia that appears with the term "inscrutable hostiles" may be a way of articulating the paradoxical danger of affection: the stronger the affective connection, the greater the threat, as if the friends secretly and inexplicably sought to dissolve him.

The Crack-Up essays imply that the disaster of identification erupted during a period of middle-aged psychic sag. But when Fitzgerald returns to the issue of identification in the 1937 remark on his mother's sorrow, the problem has come to seem primordial, rather than a midlife intrusion into a previously successful self.[6] This more radical and frightening possibility is foreshadowed, perhaps, in the first paragraph of *The Crack-Up:*

Of course all life is a process of breaking down, but the blows that
do the dramatic side of the work—the big sudden blows that come,
or seem to come, from outside—the ones you remember and blame
things on and, in moments of weakness, tell your friends about,
don't show their effect all at once. There is another sort of blow
that comes from within—that you don't feel until it's too late to do
anything about it, until you realize with finality that you will never
be as good a man again. The first sort of breakage seems to happen
quick—the second kind happens almost without your knowing it
but is realized suddenly indeed.[7]

Perhaps the remark on his mother's sorrow implies he never was
as good a man before: the fatal inner blow occurs at the commencement of the self, or rather oneself is this crack or wound of
the other's, and the "crack-up" is only the "realization" or final
manifestation of this fundamental debility that Fitzgerald felt
himself to *be.*

But what, then, gets cracked? Not a real and distinct self to
which one can return in recovering from the breakdown. But if
there is no there there, perhaps then a fantasy of a self, a fantasy
into which he has poured enough fervent belief to have sustained,
till now, work: you do not need to have a self to work; you need to
believe that you have a self to work. In "Author's House," before
leaving the basement, the author's companion notices a "too recent
mound of dirt" and, demanding an explanation, gets this:"That is
where I buried my first childish love of myself, my belief that I
would never die like other people, and that I wasn't the son of my
parents but a son of a king, a king who ruled the whole world."[8] By
imagining himself to have sprung from the Platonic conception of
himself, to borrow a phrase he had used to describe Jay Gatsby a
decade before, Fitzgerald contends, he was able to avoid having
to concede the disastrous power of his mother's emotion. Until
recently: notice that the fantasy of omnipotence is buried beneath
a *recent* mound of dirt; though the fantasy is his first childish love
of himself, it has only just lost its efficacy. The crack-up, then,
which in the earlier cluster of essays was thought of as damage
done to a true self, is now thought of as the failure of a protective
illusion. This possibility is explored again at the end of "Author's
House," when the author takes the companion up to a turret or
watchtower that seems to return to the theme of the fantasy of a
regal self:

It is small up there and full of baked silent heat until the author opens two of the glass sides that surround it and the twilight wind blows through. As far as your eye can see there is a river winding between green lawns and trees and purple buildings and red slums blended in by a merciful dusk. Even as they stand there the wind increases until it is a gale whistling around the tower and blowing birds past them.

"I lived up here once," the author said after a moment.

"Here? For a long time?"

"No. For just a little while when I was young."

"It must have been rather cramped."

"I didn't notice it."

"Would you like to try it again?"

"No. And I couldn't if I wanted to."[9]

If the towering self of Fitzgerald's early success and famous youth is now lost, the loss is not entirely regrettable, since the vistas of possibility it had offered had entailed a strict confinement. If, however, the fantasy of the tower is both broken and relinquished —that is, if it is satisfactorily mourned—self-understanding returns not to a matured or humbled real self but to the deeper and still unsolved mourning from which the fantasy was intended to distract it—the mother's grief inherited as a self, the profound puzzle of his being: "I can't look at it too closely"; "I don't know how it worked exactly."

I would like to think about how it might have worked. I have four hypotheses, none of which I strongly prefer to the others. And the four do not seem to me to be mutually exclusive. Perhaps they are four ways of stating the same thing.

1. Fitzgerald commented in a late piece that his mother was "half insane with pathological nervous worry,"[10] specifically with worry that he would develop tuberculosis: as an infant he suffered from recurrent bronchitis and his mother's father and sister had had TB. As a result of his mother's anxious attention to his health, Fitzgerald was said to have been "spoiled." But Molly McQuinlan Fitzgerald was also remembered as distracted and eccentric. Perhaps, then, the mother was recessed, as mourners tend to be, except when some turn for the worse in the boy's health excited the exorbitant anxiety that is another regular feature of unresolved mourning. If so, then, with the aptness of all children, the boy would have learned that sickness had the power to lure the mother out

from her recess and to entice her to bathe him in meticulous attention, an attention that, however immediately consoling, arose
elsewhere, in a drama that occurred before his birth, a drama in
which, when it recurred, he figured as a symbol or a cipher of the
dead, rather than as a person. Distant as such anxiety might be
from love, it has to suffice if the alternative is parental oblivious-
ness and the child's consequent intuitions of his nullity.

So love such as it can only be follows from sickness: this becomes a fundamental axiom of consciousness, and a life of insis-
tent, unyielding, deliberate self-injury commences. Self-injury, not
self-destruction, becomes Fitzgerald's "project," in the sense Sartre
uses that word: the self cannot die, because then it will cease to
attract anxiety. But what if the fountain of anxious attention dies?
Nicholas Abraham and Maria Torok suggest that a fantasy of a person can be incorporated as an inner person, that one can bring one's
notion of another within and experience what one supposes the
inner other's emotions to be.[11] So as still-a-boy Fitzgerald injures
himself, mother-within grieves for her suffering boy. The grief
that was the other's is now, though still felt as the other's, within
and one's own.

2. In several later essays, Abraham and Torok take their interest in the incorporation of an alien subjectivity toward what they
call "the phantom."[12] As a part of assimilating the parents' world
view, they contend, the child can incorporate in himself the symptoms of a neurotic structure—emotional tones, reaction patterns,
tics and rituals, physiological signals—without having undergone
the experience that generated the neurosis. As their translator
Nicholas Rand puts it:

> The concept of the phantom moves the focus of psychoanalytic
> inquiry beyond the individual being analyzed because it postulates
> that some people unwittingly inherit the secret psychic substance
> of their ancestors' lives. The "phantom" represents a radical reori-
> entation of Freudian and post-Freudian theories of psychopathology,
> since here symptoms do not spring from the individual's own life
> experiences but from someone else's psychic conflicts, traumas, or
> secrets. . . . Though manifest in one individual's psyche, the phantom
> eventually leads to the psychoanalysis in absentia of several gener-
> ations (parents, grandparents, uncles, *et al.*) through the symptoms
> of a descendant.[13]

The difference between hypothesis 1 and hypothesis 2 is that in
the first case the child builds up within himself a fantasy of a feel-

ing mother within—he believes himself to be reproducing a subjectivity he supposes he deeply comprehends. In the second case,
the child reproduces an actual, rather than a fantastic, psychoso-
matic array, but with a blank or a secret at its core. This sense of
the blankness at the heart of the inheritance might bring us closer
to Fitzgerald's feeling that he is unable to explain his emotional
inheritance, because the idea of the phantom supposes an absent
core, rather than a ferociously repressed core. The phantom, according to Abraham and Torok, "cannot even be recognized by the
subject as evident in an 'aha' experience."[14] Rather, one can only
hope to recognize the presence of an inexplicable intruder, to
chart the boundary between the self and an intrinsic accident.

3. Christopher Bollas contends that moods may represent attempts to preserve a feeling of mutuality with a parental presence
even after the actual parent departs or dies:

> Some analysands feel that their moods are the most important au-
> thentic memories of their childhood, often because through mood
> the person feels in contact with a true self experience. A conserva-
> tive object frequently serves an important function in analysis
> when it preserves a self state that prevailed in the child's life just at
> the moment when the child felt he lost contact with the parents.
> When this is the case, a conservative object preserves the child's
> relation to the parents at the moment of a breakdown in parent-
> child engagement. Adult analysands may form intense resistances
> to psychoanalytic knowing of the conservative object, as they feel
> the analyst is endeavoring to remove their preserved relationship to
> their parent.[15]

If aggression, say, is the parents' mode of being together, then the
child's creation of aggressive moods might be seen as an attempt
to reconstitute the parents' presence, despite the damage done to
all participants by aggression. Grief such as Fitzgerald imputed to
his mother is seclusive—the sufferer disappears into it frequently,
abandons the world—and perhaps the child learns to lure the
mother from her caverns by being melancholy with her, thereby
mirroring her emotion in a world that otherwise seems to her only
so much broken glass. By consoling her with the equality of their
emotions, rather than by exciting her anxiety as in hypothesis 1,
Fitzgerald might achieve recognition of his being as a person and
might revisit that mood even in the absence of the original part-
ner, because the atmosphere of the mood seems to re-create the
somber paradise. In that case, feeling mournful might be a way of

avoiding having to mourn, the reconstituted feel of the relation with the mother distracting the boy from the thought of her real absence, a strategy of denial to which the subject tends to turn desperately, hopelessly, and pathetically when doubts about his own existence assert themselves over the course of life's hard journey.

4. Eric Santner and Michael Schneider, in their expansions of the Mitscherlichs' analysis of postwar German culture, argue that the disturbed mourning of parents can lead to a tormented self-absorption so complete that the child never experiences a true primordial bond. As Santner puts it:

> the second [postwar] generation inherited not only the unmourned traumas of the parents but also the psychic structures that impeded mourning in the first place. That is, since so many members of the second generation never really had access to the full attention and care of the parents, who were expending enormous amounts of psychic energy to ward off melancholy (these were parents who were, psychologically speaking, always elsewhere), their own psychological growth has in large measure been disrupted. They have tended, as Schneider notes, to fixate on their parents to a remarkable degree. This fixation is the flip side of a "depressive self-obsession," a state of melancholy "which can be attributed less to a sense of sorrow that something has been lost than to an existential feeling that something is missing—a sense of disappointment over something which was never received."[16]

Rather than a lost thing, a thing never had, and therefore a sense of lacking without the ability to know what it is that is lacked.

In all four of my hypothetical scenarios, the son ends up a griever—desolate, anxious, sorrowful, empty, cracked, cursed, and furious—exiled from the possibility of representing either the loss or the lost. If, as Freud suggests, the work of mourning lies in the incremental construction in conscious memory of an adequate representation of the lost thing, a representation that delineates a representer who survives, then the inheritor of mourning is doomed to an inability to mourn—a true inability, not a deep or insurmountable unwillingness, which is what the Mitscherlichs described—not because the requisite knowledge is too awful but because it is nonexistent. An inability, but not for want or trying, in fact trying all the more intensely, in a series of attempted approximations of the lost object in the imagination, in a writer's life devoted to the pursuit of what Nick Carraway supposes he hears in Gatsby's longing: "Through all he said, even through his appalling sentimentality, I was reminded of something—an elusive rhythm, a fragment of lost words, that I had heard somewhere a long time ago. For a moment a phrase tried to take shape in my mouth and my lips parted like a dumb man's, as though there was more struggling upon them than a wisp of startled air. But they made no sound, and what I had almost remembered was incommunicable forever."[17]

THE DIFFERENCE between Kerouac's writing and Fitzgerald's writing is plain to all readers, Fitzgerald's deliberate elegance seeming to originate aesthetic worlds away from Kerouac's strenuous and variably interesting forays into automatic writing. But Fitzgerald had a taste for profuse and roughhewn writers such as Frank Norris and Thomas Wolfe, the latter one of Kerouac's early models, so it is not certain that, had he had the chance to comment, Fitzgerald would have rejected Kerouac's style out of hand. Despite the severe difference of literary manner, there are many other affinities between the two men's lives, and some between their aesthetic projects: born into non-WASP Catholic families, they came of age in energetic but rather vapid decades, the twenties and the fifties; absorbing the vigor but refusing the priggishness of public life, they wrote restless, edgy books that affirmed the superiority of visionary countercultural fulfillments over stodgy social prohibitions; on the basis of those books, both men arrived quickly at a thrilling and confusing celebrity, the reading public requiring them to exemplify a notorious and avant-garde lifestyle, the lifestyle of a lost generation or a beat generation; and, of course, in the wake of celebrity and the pursuit of fulfillment, both died in early middle age as a consequence of alcoholism. In the popular imagination, the darkness of the ends of their lives tends to be seen as a bleak sequel to the affirmations of the young men, as if the fireworks that burn twice as bright burn half as long, or perhaps as confirmation of an especially American insistence that the books have to balance eventually. But this narrative of fulfillment followed by destruction, preserving the separation of light and darkness by casting them as successive phases, obscures a key feature of the two writers' world views, the fact that for them grief is the propulsive force beneath affirmation from the beginning.

When Kerouac was four, his brother Gerard, eight, died from rheumatic fever. In her biography, Ann Charters suggests that Kerouac was too young to comprehend the event, and my own memories of a death and a funeral from that period of my life support her speculation, though I would say that children understand death differently rather than not at all, as a perplexing metamorphosis rather than as a sorrowful ending. At the end of *Visions of Gerard*, his memoir of this period of his life, Kerouac recalls turning to his mother and sister to ask why they are weeping during the brother's funeral:

> "Ti Jean you don't understand, you're too young to understand!" they wail, seeing my rosy face, my questioning eyes.
> I look again, the men have stepped a pace aback, expectant, old gravedigger picks up his shovel and closes the book.[18]

His own lack of grief contrasts sharply with his memory of his mother's grief, depicted throughout the book, her attention to the brother during the weeks before his death, her neglect of her own health and well-being, her blasphemous explosions of despair the night he dies, and, most importantly, the legend of Gerard she composes as her means of terminating mourning. Availing herself of a generic template that was a basic element of a French Canadian religious upbringing, *memere,* Gabrielle *Ange* Kerouac, spun out a saint's life, complete with birds coming to the sick boy's window, even hopping onto his shoulders, prodigiously sweet words whispered to amazed nuns at his deathbed, and so on. The saintly Gerard, too good for the world, had to leave it, his death a melancholy indictment of his actual world—an indictment of the brick-factory-and-tenement world of Lowell and of Quebecois proletarian culture:

> I don't count Gerard in that seedy lot, that crew of bulls—that particular bleak gray jowled pale eyed sneaky fearful French Canadian quality of man, with his black store, his bags of produce, his bottomless mean and secret cellar, his herrings in a barrel, his hidden gold rings, his wife and daughter jongling in another dumb room, his dirty broom in the corner, his piousness, his cold hands, his hot bowels, his well-used whip, his easy greeting and hard opinion—lay me down in sweet India or old Tahiti, I don't want to be buried in *their* cemetery.[19]

By remembering Gerard as not-yet-canonized saint, *memere* rationalized and affirmed his death, emanating an unmodulating melancholy idealism and a scornful indictment of the survivors: had

you not been such as you are—vulgar, coarse, brutal, licentious—
he might have remained.

The book might therefore have been better titled *Her Visions of
Gerard*, since it is primarily about the potent and toxic legacy of
memere's grief, and about the part her grief played in his genesis:

> the whole reason why I ever wrote at all and drew breath to bite in
> vain with pen of ink, great gad with indefensible Usable pencil, be-
> cause of Gerard, the idealism, Gerard the religious hero—"*Write in
> honor of his death*" (*Ecrivez pour l'amour de son mort*) (as one
> would say, write for the love of God)—for by his pain, the birds were
> saved, and the cats and mice, and the poor relatives crying, and my
> mother losing all her teeth in the six terrible weeks prior to his
> death during which she stayed up all night every night and grew
> such a mess of nerves in her stomach that her teeth began falling
> one by one, might sight funny to some hunters of conceit, but this
> wit has had it.[20]

In its nervous contortions this passage both defends and satirizes
the obligation of memory demanded in the legend: notice that
he first quotes an introjected instruction from his mother, then
analyzes that charge (in honor of his death = for the love of his
death = for the love of God; the conversion of grief into fervor), and
finally recalls the maternal suffering that cemented his compliance. Notice, too, that, as with Fitzgerald, her grief, not his, made
him a writer—his feelings about the dead brother do not appear in
this passage, and they are in fact rather infrequently expressed in
the book as a whole. Instead, the book chronicles the early effects
of his mother's melancholy idealism, the division of the world
into the two categories of offal and the sacred that she adopted in
order to avoid mourning. To avoid mourning: rather than an incremental exercise of memory in which one brings to conscious self-
representation a complex and adequate image of the lost, thereby
producing an understanding and acceptance of the boundary that
death has drawn between the dead and the survivor, enshrine-
ment sets up a ready-made and abstract statuette, prohibits further amendment—further repercussion of loss—freezing life at
the instant of loss. In such a frozen universe, the survivor son
cannot become and therefore cannot *be*, he can only *epitomize* a
generic trait, either the saintliness of the dead brother or the
abomination of the world the brother was compelled to reject.
Much of *Visions of Gerard*, in fact, is an attempt to rescue his

memories of an emigré French Canadian childhood from the disgust
his mother directed against that remembered world. Rather than
remembering Gerard, he is struggling to free memory from the
mandatory forms his mother imposed upon it as her way of escap-
ing from the truth.

I have been hovering over Fitzgerald's and Kerouac's theories
concerning the causes of their writing, not to psychoanalyze the two
men, but rather to elucidate their acts of attempted self-analysis.
Such self-attention was, of course, not a rare feature of their writing: perhaps the plainest literary affinity between them is that
they both wrote glaringly autobiographical fiction, seeming at
times, especially in Kerouac's case, to avoid autobiography *per se*
only with a sprinkling of name and date changes. But, however
slight the distinction between autobiography and autobiographical fiction in actual practice, the two writers chose to maintain it,
to be authors rather than autobiographers, to retain as an option
the alterations of fact that the ethics of autobiography prohibit
(though rarely really prevent). To understand this preference for
the leeway of fiction, we might go back to boyhood and adolescence, during which Fitzgerald and Kerouac composed and staged
little dramas, creating worlds that were purely receptive to their
design and manipulation, as opposed to the real world, in which
they were designed by the fixation of another; worlds with themselves at the center, where they were witnessed, at least in fantasy,
by those whose acknowledging eyes they desired to attract. You
will recall that Fitzgerald and Kerouac did not say that their
mothers' grief had made them mournful, but rather that their
mothers' grief had made them writers. In their young lives they
seem seldom to have found what Carraway thinks he finds in
Gatsby, the smile that "faced—or seemed to face—the whole external world for an instant, and then concentrated on you with an
irresistible prejudice in your favor. It understood you just as far as
you wanted to be understood, believed in you as you would like to
believe in yourself, and assured you that it had precisely the impression of you that, at your best, you hoped to convey."[21]

Though such recognition proved to be uncontrollably fitful in
their family's lives, performance within a constructed dramatic
space, or later within the writer-reader space, seemed to offer a
more reliably or predictably accessible recognition. If Fitzgerald and
Kerouac strike us as uncommonly self-absorbed, we might more
precisely say that they are absorbed by the attempt to manufac-
ture a self to be witnessed and affirmed, and thereby brought into

being. But a writer's career can have several trajectories: though Fitzgerald's and Kerouac's writings may have begun as juvenile and adolescent fantasy compensations, self-analytical remarks such as those I discuss are not wish-fulfillments; they are attempts to understand the predicament of consciousness, not to escape it. Writing, for Fitzgerald and Kerouac, is therefore a mixture of compensation and analysis.

But writing is not simply a mixture, because there is a causal connection between fantasy and analysis: disappointment after the failure of fantasy provokes an inquiry into the initial credulity. To understand the development of Fitzgerald's and Kerouac's careers we must attend to their affirmations, an attention that will bring us to what the common reader is apt to remember—not sorrow, but energy, velocity, longing, fulfillment, and intense affirmation, the experience of which accounts for the fierce loyalty toward and abiding celebrity of *The Great Gatsby* and *On the Road* in the general culture, and perhaps also accounts for the secondary status of both books in academic culture. Noting the vigor of affirmation in these bright books does not, however, preclude noticing as well the atmosphere of loss and decay that is intertwined with affirmation: "He had come a long way to this blue lawn, and his dream must have seemed so close that he could hardly fail to grasp it. He did not know that it was already behind him, somewhere back in the vast obscurity beyond the city, where the dark fields of the republic rolled on under the night."[22] Fitzgerald here asserts that longing and mourning can be confused and therefore substituted for one another, a convertibility Kerouac discussed in a 1949 letter that echoes Fitzgerald's passage:

> Lowell, like Winesburg, Ohio or Asheville, North Carolina or Fresno, California or Hawthorne's Salem, is always the place where the darkness of the trees by the river, on a starry night, gives hint of that inscrutable future Americans are always longing and longing for. And when they find that *future*, they begin looking *back*, with sorrows, and an understanding of how man haunts the earth, pacing, prowling, circling in the shades, and the intelligence of the compass, pointing to nothing in sight save starry passion. . . . Strange, is strange, how we be-dot infinity with our thoughts and poor rooftops and home-towns, then go away forever.[23]

Despite their opposed temporal orientations, mourning and longing are both experiences of an inner lack—I lack what I had but which is now dead / I lack what I do not yet have. Beneath the differing temporal orientations, of course, there is a significant difference in the severity of the cause of the lacking: in the case of mourning, one is irremediably exiled; but longing is based on possibility—it is only a matter of time, of devotion to the cause, or overcoming narrow-minded inhibitions, of having enough money, of getting to the right city, and so on. Both mourning and longing are experiences of being exiled from presence, but there is a significant difference between the two kinds of exile and the two kinds of unhappiness they excite.

The substitution of longing for sorrow is therefore rather like myth as Levi-Strauss described it, something that is not truly equivalent to another thing but that can seem to be—slipping into its place, supplying a feeling of resolution and possibility where there had been impasse and futility, but only a feeling of possibility, not the thing itself. (Cool jazz, from Bix Beiderbecke to Chet Baker and Art Pepper, is a kind of flickering, often from moment to moment, between sorrow and longing. This may be why Gerry Mulligan is referred to so frequently in Kerouac's *The Subterraneans*, a book that prolongs such flickering across its full length.) The prime obstacle to such a conversion of mourning into hope is succinctly stated by Emily Dickinson: "To fill a gap, / insert the thing that caused it." A dead thing is removed from the field of the possible, and longing can posit a future object as a sufficient resolution of lack only if it can distract memory from the particular features of the lost thing: but if the lost thing is remembered sharply and in its particularity, the substitution of longing for grief is not a compelling option.

If, however, mourning is inherited, there is no sharp memory of the lost thing because the heir to the mourning did not suffer the loss, and there is thus no knowledge of the loss to restrain the conversion of grief to longing: the object that longing seizes upon does not have to coexist in proximity to the memory of the lost object, and the utter incommensurability of the two is therefore not readily apparent; the success of the conversion does not depend upon the success of a prior repression of sharp memory because there is no remembered thing. But if fulfillment in this way seems more credible to one who has inherited mourning, it is not in fact more possible—the object acquired and incorporated, the sense of lack remains; having failed at its mission, the object is abruptly de-idealized, plummeting into an ontologically opposite state—filth, abomination, decay. If ordinary grief tends to be skeptical toward new worlds, inherited grief may be prone to an extended chain of uncomprehended disappointments, sensations of absolute possibility followed by plunges into disgust and perhaps into paranoid scenarios of occult, deliberate betrayal.

Space prevents me from working through the narrative lines of *The Great Gatsby* and *On the Road*, but if readers recall or even reread these novels, they will see this cycle of elevation and decay governing both novels, at least until Nick Carraway meets Gatsby and Sal Paradise meets Dean Moriarty. In both novels, disappointment shadows hope necessarily and absolutely because there is no extant object that can redeem mourning. Disappointment therefore signifies the inescapability of the work of mourning, in which one relinquishes the hope for a simple annulment of disaster; mourning arising from disappointment is a practical critique of the hope for simple compensation and a call to return to the task of accumulating an adequate conscious representation of the lost. But when such memory work is by definition impossible, as I argue concerning inherited mourning, the lesson of disappointment is tremendously harsher because there is no apparent means for exiting the hell to which the subject is remanded except new acts of self-delusion. To avoid this predicament, Carraway and Paradise posit a flaw in themselves as desirers rather than in desire itself: they imagine themselves to be only fitfully loyal to their own desire, incapable of sustained devotion. If, as Kierkegaard wrote, purity of heart is to will one thing, our narrators add that purity of desire is to desire one thing without variation or diminution. Hence their attraction to two charismatic men who do desire without intermission. Both characters are rather blank, because Fitzgerald and Kerouac cannot *imagine* a desiring subject immune to disappointment: they can only *posit* such a being. Such a blank hypothesis marks the strength with which the narrators desire to believe that there is an escape from inherited mourning, a desire so strong that the possibility that Gatsby or Moriarty might waver is the great unthinkable of the two novels—Gatsby is shot in a case of mistaken identity, and Dean Moriarty's body runs down, but neither is disloyal to his desire. The physical failure of the faithful desirer in fact spares the two narrators from having to represent their heroes as credible persons over the course of time, developing, getting old, discovering that Daisy was not so remarkable after all. Their desire intact at the moment of the last glimpse, they are images sealed in place, so that the narrators can be loyal to an elevated and simple memory. (Kerouac's statements concerning good writing as a kind of "snapshot," his interest in the imagistic brevity of haikus, and his frequent mention of the way people look as he drives away from them all testify to his attraction to this sort of preservative internalization.) They can be loyal in memory to the other's loyalty to desire, consistent in their contemplative allegiance to someone else's consistency, a second-order consistency that in fact allows them to reject the excitement the lost friend stood for, marrying the girl back in the Midwest, going off to a Duke Ellington concert rather than back on the road. The melancholy pseudo-fidelity of the two endings—and I am sure Kerouac modeled his on Fitzgerald's—represents a sonorous outbreak of bad faith, a failure to confront the issue of longing and its perpetual collapse, an issue both authors raise only to swerve from.

As I have tried to understand the course of Fitzgerald's and Kerouac's subsequent writings, I have come to focus on their increasingly open explorations of the significance of recurring disappointment: each time the object fails, one might suppose he simply chose the wrong object—that Daisy was just too callow for Gatsby, for example; or that all objects are too slight to support a noble but impossible desire. But as the series of failures prolongs itself, both writers begin to focus their attention on the demand itself and away from the objects that had failed to satisfy that demand. Once such a meditation is begun, the demand comes to seem anachronistic and irrelevant to the present world, and the world then is a scene of uniform unfulfillment, permanently lacking the originally lost object, whatever it might have been. Expectant desire collapses back into grief, but the exoneration of the actual world from indictment by grievous demand proves to be an odd mercy, not a substitution of a new thing for the lost thing, but the substitution of the possibility of true discovery for the romance of rediscovery: released from the demand that it be a factory for manufacturing simulations of the dead, the actual world manifests itself in the mode of wonder, a capacious and heterogeneous feeling that can include fear and perplexity but that has little connection with the binary claustrophobia of fulfillment and disappointment.

At such a point of altered insight, the emptiness of the world becomes the source of its allure and opportunity, an explicit premise in Kerouac's Zen writings and a fugitive tone in a number of Fitzgerald's later writings, such as this passage from *Tender Is the Night:* "On the centre of the lake, cooled by the piercing current of the Rhone, lay the true centre of the Western World. Upon it floated swans like boats and boats like swans, both lost in the nothingness of the heartless beauty. It was a bright day, with sun glinting on the grass beach below and the white courts of the Kursal. The figures on the courts threw no shadows."[24] Such is not the Christian mysticism discussed by William James and Michel de Certeau, the infilling of lack by the positive substance of grace, but instead the understanding of emptiness—grief's radical lesson —as the precondition for the adventure of the subject in a real world. Emptiness, of course, is an imposed feature—a scene is always empty of some specific thing or trait or tone, expected, hoped for, or dreaded by a particular observer. Emptiness is produced by the encounter of the scene and the observer, and it is the mode in which the scene's autonomy and consequent mystery present themselves to the observer's attention: should one insist that the scene respond to demand, its autonomy will be experienced as debasement and betrayal; but should the experience of emptiness —of the world as stranger, rather than as other—be viewed as a strange announcement rather than as the end of all hope, there is the chance that the observer might come across an unsettling something, streaked with fatality and therefore lonely, but also interesting and mysteriously companionable. I am trying here to communicate the tone I find, often in late Fitzgerald and some-times in Kerouac, a tone that is for me now quite moving, and more beautiful than the familiar strenuousness of the passages I found so irresistible when I was younger. This passage, for exam-ple, from Fitzgerald's unfinished novel, now called *The Love of the Last Tycoon*, demonstrates that tone:

> They sat on high stools and had tomato broth and hot sandwiches. It was more intimate than anything they had done, and they both felt a dangerous sort of loneliness, and felt it in each other. They shared in varied scents of the drug-store, bitter and sweet and sour, and the mystery of the waitress, with only the outer part of her hair dyed and black beneath, and, when it was over, the still life of their empty plates—a sliver of potato, a sliced pickle and an olive stone.[25]

But, of course, there is no happy ending here. For Fitzgerald, the ability to experience the world in this exquisitely ordinary way depended upon stopping his drinking. Perhaps this is the final affinity between the two writers, the disastrous attunement of

their souls to liquor's song, to the fluency of its promise of fulfillment, and its putative annulment of the world's alien features—to
the horrible and perfect eloquence of its conversation with grief. I
want to end this essay thinking of this attunement and of all that
that song drowned out, of all the writing we do not have.

Notes

1. F. Scott Fitzgerald, *Afternoon of an Author: A Selection of Uncollected Sto-ries and Essays*, with an introduction and notes by Arthur Mizener (New York: Charles Scribner's Sons, 1957), 184.
2. Ibid., 184.
3. F. Scott Fitzgerald, *The Crack-Up*, ed. Edmund Wilson (New York: New Directions, 1945), 80–81.
4. Ibid., 81, 81, 79.
5. Ibid., 71.
6. Arthur Mizener, in fact, considers "Author's House" to be a continuation of the same urgent meditation that produced *The Crack-Up* essays. Fitzgerald, *Afternoon*, 183.
7. Ibid., 69.
8. Ibid., 185.
9. Ibid., 189.
10. Quoted in Matthew J. Bruccoli, *Some Sort of Epic Grandeur: The Life of F. Scott Fitzgerald* (New York: Harcourt Brace Jovanovitch, 1981), 15.
11. Nicholas Abraham and Maria Torok, *The Shell and the Kernel*, vol. 1, trans. Nicholas T. Rand (Chicago: University of Chicago Press, 1994), 99–165.
12. Ibid., 165–207.
13. Nicholas T. Rand, "Secrets and Posterity: The Theory of the Transgenera-tional Phantom," in ibid., 166, 168.
14. Abraham and Torok, *Shell and the Kernel*, 174.
15. Christopher Bollas, "Moods and the Conservative Process," *The Shadow of the Object: Psychoanalysis of the Unthought Known* (New York: Columbia University Press, 1987), 113. Thanks to Kathleen Woodward for introducing me to Bollas's essay.
16. Eric L. Santner, *Stranded Objects: Mourning, Memory, and Film in Postwar Germany* (Ithaca: Cornell University Press, 1990), 37–38. Santner is quoting from Michael Schneider, "Fathers and Sons, Retrospectively: The Damaged Relationship between Two Generations," *New German Critique* 59 (winter 1984): 43.
17. Fitzgerald, *The Great Gatsby* (1925; reprint, New York: Charles Scribner's Sons, 1980), 112.
18. Jack Kerouac, *Visions of Gerard* (1958; reprint, New York: Penguin, 1987), 129.
19. Ibid., 9.
20. Ibid., 112.
21. Fitzgerald, *The Great Gatsby*, 48.
22. Ibid., 182.
23. Ann Charters, ed., *A Bibliography of Works by Jack Kerouac, 1939–1975* (New York City: Phoenix Bookshop, 1975), 16–17.
24. F. Scott Fitzgerald, *Tender Is the Night* (1933; reprint, New York: Charles Scribner's Sons, 1962), 147–48.
25. F. Scott Fitzgerald, *The Last Tycoon* (New York: Charles Scribner's Sons, 1941), 85.

Further Reading

Abraham, Nicholas, and Maria Torok. *The Shell and the Kernel.* Vol. 1, trans. Nicholas T. Rand. Chicago: University of Chicago Press, 1994.
    Abraham and Torok represent the furthest development of the exploration of introjection and melancholia in contemporary French thought, especially in their concept of the phantom of inherited mourning.

Bollas, Christopher. *The Shadow of the Object: Psychoanalysis of the Unthought Known.* New York: Columbia University Press, 1987.
    A subtle study of psychic ephemera such as moods in relation to grieving.

Lacan, Jacques. *The Seminar of Jacques Lacan.* Book 7, *The Ethics of Psychoanalysis,* trans. Dennis Porter. New York: Norton, 1992.
    Lacan's frustrating but extraordinary exploration of the relation between mourning and law in Sophocles' *Antigone,* and in the analysis of the play in Hegel's *Phenomenology of Spirit.*

Mitscherlich, Alexander, and Margarete Mitscherlich. *The Inability to Mourn: Principles of Collective Behavior,* trans. Beverley R. Placzek. New York: Grove Press, 1975.
    A landmark work demonstrating the extension of psychological concepts of mourning into the analysis of society and collective emotion.

Santner, Eric L. *Stranded Objects: Mourning, Memory, and Film in Postwar Germany.* Ithaca: Cornell University Press, 1990.
    A brilliant extension of the Mitscherlichs' concept into the analysis of postwar German film as an exploration of mourning and its refusal.

Spillius, Elizabeth Bott, ed. *Melanie Klein Today: Developments in Theory and Practice.* Vol. 1, *Mainly Theory,* and Vol. 2, *Mainly Practice.* New York: Routledge, 1988.
    Two invaluable volumes demonstrating the persistent vitality of Klein's understanding of the psychologically constitutive role of loss.

JULIA STERN

LIVE BURIAL AND ITS DISCONTENTS

MOURNING BECOMES MELANCHOLIA IN HARRIET JACOBS'S *INCIDENTS*

AUTOBIOGRAPHICAL ACCOUNTS of African American life under slavery, like Holocaust testimonies and the works of art they have inspired, seemingly give proof to Peter Homans's eloquent assertion that memory is a work of mourning and mourning a work of memory.[1] Both black slaves in colonial and antebellum America and Jewish inmates of Nazi labor and death camps endured what sociologist Orlando Paterson identifies as two defining features of the slave's ontological condition: "natal alienation," or the obliteration of organic family ties, and "social death," or the disenfranchisement from and actual erasure of any place in the free community.[2] For liberated slaves and survivors alike, life-writing becomes an act of meta-mourning; the painful sifting that enables both remembering and grieving must be performed anew in the act of literary production. In this essay I take up three neglected passages from Harriet Jacobs's 1861 *Incidents in the Life of a Slave Girl, Written by Herself,* arguably the most haunting and lyrical testament to a woman's life under slavery bequeathed to American letters from the nineteenth century.[3] Driven by the losses that mark its author's history, *Incidents* would seem to be enabled by the "great creativity" that Homans views as one outcome of "successful" mourning.

But how "successful" can such grief-work be if its implications extend beyond the purview of personal suffering into the realm of mass trauma? When entire groups endure unrelenting experiences of dehumanizing, disabling treatment and recurrent separation and death, the notion of mourning itself might be better understood as collective melancholia. In "Mourning and Melancholia," Freud compares so-called normal grief to a "morbidly pathological disposition" in which response to bereavement comes to subsume the daily business of living. Freud identifies such a state as "melancholia."[4] In light of these definitions that, eighty years after their initial formulation, remain vital for contemporary therapists, how do we account for the affect experienced—and in Jacobs's case, *imaginatively represented*—in the wake of unceasing personal and transpersonal devastation?

Publishing her narrative in 1861, one year before the United States emancipates its slaves, Jacobs accounts for the very sort of extraordinary, durative, and physically debilitating experiences of brutality categorized by both twentieth-century historians and psychologists as "collective traumas"; these would include among other cases the Nazi extermination of 6 million European Jews, an equal number of Russians, and untold gypsies, homosexuals, and political dissenters; and white owners' and traders' enslavement, torture, and familial destruction of nearly 60 million Africans and African Americans over a period of more than two hundred years. Far from being "successfully" mourned, such ongoing legacies of trauma are memorialized—encrypted rather than worked through and eventually, under optimal conditions, released—in the very sort of melancholic creative formation of which Jacobs's narrative proves a primary example.[5]

Why Incidents *and Mourning?*

In the twelve years since Jean Fagan Yellin authenticated and documented the material history of Harriet Jacobs's life in the introduction and editorial apparatus of her monumental, definitive 1987 Harvard edition of Jacobs's *Incidents*, literary critics have created a virtual Jacobs industry. Americanists, feminists, historicists, and race theorists, as well as scholars of autobiography, gender, and sexuality, have contributed to an ever-growing, interdisciplinary conversation about this text. Yet beyond a few undeveloped remarks made about the grief motivating Jacobs's story, little to none of the secondary literature deals directly with the relation of mourning or melancholia to writing in her autobiography.[6] Such oversight of what I consider to be *the* affective undercurrent organizing *Incidents* may be the result of the reluctance of many scholars of African American literature to bring psychoanalytic theory—in either its Freudian or numerous post-Freudian (Winnicottian, Lacanian,

Kohutian, feminist) incarnations—to bear on the reading of slave narratives.

This rejection of psychoanalysis as a viable method for explicating African American literature arose, nearly forty years ago, in response to Stanley Elkins's controversial study *Slavery: A Problem in American Institutional and Intellectual Life* (1959). As Jennifer Fleischner notes, Elkins's argument was sociological rather than psychoanalytic in orientation, turning on a factitious taxonomy of slave personality "types" such as the much maligned, purportedly docile, "Sambo" figure.[7] Far from providing a deep or searching account of the interiority of slave experience— what in the late 1950s and early 1960s might have been called the "psychological profiles" of individual slaves—Elkins based his composite analyses on secondary sources; he made no use of the artifacts that were to revolutionize the historical study of slavery: narratives, letters, speeches, and interviews produced by slaves themselves.[8] The inflammatory nature of Elkins's work led scholars of African American history and culture to reject *tout court* such seemingly "psychological" analyses. The result was a swerve toward materialist readings that left slave affect—with its own history—out of the scholarly equation.

Marking an absolute break with the anti-analytic impulse governing contemporary treatment of African American narrative, Fleischner's *Mastering Slavery: Memory, Family, and Identity in Women's Slave Narratives* (1996) recuperates a powerful history of slave feeling based on the autobiographical evidence of five black women writers. Henry Louis Gates Jr., perhaps the most influential contemporary scholar of this tradition, notes the startling persuasiveness of Fleischner's psychoanalytic method, identifying her contribution as "a stunning achievement, an instance in which a heretofore 'marginal' literature is revealed in its astonishing complexity by a critical method not before applied to those very texts."[9]

Compelled by the conjunction of "memory, abuse, and narrative," Fleischner reads the nineteenth-century slave family as an entity constituted and reconstituted by losses, substitutions, displaced griefs, and interdicted acts of mourning.[10] In so doing, she complicates an earlier vision of African American domesticity under slavery as the story of the violation, fracture, and dispersal of kin. Fleischner thus salvages and redeploys for African American literary studies the heretofore reprobated psychoanalytic concepts of repression, displacement, screen memory, idealization, the incorporation of parental imagoes, and mourning for objects rather than for object-relations—what, following Freud, I would call fetishism.

Taking off from Fleischner, who emphasizes Jacobs's heretofore untheorized masculine identification with her father and brother, two heroic men who made resistance to slavery the abiding fact of their lives, I also put psychoanalytic theory at the center of my inquiry.[11] But unlike Fleischner, who stresses the significance of an internal, idealized male object world for Jacobs's personal and autobiographical vision, I am interested in the way that mourning-become-melancholia informs the former slave's material and narrative self-representations. To explore this claim, I return to three scenes from *Incidents:* the episode detailing Jacobs's terror and grief over the thought of losing her small daughter who, desperate for the mother who cannot tend to her needs, disappears for several hours under the master's house; the passage detailing Jacobs's fanciful, revised account of the broadside advertisement with which her demented master, driven by sexual obsession upon her escape, has plastered the local countryside; and the semi-penultimate paragraph of the last chapter of the autobiography, marked by Jacobs's odd narrative displacements, which center upon death rather than freedom, and which inform the manner in which she brings closure to her tale.

In the first instance, mournful ruminations quickly shift into infanticidal fantasies during the brief period in which "Linda Brent" (Jacobs's pseudonym) mistakenly believes that her missing child somehow has died on the plantation of her master's son. After having served as an urban house slave in the "Flint" (Norcom) family for over fifteen years, Jacobs is exiled by her sexually insatiable master for the "crime" of refusing to consent to his advances; it is against this backdrop of physical isolation and unexpected threat —Norcom's son has expressed his untoward lust for Jacobs as well—that the author imagines the death of her daughter.

The second passage recounts the narrator's imaginative experience of "working-through" via the act of rewriting: here, to obviate the grief necessarily provoked by her evil master's debasing reduction of her selfhood to sheer voluptuous physicality, Jacobs rescripts Norcom's dehumanizing broadside advertisement for her capture into a celebration of her superior mind. What she deploys in place of the broadside text—for the benefit of virtuous white middle-class women readers of the autobiography—is her own, decorporalizing self-portrait, motivated as much by wish fulfillment as it is by fact.

Supplementing this intranarrative substitution to fascinating extranarrative effect is the editorial apparatus Yellin herself deploys in the Harvard edition; since broadsides for the capture of runaway slaves number among the more ephemeral artifacts of the "peculiar institution," rarely surviving exposure to the elements, Yellin appends an even more remarkable document in its stead: a facsimile photograph of the actual newspaper advertisement James Norcom placed in the *American Beacon* of Norfolk, Virginia, on 4 July 1835, offering a reward for the fugitive Jacobs.[12]

Given the doctor's grandiose, exhibitionistic entanglement with the slave woman's grandmother, uncles, aunts, and children, and his penchant for triumphantly assaulting her traumatized family with letters and other documents pertaining to "Linda Brent's" alleged whereabouts, it is likely that Jacobs's beloved grandmother Molly Hornblow ("Aunt Martha") and her uncle Mark Ramsey ("Uncle Phillip"—purchased by Molly Hornblow and, of all her children, the only son to remain a constant presence in Molly's life) actually read and retained the newspaper clipping in question. Under the precarious circumstances of Jacobs's seven-year-long interment in the coffin-sized crawl space of her grandmother's attic, it is more than probable that "Aunt Martha" and "Uncle Phillip" would have shared the advertisement with Jacobs, who anxiously awaited any details about her miserable fate, suspended as she was between the social death of slavery and the live burial of her hiding place, which she termed the "loophole of retreat."[13]

In creating the narrative that became *Incidents* almost two decades after the conclusion of the events it recounts, it is likely that Jacobs underwent an extended, arduous process of self-reflection; given the permanently crippling physical effects of her self-willed incarceration under Dr. Norcom's very nose, such ruminations could not help but be informed, to whatever degree and however subliminally, in reaction to the maniacal master's quasi-pornographic newspaper portrait of herself as a younger, fully able woman. I examine Jacobs's acts of reading, reflection, substitution, and rewriting as phantasmagoric miniatures for her autobiographical impulse writ large: both part and whole are inflected by unstaunched grief for a self that has been overwritten by slavery's violent inscriptions.[14]

Finally, I explore the displacement and substitution that guide Jacobs's rhetorical strategy for the paragraph that inaugurates her conclusion. Other scholars have focused on the larger shape of the final chapter, particularly the section that her abolitionist-minded novelist-editor Lydia Maria Child convinced Jacobs to drop because she felt it was too politically incendiary. (The chapter closed on a revolutionary note, with a sketch of John Brown's raid on Harpers Ferry.) Working on a smaller scale, I examine, instead, the obituary of Jacobs's "Uncle Philip," with which she draws her published account to its virtual close. The author pointedly says that she could have terminated her tale with a discussion of the bill of sale that led to her eventual freedom, a document that appalls the fugitive Jacobs rather than affords her relief. Having been purchased by the devoted northern mother of the baby for whom she cares so that this mistress (Cornelia Grinnell Willis, "Mrs. Bruce") can ensure Jacobs's manumission, the author, horrified by such a method of gaining "freedom," to which she has not consented, lets the documents marking the putative end to her legal invisibility go unrepresented.[15] Instead, Jacobs substitutes for such testimonials to her former social death a movingly celebratory account of her uncle's life and passing. Mourning circulating legitimately through the public sphere of print—the obituary appeared in a local newspaper—thus becomes a screen for the unspeakable and immaterial melancholia provoked by slavery itself, an affective reality that the autobiography rearticulates in its uncanny form.[16]

Trauma, Convention, and Form

Such scholars of African American literature as Henry Louis Gates Jr., Charles T. Davis, Robert Stepto, Houston A. Baker Jr., William Andrews, Valerie Smith, and Hazel Carby have identified and explicated the various literary imperatives under which former slaves labored while composing their memoirs of life in bondage. Like Renaissance verse, slave narratives unfold according to received historical notions of form. Just as the Shakespearean sonnet has fourteen lines, most often divided into two quatrains and a sestet, so late-eighteenth- and nineteenth-century slave narratives are introduced by white editors, framed by authenticating documents, and prefaced or appended with letters written by famous abolitionists; according to convention, they begin with a story of early familial loss and culminate with occluded accounts of escape. Those who aid and abet runaway narrators are never named; Underground Railway routes go unidentified; and strategies for final leave-taking constitute the most vital—necessarily suppressed—details of all that goes "unspoken" by such texts.

These formal features of Jacobs's narrative resonate politically, and so they have been read. But little attention has been paid to a set of affective gaps or displacements that dapple *Incidents* and mark its uniqueness in the genre; it is to these episodes that I now turn. In each of the following scenes, transformed bodies substitute for abject ones: a child wished dead returns alive and is mysteriously replaced by a slaughtered snake; the image of a hyper-eroticized female slave becomes a thoughtful, literate talking head; and, standing in for nonexistent manumission papers, the notorious bill of sale, documenting an African American woman's legal, economic, and political condition as the property of "Mrs. Bruce," itself goes unrepresented; in its place, Jacobs inserts the obituary notice of her uncle, testifying to the spiritual liberation of a black man. In the pages that follow, I hope to offer some tentative speculations about the meaning of these melancholic displacements and identifications and, so, to return affect to politics in our understanding of *Incidents.*

"Scenes at the Plantation"; or, Live Burial

In chapter 16 of her autobiography, Jacobs narrates an ostensibly minor "incident" that emblematizes her insights about the "human parasitism" marking the master-slave relation, the way that black labor is devoured and black bodies are wasted by the white owners who purportedly have African Americans' well-being in mind according to the specious logic of paternalism.[17] Under the trials of plantation life, Jacobs's daughter "Ellen" (Louisa Matilda) breaks down and disappears:

> As it was noon, I ventured to go down and search for her. The great house was raised two feet above the ground. I looked under it, and saw her about midway, fast asleep. I crept under and drew her out. As I held in my arms, I thought about how well it would be for her if she never waked up; and I uttered my thought aloud. I was startled to hear someone say "Did you speak to me?" I looked up, and saw Mr. Flint standing beside me. He said nothing further, but turned, frowning, away. That night he sent Ellen a biscuit and a cup of sweetened milk. This generosity surprised me. I learned afterwards, that in the afternoon he had killed a large snake, which crept from under the house; I suppose that incident prompted his unusual kindness. (187)

This evocative passages begins by reinscribing what Patterson characterizes as the natal alienation so crucial to the success of slavery; plantation life produces the condition of motherlessness in a child whose female parent, though very much alive, is forced to endure the fate of the socially dead. Far from the first time she has uttered such fatal thoughts regarding her child's welfare, these words recur throughout the narrative as a melancholic refrain;[18] under such particular circumstances, *at the level of the wish,* Jacobs's infanticidal fantasy seeks to literalize, so as to put to an end, that which the slave mother intuits to be true in the operations of reality. It is no accident that young "Mr. Flint" will mistake himself as the referent of the unrecorded malediction he overhears ("how I wish you were dead!"), for he is a man with a guilty conscience, a subject that I discuss shortly.

Before doing so, however, it is crucial to note that slavery's gothic dynamics, described by Eric Sundquist in his literary elaboration of Patterson's work, spring to material life in this chilling scene.[19] In fact, the poetics of space at work in the passage brilliantly replay the physical subordination of black females under slavery and emphasize their problems of place. "Ellen's" concealment outside, underneath, but also on the margins of the big house enacts the notion of slavery as social death by rehearsing its dynamic of live burial. Such encryptment also foreshadows Jacobs's own furtive act of self-positioning at the beginning of her protracted escape from slavery, when she secretes herself in her grandmother's attic for seven seemingly endless years.

Appearing on the scene of this alienated domesticity is the paranoid "Mr. Flint" (James Norcom Jr.), a weak facsimile of his evil father. His appearance raises disturbing questions. What does he mistakenly infer from eavesdropping upon Jacobs's muttered death wish for her daughter? In addition to the metaphysical injustice underlying their relationship as master and slave, of what additional criminal impulses can the man be accused? What potentially unspeakable deeds has he meditated, so heinous that, in the face of them, six-year-old "Ellen" would be better off not just symbolically, but physically, dead? Jacobs's perplexity about the master's uncharacteristically kind behavior toward "Ellen" in the wake of her disappearance and recovery signals nothing less than these suspicions: indeed, his gifts of food remain inexplicable to the slave mother until she learns about the killing of the snake and speculates that such dangerous "sport" (sexual or predatory?) has elevated his mood.

An even darker picture of the young master emerges as we begin to decode the meaning of "Mr. Flint's" edible offering. Its first component, the biscuit, would have been a staple of southern fare by midcentury, with the wide availability and improved distribution of white flour, eaten by the white master class and, occasionally, by elite house slaves as well. This breadstuff is significant as an emblem of class, reaffirming the status of Jacobs's high-ranking African American family or serving as a token of the master's beneficence, his extension of an occasional privilege to a favored slave. The sweetened milk, in contrast, carries more ominous symbolic weight. Most often associated with slave mothers in Jacobs's narrative, maternal milk devolves virtually without exception into the property of the mistress, who alienates the precious stuff from its primary biological telos and reroutes it to the mouths of white babies. To give a black child milk, even cow's milk, then, is an ironic gesture: it is to offer as a luxury a foodstuff whose naturalness has been perverted by the institution of slavery. Even more significant than "Mr. Flint's" co-optation of maternal nurture in the tendering of milk is the adulterated form his tribute takes: an inadequate venue through which he can convey his message, the merely maternal must be supplemented, sugared, to be made sufficient for his purposes. In light of this, how might we come to understand the nature of a deal that must be sweetened? Surely the taste of such a bargain is bitter to swallow indeed.

We can begin to read these symbols politically by considering the connection, to borrow the words of Sidney Mintz, between "sweetness and power."[20] Sugar was the ultimate comestible artifact of slavery; it was largely for this priceless good that America's slave trade with the West Indies became established. Understood in these terms, "Mr. Flint's" supplement, the sweetened milk, reinscribes in the mystified form of a gift the parasitic dynamic that obtains between "Ellen" and himself. A more local and speculative reading identifies an additional level of menace in the scene. "Mr. Flint" has been stopped from harming the sleeping child, first, by the presence of the large snake that dwells beneath the big house, and second, by the advent of "Ellen's" mother, who rescues the child from both the visible reptile and the invisible viper who lurks in the shadows and then suddenly materializes. Through the gift of food, "Mr. Flint" rewards "Ellen" for her response to—most likely her silence in the face of—an act that I would suggest is distinctly unsavory. Co-opting what by rights is only the mother's to offer, the young master attempts to palliate the slave child's potential disgust.

Explicating the scene figuratively, we might see the snake as an emblem of the "Flints'" diabolical sexuality: Jacobs repeatedly describes "Dr. Flint" as a hissing demon who whispers foul thoughts into her ears and who seeks her fall from innocence into the corruption of his embrace.[21] According to these associations, we can view Jacobs's deliverance of "Ellen" from under the house as an intervention that breaks the cycle of sexual abuse that young "Mr. Flint" would like to repeat, in masterly fashion, on the body of Jacobs's preadolescent daughter. The murder of the snake can be seen as an enactment of the son's Oedipal drama, in which young "Mr. Flint" assumes the power of his father by slaying the doctor's symbolic totem. The killing also functions as a diversionary tactic, expressing the son's rage over a conquest lost and simultaneously covering up the real nature of his dirty "business" underneath the house.

Finally, the scene functions emblematically, telegraphing a basic axiom of antislavery thought: the snake under the plantation house, coexisting with the sleeping black girl child, forms a natural image of a practice that is tragically cultural. The serpent stands for slavery, the deadly doppelgänger of nineteenth-century American domesticity. Threatening the safety of all those who dwell within the house—both white and black—and menacing the innocence of African American girls in particular, slavery is a hungry viper, making parasites of human beings.[22] That in the face of this monster the slave mother believes her daughter would be better off dead only emphasizes the hideous dilemma confronting those whom slavery has buried alive: if social death produces in its victims a chronic melancholia, then real death, with its promise of endurable—because it is actual—mourning, would seem to offer the only cure.

Advertisement for Myself, or the Melancholic Mirror

"Ellen's" hiatus beneath and reemergence from the plantation house uncannily prefigure her mother's disappearance and eventual resurrection from the living death of slavery. This motif of repression and return, the refrain of Jacobs's story, would seem to rehearse the very movements of mourning itself: when a beloved object disappears as a result of separation or death, the survivor conjures imaginative representations of the lost object and, over time, comes to reconstitute that figure in full, contradictory complexity, internalizing a multifaceted image that releases the sufferer from fixation upon an idealized singularity that, over time, could lead to melancholia.

James Norcom's newspaper advertisement for the runaway Jacobs testifies to one such perversely idealized melancholic obsession. Keeping in mind that the doctor would have been charged by the line, if not by the word, for the notice regarding his fugitive slave, that he would have had to "pay," as it were, a material price for his madness, I quote the text in full:

$100 REWARD

Will be given for the apprehension and delivery of my Servant Girl HARRIET. She is a light mulatto, 21 years of age, about 5 feet 4 inches high, of a thick and corpulent habit, having on her head a thick covering of black hair that curls naturally, but which can be easily combed straight. She speaks easily and fluently, and has an agreeable carriage and address. Being a good seamstress, she has been accustomed to dress well, has a variety of very fine clothes, made in the prevailing fashion, and will probably appear, if abroad, tricked out in gay and fashionable finery. As this girl absconded from the plantation of my son without any known cause or provocation, it is probable that she designs to transport herself to the North.

The above reward, with all reasonable charges, will be given for apprehending her, or securing her in any prison or jail within the U. States.

All persons are hereby forewarned against harboring or entertaining her or being in any way instrumental to her escape, under the most rigorous penalties of the law.

JAMES NORCOM
Edenton, N.C. June 30 (215)

If "delivery" in the context of Norcom's ad pertains to the transfer of property, then it is telling that Norcom immediately refers to Jacobs as his "servant girl," rather than as his bondswoman. Does the fact that she is a "light mulatto" "serving" in the antebellum

South simply telegraph, in nineteenth-century code, that Jacobs is enslaved? Or does Norcom disingenuously intend to suggest that the runaway enjoys a more privileged status than that of a common slave woman, implying at the level of his prose a relation that he has been, in reality, denied? If so, one cannot help but read the advertisement as directed not only to potential slave hunters in the newspaper audience, but also to Jacobs herself.

The rhetorical symptoms of Norcom's compulsion are far from subtle: redundant, and therefore costly, diction underscores the doctor's fetishization of Jacobs's fleshiness: both "thick" and "corpulent," her body, according to the master, speaks both of relative privilege and erotic appeal. Norcom's extravagant description of the slave woman's hair is equally interpretable and actually borders on the lurid: why does he specify that the locks in question lie on Jacobs's *head*? What does this imply about the master's obscene imagination of the hair that covers other parts of her body? Such an overdetailed account (what we in the twentieth century call "too much information") suggests something that readers of *Incidents* already know, a fact that does not work to the advantage of Norcom's reputation: earlier in the narrative, Jacobs has recorded that her master, driven to distraction by the news that his slave is to become the mother of another man's child, orders the pregnant Jacobs to bring him a pair of shears and performs upon her a rape-like haircut (77), during which the author fears for her life.

In James Norcom's demented obsession with Jacobs, displaced forms of violence like the assault on her hair stand in for more permanently damaging forms of sexual abuse. Despite the lengths he has gone to disavow her resistance, at times even in public, Norcom refuses to acknowledge Jacobs's nonconsent. Instead, recounting her "agreeable carriage and address," Norcom actually seems to suggest that the slave woman comports herself to arouse his desire. Certainly the doctor's extravagant interlude on the subject of her "fine clothes" would appear to support his insidious claim that Jacobs has enjoyed relative luxury at his hands as a function of their purported relation; but such sartorial splendor is meant for his eyes alone: beyond the purview of his lurid gaze, the well-dressed Jacobs devolves into nothing less than a prostitute, "tricked out in gay or fashionable finery." Most remarkable is his claim that Jacobs has "absconded" "without known cause or provocation." The profound sexual delusion under which Dr. Norcom labors makes it impossible for him to see the effects of his so-called desire for Jacobs,[23] though the final lines of his ad bring this truth home: "forewarning" all persons who might abet, much less "entertain," the fugitive that they will be rigorously prosecuted, the man virtually confesses that erotomania, rather than economic interest, drives his madness.

Tellingly, Jacobs rescripts the pornographic portrait over which we can imagine Norcom luxuriating into an image so chaste that its visual tableau does not venture below the neck; indeed, the "Linda" described in Jacobs's version of the broadside is so evidently superior to her degraded enemy that it is as if she were disembodied:

> *$300 REWARD!* Ran away from the subscriber, an intelligent, bright, mulatto girl, named Linda, 21 years of age. Five feet four inches high. Dark eyes, and black hair inclined to curl; but it can be made straight. Has a decayed spot on a front tooth. She can read and write, and in all probability will try to get to the Free States. All persons are forbidden, under penalty of law, to harbor or employ said slave. $150 will be given to whoever takes her in the state, and $300 if taken out of the state and delivered to me, or lodged in jail.
>
>   Dr. Flint (97)

By the time he had placed the ad for Jacobs's capture in the Virginia paper, sometime after the broadside poster had appeared locally in North Carolina, James Norcom might have become unwilling to offer as large a reward for Jacobs's capture as the sum indicated in the broadside, a fact that would explain the discrepancy in bounty money in the two texts; it is also possible that Jacobs, attempting to relocate her value from sexual body to searching mind, emphasizes, in a redundant manner worthy of "Dr. Flint," her "intellig"[ence] and "bright"[ness]; Jacobs calculates that a potential captor would deserve three times what her master imagines as a fair reward for redeeming such a prized slave.

When she turns from mind to body in order to describe how her hair might be dressed to enhance a potential disguise as a white woman, Jacobs utterly avoids James Norcom's perversely visceral account: in her version, the curly hair "can be made straight," a locution that avoids any trace of personal, potentially erotic, agency; it is as if, by sheer force of will, without raising hand to head, the fugitive can alter her appearance. But the most emblematic detail in the entire account involves Jacobs's description of a "decayed spot on a front tooth." Remarkably, Norcom omits this striking blemish; perhaps in his fatal attraction to Jacobs, he has not even noticed it.

Why, then, does Jacobs place the rotten tooth front and center in her revisionist account of Norcom's broadside? What does this small, soft, black absence, overshadowing a relatively large, hard, white, presence, have to do with either the politics or the affect underwriting Jacobs's self-portrait? As I argue in my work on Edgar Allan Poe, teeth are a corporeal hinge, bridging the gap between life and death: while dental whiteness symbolizes youth and vigor, rotten teeth evoke (premature) age and imminent decay.[24] Foregrounding the blackened tooth in her revised version of the broadside portrait, thrusting her least attractive feature directly in his face, Jacobs strategically explodes Norcom's pornographic reification; at the same time, her emphasis on the rotten tooth calls political attention to the way slavery's "paternal care" accelerates organic processes that signal the onset of death.

Immediately following the abrupt insertion of this de-idealizing detail, Jacobs returns again to assertions of her superior mind. Not only can she read, a skill that, under southern law, was punishable for both slaves and those who taught them; she can write as well, a talent that poignantly prefigures her later authorial career. Jacobs's ability to write has sociological resonance as well: scholars of literacy in eighteenth- and nineteenth-century America note a significant discrepancy between the numbers of Americans who could read and perhaps "sign" their names (there were many) and those who could read and write (there were far fewer).[25] That Jacobs falls into the latter category is an index of both her intelligence and her ambition; that James Norcom suppresses this fact, emphasizing instead her pleasant vocal powers speaks volumes about how his racism, his sexism, and, most of all, his madness delude him into underestimating the intellectual resourcefulness of the fugitive who comes to outwit him.

The slave woman is certainly more eloquent and politically astute than her master; in reworking Norcom's crudely clinical portrait, the slightest noncorporeal details, even geographical descriptions, themselves become politically expressive: rather than traveling "north," as Norcom has indicated she undoubtedly will do, the slave woman's "Linda" is headed to the "Free States." There, far from planning to be "entertained" according to Norcom's paranoid idea that the mere sight of Jacobs drives strange men to offer her money and aid in exchange for the pleasures of her company, the author imagines being gainfully "employed," a shift that signals her complete rejection of the doctor's compulsion to view her as a sexual body rather than as an economic agent.

And in her final, most trenchant revision of Norcom's prose, Jacobs identifies herself as "said slave," using the heretofore unspeakable term that the master cannot bring himself to deploy. Jacobs's deep political and affective insight lies in her return to and insistence upon the literal: her emphasis on the distinction between the live burial of slavery and the actual entombment in her grandmother's attic; the stress she places on her sorrowful reaction to being purchased by her northern employer, whose courage in working to free the fugitive she nevertheless admires; and her freedom itself, the quotidian reality of which receives little treatment in her autobiography, since it is 1861 and, in the ethos created by the Fugitive Slave Law, the so-called liberty of northern blacks can, at the hands of any slave catcher, come to mean less than nothing.

Trauma and the Literal:
Obituary as Autobiography

Furtively composing her autobiography at night between the years 1852 and 1858, while she lived with and cared for the children of Nathaniel Parker Willis, a pro-slavery magazine editor who was unaware of Jacobs's project, and his anti-slavery wife, Cornelia Grinnell Willis, who supported Jacobs's freedom, what did Jacobs seek to achieve? Both inspired by and indebted to the abolitionist movement that sponsored her, Jacobs created in *Incidents* a powerful political contribution to the cause, addressed to those middle-class white northern women who thought that slavery had no impact on their lives but who, upon reading her testimony, might become enlightened and even aroused to action. Less discussed is the fact that Jacobs's book makes a vital contribution to the affective history of African American life under slavery as well, and it is in this regard that we might view her re-vision of Norcom's broadside advertisement as an emotional miniature for her autobiographical ambitions. The features she highlights as she rescripts this text—her intelligence, her literacy, and her flawed physicality—attempt to correct, or overwrite, the master's pornographically debasing and reductive image, creating instead a complex self-portrait of a woman of strong mind dwelling in a radically imperfect body.

In this gesture, Jacobs attempts to mourn for the self that has been buried as a slave, and she does so in the face of a trauma so overwhelming that its most pervasive effect is melancholia. If, as Mitchell Breitwieser movingly asserts, such pathological disturbances of grief involve the painful encryptment of static, idealized representations of the lost, while mourning mandates the procession of multiple images through what he calls the mental "museum" of the dead in order that a complex image can be incorporated dynamically rather than buried alive, then I see Jacobs's microcosmic autobiography—the revised broadside—as an attempt to assert motion over against the suspended animation of slavery.[26]

The peculiar three-paragraph ending of Jacobs's narrative, a conclusion that, like melancholia itself, avoids its necessary object and thus resists real closure, presents, however, a far darker testament to Jacobs's affective state. Though the author asserts that her sympathetic employer has paid "money for [the fugitive's] freedom" (200), Jacobs recognizes the fact that in order to enable her liberty, Mrs. Bruce has had to purchase her for cash. Instead of describing hypothetical manumission papers, Jacobs alludes to, without representing, the bill of sale identifying herself as property to be bought and "sold at last in New York City" (200), where slavery ostensibly is illegal, but where, in fact, the Fugitive Slave Law makes such transactions possible.

Documents attesting to freedom are occluded entirely, and the bill of sale is mentioned in a fleeting paragraph. Instead, Jacobs draws her book to the beginning of its conclusion with a quotation from her "Uncle Phillip's" obituary. What does this bizarre displacement signify? How are we to understand the shift in Jacobs's identifications with and her nonrepresentations of live burial (the bill of sale indicating slave status) and putative life in limbo (the nonexistent receipt indicating that Jacobs will not be held as Mrs. Bruce's slave, though such a document would have no legal efficacy should she be kidnapped by a slave catcher and sold south) to the inclusion of textual evidence certifying a physical death (the obituary marking "Uncle Phillip's" passing)?

Of this notice, Jacobs writes: "It was the only case I ever knew of such an honor being conferred on a colored person" (200). Composed by one of his friends, the one-of-a-kind obituary reads, "Now that death has laid him low, they call him a good man and a useful citizen," in response to which Jacobs ironically opines: "So they called a colored man a *citizen*! Strange words to be uttered in that region!" (200). Jacobs's free black kinsman comes into public (journalistic) and political (citizenly) visibility only after, quite literally, he has been interred. But as Jacobs suggests in her phrase "strange words," and as Anita Goldman notes in her research on North Carolina's antebellum racial statutes, quoting *State vs. Elijah Newsom*, an 1844 North Carolina Supreme Court ruling, "free persons of color in this state are not to be considered as citizens."[27] Written by one black man to memorialize another, the obituary eloquently articulates the tragic distance between poetic words "they call him . . . a useful citizen" and the legal reality that would have such a man remain a nonperson as long as he lived.

The space between language and law in antebellum America is precisely the distance that haunts Jacobs's position as an African American writer, for at any time between 1850 and 1861 she could have been abducted from her life as a northern fugitive and remanded to southern slavery. It is thus with the actual death of a free black man, which *can* be mourned, and not, at an affective level, with her own freedom, which she represents as belated, that Jacobs makes her concluding identifications.[28] As Cathy Caruth observes, trauma involves "the inability to fully witness the event as it occurs, or the ability to witness the event fully only at the cost of witnessing oneself." Writing of post-traumatic stress disorder (from which, one might argue on the evidence of the autobiography, Jacobs possibly suffered), Caruth notes: "if post-traumatic-stress-disorder must be understood as a pathological symptom, then it is not so much a symptom of the unconscious, as it is a *symptom of history.*"[29]

In affective terms, both Jacobs's life and the narrative that recounts it move between what we understand as the process of mourning and the stasis of melancholia, an inevitable effect of enduring the trauma of slavery. While mourning ultimately enables the bereaved to introject the loved object and thus master loss, the melancholic, devoured by his or her grief, actually is incorporated by it. Like those survivors about whom Caruth so poetically writes, we might say that Jacobs and her autobiography "carry an impossible history within them," or that "they become themselves the symptom of a history they cannot entirely possess."[30] Borne on the tide of traumatic suffering, Jacobs gives back to American literary history what she cannot achieve for herself in life. The result is a book marked by belatedness and sorrow that nevertheless speaks the melancholy truth about America's most excruciating trauma, slavery, whose the terrible legacy perhaps cannot ever be adequately mourned.

Notes

1. Toni Morrison suggests most powerfully this connection of slavery to mourning in her gnomic dedication to *Beloved:* "Sixty million and more." See Morrison, *Beloved* (New York: New American Library, 1987). For more on memory and mourning, see Peter Homans, *The Ability to Mourn: Disillusionment and the Social Origins of Psychoanalysis* (Chicago: University of Chicago Press, 1989).
2. See Orlando Patterson, *Slavery and Social Death: A Comparative Study* (Cambridge: Harvard University Press, 1982), 334–42.
3. Harriet Jacobs, *Incidents in the Life of a Slave Girl, Written by Herself,* ed. Jean Fagin Yellin (Cambridge: Harvard University Press, 1987).
4. See Sigmund Freud, "Mourning and Melancholia," (1917), trans. Joan Riviere, in Philip Rieff, ed., *General Psychological Theory* (New York: Macmillian, 1963), 164–79.
5. In his brilliant and searching study, *American Puritanism and the Defense of Mourning: Religion, Grief, and Ethnology in Mary White Rowlandson's Captivity Narrative* (Madison: University of Wisconsin Press, 1990), Mitchell R. Breitwieser single-handedly inaugurates a new subfield of American literary and cultural studies, what other scholars have come to call the representational history of emotion. My own work on the significance of mourning in eighteenth- and nineteenth-century American narrative is deeply indebted to Breitwieser's book on Rowlandson and also to Mitchell B. Breitwieser, "*The Great Gatsby:* Grief, Jazz, and the Eye-Witness," *Arizona Quarterly* 47, no. 3 (autumn 1991): 17–70, and "Fitzgerald, Kerouac, and the Puzzle of Inherited Mourning," published in this volume.
6. See Stephanie Smith, "The Tender of Memory: Restructuring Value in Harriet Jacobs's *Incidents in the Life of a Slave Girl,"* in Deborah M. Garfield and Rafia Zafar, eds., *Harriet Jacobs and "Incidents in the Life of a Slave Girl"* (New York: Cambridge University Press, 1996): 251–74.
7. Jennifer Fleischner, *Mastering Slavery: Memory, Family, and Identity in Women's Slave Narratives* (New York: New York University Press, 1996), 12–13.
8. Ibid., 12.
9. See Gates, quoted on the back cover of ibid.
10. Ibid., 26.
11. Jacobs's father Elijah reportedly died of melancholia over remaining enslaved; her brother John Jacobs, author of his own life-narrative, a text that Fleischner illuminates with great intelligence and imagination, successfully escaped from his final master. Uncannily and gothically, this slaveholder, Congressman Samuel Tredwell Sawyer, was the very man who fathered Harriet Jacobs's two children. Jacobs turned to Sawyer in her deluded attempt to lose herself in a romantic liaison of choice with a white man she believed would protect her from the demonic, sexually maniacal clutches of her own master, Dr. James Norcom.
12. The harsh effect of exposure to the elements was emphasized in the author's conversation with George Stevenson, chief archivist, North Carolina State Archives, 2 March 1993.
13. In her notes to the Harvard edition, Jean Fagin Yellin writes that the phrase "loophole of retreat" is "a reference to William Cowper's 'The Task,' IV. 88–90": "'Tis pleasant, through the loopholes of retreat, / To peep at such a

world,—to see the stir / Of the Great Babel, and not feel the crowd." Yellin notes that "Jacobs was not the first Afro-American to use Cowper's phrase." In 1838 the phrase "From the loop-holes of Retreat" appeared as an epigraph to "The Curtain," a column in *Freedom's Journal* (New York). See 277 n. 1. All further references to the Harvard edition of Jacobs's narrative will be made parenthetically.

14. See Jacobs (14). Smith makes a similar claim for the last three paragraphs of Jacobs's narrative: "a legal bill of sale for Linda Brent," "a private letter relating Aunt Martha's death," and "another such black-bordered letter, accompanied by Uncle Phillip's newspaper obituary" taken together "provide a reified recapitulation of the whole narrative, showing the hidden connections between public and private histories." See Smith, "Tender of Memory," 269.

15. Jacobs rails against all forms of economic engagement with slave traders—even the notion of self-purchase—early on in her narrative.

16. The "uncanny," according to Freud, involves the return of the repressed, repetition, re-vision, re-view. In the conclusion of this essay, I take up the notion of return as paradox—that of movement devolving into stasis—which, dynamically, unfolds somewhere between mourning and melancholia as they are conceptualized in spatial terms by Breitwieser in *American Puritanism*.

17. Patterson, *Slavery and Social Death*, 334–42.

18. Jacobs voices death wishes in a full range of forms, particularly the infanticidal and suicidal, on the following pages: 62, 80, 81, 86, 87, 88, 91, 101, 109.

19. See Eric Sundquist, *To Wake the Nations: Race in the Making of American Literature* (Cambridge: Harvard University Press, 1993), 52 and 54.

20. See Sidney Mintz, *Sweetness and Power: The Place of Sugar in Modern History* (New York: Penguin, 1986).

21. For an imaginative elaboration of this motif, see Deborah Garfield, "Earwitness: Female Abolitionism, Sexuality, and *Incidents in the Life of a Slave Girl*," in Garfield and Zafar, eds., *Harriet Jacobs*, 100–130.

22. Mary Titus makes a similar point, arguing that "the central trope of bodily contamination in *Incidents* builds around a conventional image of abolitionist rhetoric, the slaveholder as a snake. As Jean Yellin notes, 'abolitionists, who characterized slavery as "the national sin," routinely symbolize the institution as a serpent.'" Titus cites the following examples from Jacobs's narrative: slavery is a "serpent" with "poisonous fangs" (62); "Dr. Flint" is a "venomous reprobate" (76); slavery exerts a "poisonous grasp" (76); and, most pertinent to my argument, "Hot weather brings out snakes and slaveholders" (174). See Yellin, "Notes," 269, quoted in Mary Titus, "This Poisonous System: Social Ills, Bodily Ills, and *Incidents in the Life of a Slave Girl*," in Garfield and Zafar, eds., *Harriet Jacobs*, 208.

23. According to Stevenson, James Norcom suffered from a form of madness that we would identify today as bipolar affective disorder, or manic depression. This diagnosis would account for his violent rages, the seemingly whimsical, episodic bursts of energy that enabled Norcom to resume his pursuit of the fugitive Jacobs after periods of hiatus, and what, to local white inhabitants and black slaves alike, appeared to be his outrageous lack of shame regarding his female slaves. Stevenson, conversation with author, 2 March 1993.

24. See Julia Stern, "Parsing the First-Person Plural: Gender and Voice in the Fiction of Charles Brockden Brown and Edgar Allan Poe," Ph.D. dissertation, Columbia University, 1991.

25. American Puritans and their New England descendants, both male and female, enjoyed a very high rate of reading literacy, as unmediated access to the Bible was central to Protestant worship. The skill of writing, however, was less

pertinent to reformed religious experience, though most Puritan men of business and the mothers, wives, and daughters who aided their work could write
and cipher. See Cathy Davidson, *Revolution and the Word: The Rise of the
Novel in Early America* (New York: Oxford University Press, 1986), 56–59.
26. See Breitwieser, *American Puritanism,* 41.
27. See Anita Goldman, "Harriet Jacobs, Henry Thoreau, and the Character of
   Disobedience," in Garfield and Zafar, eds., *Harriet Jacobs,* 237.
28. In asserting this, I obviously seek to trouble Jacobs's much-quoted exclama-
   tion that her story ends not with marriage "but with freedom" (200); it is
   my contention that freedom and melancholia are not incongruent.
29. See Cathy Caruth, introduction to *Trauma: Explorations in Memory,* ed.
   Cathy Caruth (Baltimore: Johns Hopkins University Press, 1995), 5.
30. Ibid., 5.

Further Reading

Breitwieser, Mitchell R. *American Puritanism and the Defense of Mourning: Religion, Grief, and Ethnology in Mary White Rowlandson's
   Captivity Narrative.* Madison: University of Wisconsin Press, 1990.
      Breitwieser's book revolutionized the study of affect in early American
   literature. Through his eclectic use of psychoanalytic and poststructuralist
   literary theory, combined with research into historical and philosophical
   texts, Breitwieser's meditation on Rowlandson changed the way literary
   scholars think about premodern narratives.
Caruth, Cathy. Introduction to *Trauma: Explorations in Memory,* ed.
   Cathy Caruth. Baltimore: Johns Hopkins University Press, 1995.
      Caruth's work joins literary to psychoanalytic theory in powerful new
   ways. Her comparative approach to trauma expands the range of applica-
   tions that literary scholars can make to the representations of trauma.
Fleischner, Jennifer. *Mastering Slavery: Memory, Family, and Identity in
   Women's Slave Narratives.* New York: New York University Press,
   1996.
      Fleischner reconfigured the field of African American literary studies by
   joining a subtle psychoanalytic practice to original historical research in the
   black archives.
Freud, Sigmund. "Mourning and Melancholia." (1917). Trans. Joan Riviere.
   In *General Psychological Theory,* ed. Philip Reiff. New York: Macmillian, 1963.
      Freud's work is, of course, the urtext of all of research in this field. I still
   admire this essay, though I appreciate the fact that the sharp distinction he
   drew between mourning and melancholia may, in reality, be more blurred
   than he suggests.
Garfield, Deborah M., and Rafia Zafar, eds. *Harriet Jacobs and "Incidents
   in the Life of a Slave Girl."* New York: Cambridge University Press,
   1996.
      This volume is the most recent and rigorously theoretical work of Jacobs's
   criticism available.
Jacobs, Harriet A. *Incidents in the Life of a Slave Girl.* Ed. Jean Fagin Yellin.
   Cambridge: Harvard University Press, 1987.
      Jacobs's narrative is the most important African American woman's
   autobiography—and, to my mind, the most important slave narrative—of
   the nineteenth century.

Morrison, Toni. *Beloved.* New York: New American Library, 1987.
> Morrison's novel transforms our understanding of slavery's quotidian horrors and their post-traumatic aftermath better than any novel written in this century.

Patterson, Orlando. *Slavery and Social Death: A Comparative Study.* Cambridge: Harvard University Press, 1982.
> I find Patterson's work the most theoretically searching account of slavery I have seen to date. Particularly valuable are his ideas of "social death" and "parasitism."

PAUL A. ANDERSON

"MY LORD, WHAT A MORNING"

THE "SORROW SONGS" IN HARLEM RENAISSANCE THOUGHT

IN THE PREFACE to her collection of poetry, *A Woman's Mourning Song*, bell hooks recalls the black community she was a part of as a working-class girl in rural Kentucky. It was a tightly knit world where the ritual of "passing on," the natural death of the elderly and infirm, followed a lively public spirit that blended grief with celebration. Individual and communal assumptions of spiritual continuity lessened the immobilizing sense of grief among survivors. "One celebrates the passing of life," hooks writes, "not only to ease the transition of the dead but to make it known that the moment is also a time of reunion, when those who have been long separated come together."[1] Where ascension into the ancestral spirit-world is assumed, the threshold between the natural and supernatural worlds can be approached as a benign passageway rather than as a site of horror.

A Woman's Mourning Song, with its attentiveness to folk responses to death in the black diaspora, brings to mind the ritualized "tame death" that Phillipe Ariès attributed to traditional European culture before the medical privatization of death and the tidal wave of cultural modernization.[2] Sigmund Freud represented a new wave of modernization when he formulated his psychoanalytic models of mourning and melancholia under the assumption that mourning had become a secular and largely individualized process. He wrote of mourning as a kind of work undertaken by an individual's psychic economy; it was a difficult but usually successful process, combining grief, memorialization, reality testing, and decathexis or disattachment. According to Freud's definition in "Mourning and Melancholia," mourning "is regularly the reaction to the loss of a loved person, or to the loss of some abstraction which has taken the place of one, such as one's country, liberty, an ideal, and so on."[3] Although the lost object being mourned might be a collective identification, the real work of mourning still took place on an individual level. If an individual's mourning process lost its progressive thrust and became stalled or ensnared, the psychoanalyst could offer clinical assistance by probing for the pathologies blocking forward movement. The pathological melancholic, for example, suffered in remaining affectively fixated on a desire for some known or unknown lost object. Thus, Freud interpreted melancholia as an ultimately regressive and narcissistic identification. He left to later generations the task of exploring how collective processes of mourning could be set in motion by the shared loss of an abstract ideal, collective practice, or identification.

One might map an arc or spectrum for the varieties of mourning summoned in *A Woman's Mourning Song.* At one point of the spectrum there is a gentle acceptance of death fueled by a community's assurance of sacred restitution. In her poetry and prose, hooks stages a personal scene of mourning over her weakened ties to these older traditions. In the book's cover photograph, Billie Holiday (1915–59) stands before a stage microphone singing with arms crossed and eyes closed. Holiday was raised Catholic, an outsider to the full-throated gospel shouts and dramatic catharses of the black evangelical church. Holiday's mature singing voice often evoked an affective world far removed from the sacred mourning practices hooks remembers from her childhood community and longs to incorporate into the work of what she calls black "self-recovery."[4] Today, forty years after her death, Holiday's reputation as an unparalleled jazz vocal artist is especially linked to her balladry and its demanding testimonies about romantic love and loss. In her later years, Holiday often entranced audiences with theatrical renderings of popular songs that approached sorrowful inconsolability. Holiday's greatest music, fans concur, has the potential to light the path out of bleak solipsism and despair even as it illuminates the darkest corners of heartbreak. "Lady Day," Leon Forrest wrote, "prophetically read out the terrorized terms of the heart, more than any other national black female artist in American culture."[5]

As a public intellectual, hooks asks how black diasporic practices for the overcoming of loss and grief can be nurtured under present historical conditions. She has written that traditional and "healthy approaches to death and dying made it possible for black people to confront and cope with loss." Although hooks perceives a weakening of these traditions, she asserts that "Many southern black people have held to the belief that a human being possesses body, soul, and spirit—that death may take one part even as the others remain."[6] *A Woman's Mourning Song* uses images of music as sites of mourning that speak to hopes for black "self-recovery" through reattachment and reconnection rather than through a Freudian decathexis and disconnection from highly energized sites of loss and identification. With its deep traditions and long memory —and because it is varied enough to appeal to so many needs and constituencies—music may be the most intensely developed of all sites of black diasporic memory.[7]

The slave spirituals have long occupied sacred ground as a place of memory among African Americans. The writer and activist W. E. B. Du Bois articulated an especially resonant image of the spirituals as "sorrow songs" a century ago. Through his influential writings, Du Bois hoped to manage and reframe this site of memory according to his own very ambitious agenda for social transformation. A long debate over the inheritance of the spirituals took on a particular urgency in the 1920s context of the "New Negro" Renaissance or Harlem Renaissance. This essay contrasts Du Bois's image of the "sorrow songs" as a site of memory with the responses of Jean Toomer, Alain Locke, and Zora Neale Hurston, three prominent voices of the Harlem Renaissance era. Toomer, an avant-garde writer, and Locke, a philosopher and cultural critic, responded to Du Bois's paradigm by encouraging modernist postures of mourning toward black folk culture. Locke's sponsorship of "New Negro" art as, in part, a commemorative project resembled Du Bois's dialectic of black continuity in cosmopolitan development. Toomer, on the other hand, gestures toward a more radical and post-racial view of mourning. Zora Neale Hurston, an ethnographer and novelist, refused the "New Negro" rhetoric of mourning the loss or immanent obsolescence of black folk culture and offered an alternative conception of black cultural continuity.

In his 1888 valedictory address at Fisk University in Nashville, the graduating college senior William Edward Burghardt Du Bois celebrated Otto von Bismarck, the long-time chancellor to Wilhelm I and the political architect of a newly united German nation. Bismarck's glory was in making a nation "out of bickering peoples." "The life of this powerful Chancellor illustrates the power and purpose, the force of an idea," the young Du Bois explained.[8]

The great idea that so gripped Du Bois's imagination was modern nationhood, though he would later repudiate Bismarck's imperialism. After receiving a doctorate in sociology from Harvard and publishing several important scholarly studies, including *The Philadelphia Negro* (1899), Du Bois fashioned a more personal voice in *The Souls of Black Folk* (1903). The book, an autobiographically influenced account of "the problem of the color line," described the struggle for racial equality and the recognition of black contributions to America's growth. Du Bois took hold of the "sorrow songs" in order to dig deep into the southern past and the legacy of slavery. His goal was to distill the power of the most solemn spirituals and capture that power in his own intensely lyrical prose. He would then wield a transformed fragment of the black past as a tool for social transformation. One might view his strategy of redemptive recontextualization in the light of a later messianic formulation from Walter Benjamin: "Only that historian will have the gift of fanning the spark of hope in the past who is convinced that *even the dead* will not be safe from the enemy if he wins."[9] To fan the embers of "hope in the past" Du Bois had to evoke the traumatic wounds of displacement and subjugation that first inspired black slaves in America to express their grievances, joys, and dreams in collective song.

Du Bois explained in the "Sorrow Songs" chapter of *The Souls of Black Folk* that he first heard some of the old slave spirituals during his western Massachusetts childhood. He had always been moved by them but only came to grasp their meaning in the southern black world of Fisk. "Then in after years when I came to Nashville," he wrote, "I saw the great temple builded of these songs towering over the pale city. To me Jubilee Hall seemed ever made of the songs themselves, and its bricks were red with the blood and dust of toil." In the 1870s, the Fisk Jubilee Singers took "those weird old songs in which the soul of the black slave spoke to men" to the wider world and raised funds for the school.[10] The singing group of black college students presented an arranged and somewhat Europeanized version of the folk music to concert hall and church audiences in the United States, the British Isles, and Western Europe. Their tours' unexpected success funded, among other things, the construction of Jubilee Hall on the Fisk campus. Other black colleges soon followed suit and pursued this unique fund-raising opportunity. "Making black expressiveness a commodity . . . is not simply a gesture in a bourgeois economics of art," the literary critic Houston A. Baker has noted, but "is a crucial move in a repertoire of black survival motions in the United States." "Afro-America's exchange power," Baker concludes," has always been coextensive with its stock of expressive resources."[11] Du Bois's reflection on the "sorrow songs" emphasized the uplifting commemorative work of the Fisk Jubilee Singers as a repudiation of minstrelsy.

The spirituals inspired minstrel parodies and crude imitations both before and after the Fisk Jubilee Singers' vogue in the twilight of Reconstruction. Du Bois distinguished the real "sorrow songs" from variations that ridiculed or improperly memorialized the slaves' millennial hopes and collective sorrow. "Caricature," he exclaimed, "has sought to spoil the quaint beauty of the music, and has filled the air with many debased melodies which vulgar ears scarce know from the real." Du Bois held up the "sorrow song" legacy as proof that African Americans were not bereft of collective memory or valuable folk cultural traditions. His childhood memory of an ancestral African lullaby, passed on for generations, demonstrated that the "sorrow songs" bound Americans to a barely known African past. A mixture of African and diasporic memories had congealed into musical form, as the haunting music of the "sorrow songs" was "far more ancient than the words."[12]

The double meanings of spirituals like "My Lord, What a Morning," "Go Down, Moses," "Swing Low, Sweet Chariot," "Deep River," and "Were You There (When They Crucified My Lord)?" were not to be forgotten. To mask the dangerous messages from the ears of whites, song lyrics wove together motifs of spiritual and secular liberation through frequent identification of the tribulations of American slaves with the sacred trials of earlier "suffering servants," whether Christ or the Israelites in bondage. The songs' most rebellious strains—"naturally veiled and half articulate," Du Bois noted—remained obscure to outsiders. Du Bois usually concentrated on the worldliness of the "sorrow songs" and referred to Christianity as a "dimly understood theology" among the slaves. Moreover, he expressed no great sympathy for religious emotionalism and "frenzy," whether in animistic spirit-worship or evangelical enthusiasm.[13] His understanding of the "sorrow songs" beckoned instead toward a social and political transformation of this world:

> Through all the sorrow of the Sorrow Songs there breathes a hope—a faith in the ultimate justice of things. The minor cadences of despair change often to triumph and calm confidence. Sometimes it is faith

in life, sometimes a faith in death, sometimes assurance of bound-
less justice in some fair world beyond. But whichever it is, the meaning is always clear; that sometime, somewhere, men will judge men
by their souls and not by their skins. Is such a hope justified? Do
the Sorrow Songs ring true?[14]

Du Bois wanted readers to apprehend a chain of logic linking his
sense of the Fisk Jubilee Singers as placeholders for the "sorrow
songs" to his demands for a new paradigm in civil rights agitation
and black nationalist consciousness. The success of the Fisk Jubilee Singers, like the adaptation of motifs from the spirituals in
Antonin Dvorak's symphony *From the New World* (No. 9 in E
minor) of 1893, called for a new aesthetic of cultural nationalism.
For Du Bois, the "sorrow songs" crystallized the deepest collective longings of the African American slaves. "They are the music
of an unhappy people," he wrote, "of the children of disappointment; they tell of death and suffering and unvoiced longing toward
a truer world, of misty wanderings and hidden ways." Du Bois's
emphasis on "sadness, disappointment . . . [and] unvoiced longing" invites us to revisit Freud's "Mourning and Melancholia."
For Freud, melancholic grief is usually incapable of fully identifying its own cause; with no clear origin for the pain, the sufferer
can find no path away from it and toward reparation. Instead, the
horizon is bereft and emptied of worthy new love objects or ideals.
"The complex of melancholia," Freud argued, "behaves like an
open wound, drawing to itself cathectic energies . . . from all directions, and emptying the ego until it is totally impoverished."[15]
The Du Boisian image of the "sorrow song" differs in important
ways from Freud's depiction of the melancholic's "open wound."
Although Du Bois's "sorrow songs" constitute a perennial site of
loss and memory, they do not emphasize self-directed aggression
or a static repetition of ego impoverishment. When performed,
the songs can instead address "open wounds" and memories of
subjugation through a more subtle dynamic of repetition, artifice,
and mournful reparation. Sacred and secular hopes for deliverance,
along with the ritualized demonstration of communal support,
can counteract a vertiginous fall into inconsolable melancholia at
the traumatic site of a collective "open wound." Du Bois's image of
the "sorrow songs" represented something more than a melancholy
inducing memorial to undifferentiated trauma. His reparative and
forward-looking model of black cultural development insisted that

the pull of despair could be met and intertwined with restitutive memories and an idealism that began to articulate the spirituals' "unvoiced longing toward a truer world." Freud's avowedly secular ideal of successful mourning meant coming to terms with or "working-through" the loss of the beloved person, object, or ideal through a gradual and ultimately complete decathexis of libidinal investment. Public performances of the "sorrow songs" respectfully staged and remembered the sadness addressed in the original songs; these same performances could recuperate the slaves' millennial hopes as contexts for new collective ideals in the post-slavery era.

It should be noted that the cultural logic of mourning in Du Bois's "sorrow song" ideal appears only implicitly in his writings.[16] As a historical frame for the present interpretation, one might consider the general predicament of folkloric cultural nationalism.[17] Countless varieties of romantic nationalism in the modern era have presented idealized and lyrical images of the rural folk. Often distinctly pastoral, these images serve as abstract love objects for bourgeois audiences dissociated from the texture of everyday rural life and alienated from, if not outrightly critical of, the urban "masses." The ideal of the national folk allows for a mythic reconciliation between the urban bourgeoisie and the peasantry qua specters of "pre-modernity" and insurers of the nation's archaic authenticity.[18] The cosmopolitan Du Bois urged the preservation of some elements of the black folk inheritance for the sake of a black nationalist wing in the "kingdom of culture." His famous notion of black "double-consciousness" depicted a racialized form of psychic alienation among African Americans that was felt most acutely by highly assimilated intellectuals like himself. "One ever feels his two-ness," Du Bois wrote, "—an American, a Negro; two souls, two thoughts, two unreconciled strivings, two warring ideals in one dark body, whose dogged strength alone keeps it from being torn asunder. . . . The history of the American Negro is the history of this strife,—this longing to attain self-conscious manhood, to merge his double self into a better and truer self. In this merging he wishes neither of the old selves to be lost."[19] Du Bois's vision of black liberation, influenced by Hegelian idealism and Herderian nationalism, took shape as a dialectical conception of individual and collective self-consciousness and disalienation. Moreover, the logic of *Aufhebung* or dialectical sublation (the intertwined developmental work of cancellation, preservation, and elevation) might be likened to Freud's normative vision of successful mourning. Mitchell Breitwieser argues in *American Puritanism and the Defense of Mourning* that Freud's model of ideal mourning "may be dialectic's purest case."[20] Apropos of critical theory in the wake of deconstruction, Breitwieser illuminates a relationship between the evasion of the unsublated remainder in Hegelian dialectics and the disavowal or repression of the leftover of melancholic identification in Freud's model of ideal mourning.

Du Bois crafted a usable past out of idealized images of the black folk and the "sorrow songs" even as he de-emphasized the songs' role in a living religious tradition. He believed that the songs' innermost nugget of folk authenticity and moral seriousness could be preserved while their musical forms were dialectically lifted into more refined concert idioms appropriate to the cosmopolitan "kingdom of culture." The dialectical aspects of both Du Bois's "sorrow song" ideal and his implicit cultural logic of mourning assumed an abstract negation or casting off of those aspects he considered vulgar, counterprogressive, or simply backward in black culture. "As a highly educated Western black intellectual," the philosopher Cornel West has noted, "Du Bois himself often scorns the 'barbarisms' (sometimes confused with Africanisms) shot through Afro-American culture." A mixture of folk romanticism and bourgeois self-righteousness courses through *The Souls of Black Folk*. West counts "eighteen allusions to the 'backwardness' of black folk."[21] The "talented tenth," as Du Bois referred to the prospective race leaders, was to reach backward and capture the heroic memories crystallized in the expressive products of black slave culture. Throughout his very long and active life, Du Bois (1868–1963) sternly evaluated African American art and cultural thought in terms of services or disservices to the long campaign for black liberation, as he understood it. During the 1920s Harlem Renaissance, younger African American writers (including Zora Neale Hurston, Langston Hughes, and Sterling Brown) came to the defense of the dialectical residue within black vernacular culture that Du Bois judged backward or counterprogressive. Before we move to Hurston's particular critique of Du Bois's "sorrow song" ideal, it is instructive to sketch two 1920s variations on the spirituals offered by Jean Toomer and Alain Locke.[22]

James Weldon Johnson, field secretary of the NAACP, looked back on *The Souls of Black Folk* as "a work which, I think, has had a greater effect upon and within the Negro race in America than any other single book published in this country since *Uncle Tom's Cabin*."[23] For an example of Du Bois's influence upon black modernist writing, one might look to Jean Toomer's poem "Song of the Son." Toomer (1894–1967) first published the poem in *The Crisis* (the NAACP monthly under Du Bois's editorial leadership) in June of 1922. "Song of the Son" appeared the next year in Toomer's book *Cane* and then again in *The New Negro* (1925), a landmark anthology of fiction, poetry, and nonfiction edited by Alain Locke. "Song of the Son," like other stories and poems with rural settings in *Cane,* mimics the plaintive tone and unrushed tempo of the most mournful spirituals:

> Pour O pour that parting soul in song,
> O pour it in the sawdust glow of night
> Into the velvet pine-smoke air to-night,
> And let the valley carry it along.
> And let the valley carry it along.
>
> O land and soil, red soil and sweet-gum tree,
> So scant of grass, so profligate of pines,
> Now just before an epoch's sun declines
> Thy son, in time, I have returned to thee,
> Thy son, I have in time returned to thee.
>
> In time, for though the sun is setting on
> A song-lit race of slaves, it has not set;
> Though late, O soil, it is not too late yet
> To catch thy plaintive soul, leaving, soon gone,
> Leaving, to catch thy plaintive soul soon gone.
>
> O Negro slaves, dark purple ripened plums,
> Squeezed, and bursting in the pine-wood air,
> Passing, before they stripped the old tree bare
> One plum was saved for me, one seed becomes
>
> An everlasting song, a singing tree,
> Caroling softly souls of slavery,
> What they were, and what they are to me,
> Caroling softly souls of slavery.[24]

The elegiac poem evokes the "sorrow songs" as a haunting music that reaches out from the past to confront and challenge the present. The exhausted culture of a "song-lit race of slaves" slowly winds down as an "epoch's sun declines." "Caroling softly souls of slavery," the apparitional song echoes through the rural Georgia valley. The eulogizing son, poised to receive his ancestral heritage at a tragic site of memory, responds by catching and rehearsing the song's cadence as if it may be his only inheritance. Within the broader context of *Cane,* the speaker who has "in time returned to thee" also represents the vast distance between urban modernity and a rural black folk culture forged in slavery.[25] A posture of nostalgic identification with that past world is not available. The collapsing epoch of a "song-lit race of slaves" is rendered as raw and brutal rather than pastoral: "O Negro slaves, dark purple ripened plums, / Squeezed, and bursting in the pine-wood air[.]"

The process of mourning becomes pathological, according to Freud, when the identification with the lost object is excessively prolonged, thus leading to heightened feelings of ego impoverishment and dejection. "In mourning," Freud contended, "it is the world which has become poor and empty; in melancholia it is the ego itself. The [melancholic] patient represents his ego to us as worthless, incapable of any achievement and morally despicable."[26] "Song of the Son," a black modernist elegy directed at a fading folk culture, suggests a logic of mourning that parts ways with Freud's ideals for "working-through" profound losses. The wind "Caroling softly songs of slavery" through the rural Georgia valley passes along memories of racial terror in slavery as well as the restitutive spiritual resources of the black folk community. Traumatic legacies, according to Du Bois's cultural logic of mourning, would be commemorated in music and other rituals and sublimated into refined expressive forms. Such commemorative mourning-work would also enable present collective solidarity and anti-racist activism. When the speaker laments the folk culture's fragile and eroding beauty in "Song of the Son," the old folk culture extends a precious remnant to him: "Passing, before they stripped the old tree bare / One plum was saved for me, one seed becomes / An everlasting song, a singing tree[.]" "Song of the Son" dramatizes the last-minute rescue of a restitutive and "everlasting song."

A two-month stay in Sparta, Georgia, first inspired the young Toomer, a native of the black bourgeoisie of Washington, D.C., to write *Cane.* In contrast to the hopeful implications of the above poem's "everlasting song," Toomer's correspondences and unpublished writings recorded a different perspective on African American folk culture's powers of endurance. He wrote the following about how the "folk-songs and spirituals" first captured his imagination:

The setting was crude in a way, but strangely rich and beautiful. . . .
A family of back-country Negroes had only recently moved into a

shack not too far away. They sang. And this was the first time I'd
ever heard the folk-songs and spirituals. They were very rich and
sad and joyous and beautiful. But I learned that the Negroes of the
town objected to them. They called them "shouting." They had
victrolas and player-pianos. So, I realized with deep regret, that the
spirituals, meeting ridicule, would be certain to die out. With Negroes
also the trend was towards the small town and then towards the
city—and industry and commerce and machines. The folk-spirit
was walking in to die on the modern desert. That spirit was so
beautiful. Its death was so tragic. Just this seemed to sum life for
me. And this was the feeling I put into *Cane*. *Cane* was a swan-
song. It was a song of an end. And why no one has seen and felt that,
why people have expected me to write a second and third and a
fourth book like "*Cane*," is one of the queer misunderstandings of
my life.[27]

Toomer's "swan-song" commentary followed a broader meta-
narrative of modernization as cultural disenchantment. The
meta-narrative of modernity as entropic decline casts an elegiac
expectation over the eradication of spiritually integrated folk and
indigenous cultures in the face of the ever-advancing monolith of
cultural and economic modernization. Toomer sounded another
note of modernist despair when he announced the pervasiveness
of cultural fragmentation and discontinuity: "The modern world
was uprooted, the modern world was breaking down, but we
couldn't go back. There was nothing to go back to. Besides, in our
hasty leaps into the future we had burned our bridges."[28] The cultural anthropologist James Clifford has written effectively about
the modern "entropologist" who mourns the "vanishing 'loop-
holes' or 'escapes' from a one-dimensional fate" in the face of the
"prophetic disintegration of all real cultural differences."[29] The
"salvage paradigm," a perennial accompaniment to the entropic
narrative of modernity, reflects a "desire to rescue 'authenticity' out
of destructive historical chance." Present "in a range of familiar
nostalgias," the "salvage paradigm" is "a pervasive ideological
complex" that reproduces distorted images of history and cultural
difference "that need to be cleared away if we are to account for the
multiple *histories* and *inventions* at work in the late 20th century."[30]

Toomer was more eager to build a new and discontinuous personal identity in the context of modernist disintegration than to
salvage black folk "'authenticity' out of destructive historical
chance." He explained his position in a letter to Waldo Frank:

> But the fact is, that if anything comes up now, pure Negro, it will be
> a swan-song. Don't let us fool ourselves, brother: the Negro of the
> folk-song has all but passed away. . . . The supreme fact of mechan-
> ical civilization is that you become part of it, or get sloughed off
> (under). Negroes have no culture to resist it with (and if they had,
> their position would be identical to the Indians), hence industrial-
> ism the more readily transforms them. . . . In those pieces [of *Cane*]
> that come nearest to the old Negro, there is nothing of the buoyant
> expression of a new race.[31]

A sense of deep discontinuity between the folk culture of the "Old
Negro" and contemporary modernity emerged from Toomer's assumption that the "Negroes have no culture to resist it [mechan-
ical civilization] with." In the end, he chose not to sustain the
"everlasting song" of "Song of the Son" as a homeopathic balm
and marker of black ancestralism and cultural continuity. For Du
Bois, the "sorrow songs" and the utopian "spark of hope in the
past" would never be abandoned. Toomer, by contrast, came to
terms with the African American past and its consequences for his
sense of selfhood by imagining a "new race": mystically constituted, radically modern, and ethnically unmarked. His personal
situation enabled this new perspective. With his light skin color,
straight hair, and Caucasian features, he easily "passed" as racially
white. Having completed his "swan-song" to the rural "Old Negro,"
Toomer felt no strong artistic or personal attachment to what he
apprehended as an altogether new urban black culture.[32] Not long
after the publication of *Cane*, he chose to no longer identify himself as black and parted ways with the "New Negro" movement
and the ascending Harlem Renaissance. Toomer instead welcomed
the opportunity for modernist re-enchantment through a mystical passage into a "new race."

Toomer interpreted his new identification not as "passing" for
white but as a refusal of dominant regimes of racialization. His
next major work, *Essentials* (1931), clustered together philosophical aphorisms emblematic of his discipleship of the spiritual master Gurdjieff. All distinctions of racial identity, along with other
fixed and local forms of identity, were no longer relevant: these
distinctions were, more precisely, inessential. The literary critic
Henry Louis Gates has described Toomer's project as an attempt
to invent "an entirely new discourse, an almost mythic discourse
. . . in which irreconcilable opposites, sexual and racial differences
were not so much reconciled as absent, unutterable, unthinkable,

and hence unpresentable."[33] Moreover, Toomer effectively hollowed out each moment of the hybridizing process outlined in Du Bois's dialectic of black "double-consciousness." Toomer left the hope of ancestralist continuity and cosmopolitan hybridization to other modernists of the "New Negro" Renaissance.

Alain Locke (1885–1954) was among those charting a cosmopolitan vision of "New Negro" artistic development in the interwar years. Armed with a doctorate in philosophy from Harvard, the Howard University professor felt confident in his self-assigned leadership responsibilities. Locke hoped to ensure the continuous development of African American expressive traditions while also shepherding them into more classicized forms. While Toomer mourned over the passing of black folk culture as an irreparable rupture and a "death [that] was so tragic," Locke saw stronger signs of continuity between particular folk forms and black achievements in modern concert music and other arts. It was inevitable, Locke held, for some residual "premodern" aspects of rural black culture to dissipate under the force of migration and industrial opportunity. His somewhat urgent tone suggested less regret about folk cultural disintegration than an eager desire to salvage the past and publicize the necessity of mourning. The Fisk Jubilee Singers "only anticipated the inevitable by a generation— for the folk that produced them is rapidly vanishing," Locke wrote.[34] The great achievement of the black college singing groups that circulated the spirituals outside the church was that the songs "were saved during that critical period in which any folk product is likely to be snuffed out by the false pride of the second generation."[35]

Locke saw it as a proper aspiration for concert music to represent a national culture. Like Du Bois and others, he looked to the "sorrow songs" as universally appealing, but nationally specific, folk ballads. The concert spiritual was fit to play an equal role in recitals of European art songs.[36] A steady evolution from folk spirituals to art songs and symphonies based on folk sources, Locke contended, demanded the presence of black artists in the most advanced circles of cosmopolitan achievement. At the same time, he approached many developments in black popular music with grave concerns about the exoticizing appeals of primitivism and neo-minstrelsy. His program for "New Negro" art shared many themes with Du Bois's more politicized dialectic of "double-consciousness," mourning, and hybridic reconstitution. The "rapidly vanishing" folk culture would be memorialized as a lost object

and divided into its perceived contingent and essential characteristics. Splitting the lost object allowed for a deliberate and permanent incorporation of its most treasured characteristics; artists
and critics did not always agree about which of the folk object's
characteristics were indispensable. A rebirthing of "the Negro" as
an idealized "New Negro," as Locke read the situation, would
sublimate a traumatic legacy through sophisticated modes of artifice and stylized expressivity and thereby evade a counterprogressive melancholic position.

Alternative voices took aim at the developmental priorities
of Du Bois and Locke and their domesticated idealizations of
black folk culture. The intellectual counteroffensive, a discursive
"return of the repressed," challenged what is being described here
as a "New Negro" cultural logic of mourning. If one might characterize Toomer's avant-garde post-racialism and Locke's "New
Negro" aesthetic in terms of a deliberate desire to mourn, then
Zora Neale Hurston's contrasting perspective might be read as a
principled refusal to mourn. Although Locke was an early sup-
porter of Hurston's fiction and ethnographic work, she refused
to join the "swan song" chorus that regarded black folk culture
as a world in inevitable decline. Instead, she critiqued "New
Negro" evolutionism as hopelessly assimilationist, Eurocentric,
and tone-deaf to the full richness of black folk culture. On the
matter of real folk spirituals, Hurston rejected Du Bois's emphasis
on slavery as the definitive context of the songs' creation: "Their
creation is not confined to the slavery period. Like the folk tales,
the spirituals are being made and forgotten every day." Hurston
contributed the short essay "Spirituals and Neo-Spirituals" to
Nancy Cunard's *Negro* (1934) anthology. The essay distinguished
between the authentic black folk spirituals (with their African-
derived traits of communal improvisation, "jagged harmony," and
intentionally "rough" tonality) and the fully scored, more Europeanized "neo-spiritual" compositions and arrangements made popular by college singing troupes and "New Negro" concert artists
like Roland Hayes and Marian Anderson. "There never has been
a presentation of genuine Negro spirituals to any audience any-
where," Hurston declared. "What is being sung by the concert artists and glee clubs are the works of Negro composers or adaptors
based on the spirituals."[37]

Most importantly, Hurston moved to invalidate the claims of
developmental necessity made in support of arranged spirituals

and art music "based on the spirituals." Du Bois, Locke, and like-minded "New Negro" spokesmen held that such formal composi-tions were often genuinely uplifting memorials to a fading folk culture. Hurston preferred to locate the "genuine Negro spiritu-als" and their function within a resilient, living continuum of Afro-Christian worship. Among the Harlem Renaissance figures discussed in the present essay, only Hurston (1891–1960) was a native of the deep South. Her fond memories of growing up in the all-black rural town of Eatonville, Florida, left her eager to prove that the difference between folk and elite culture was not a distinc-tion between the raw, untutored expressivity of the "Old Negro" and the cosmopolitan sophistication of the "New Negro." There-fore, she took pains in "Spirituals and Neo-Spirituals" to distin-guish between the primitivist myth of raw and unmediated folk expressivity and the reality of carefully crafted vernacular practices in the black church. Hurston's essay values "training," "sound effects," and formal rules not only as markers of European-style concert music but as essential characteristics of vernacular "Negro expression" as well. Far from the anarchy of "every man for him-self," the folk church service involved numerous formalities that helped shape a highly stylized and aesthetically impressive event. Especially in the service's most spontaneous and improvised moments, Hurston insisted, "ability is recognized as definitely as in any other art." She explained the dynamic interplay between individual and group spontaneity and preexisting formalized con-straints: the "individual may hang as many new ornaments upon the traditional forms as he likes, but the audience would be disagree-ably surprised if the form were abandoned." In short, elite "New Negro" assumptions that rural folk lacked rigorous aesthetic criteria were simply mistaken. "The truth is," Hurston asserted, "that the religious service is a conscious art expression. The artist is consciously creating—carefully choosing every syllable and every breath."[38]

Hurston's argument in "Spirituals and Neo-Spirituals" also dis-rupted the logic of continuity underwriting Du Bois's inheritance claims to the "sorrow songs" as a self-styled patriarch of early-twentieth-century black nationalism. As a student of folk culture, she insisted that any "idea that [the] whole body of spirituals are 'sorrow songs' is ridiculous. They cover a wide range of subjects from a peeve at gossipers to Death and the Judgment."[39] Du Bois's "sorrow song" concept, in other words, struck Hurston as vastly

misleading about most spirituals and their ritual functions. She
especially disliked seeing the spirituals understood only according to their "minor cadences of despair." In contrast to the stress
put on alienation and dialectical progress in Du Bois's sense of
"double-consciousness," Hurston preferred to celebrate the humor,
playfulness, and immanent pleasures of black folk traditions. She
argued that black folk culture's many positive traits, including
the skill of cultivating joy through ritualized vernacular practices,
needed to emerge from beneath the ultimately counterproductive
anti-racist imagery of black alienation, sorrow, and victimization
under segregation. Reclaiming the joyful folk spiritual and religious "shout" as a celebratory rather than mournful site of memory was one strategy in Hurston's iconoclastic campaign to repeal
the anti-racist rhetoric of black suffering and damage. She explained in the essay "How It Feels to Be Colored Me" (1928) that
"I am not tragically colored. There is no great sorrow dammed up
in my soul, nor lurking behind my eyes. I do not mind at all. I do
not belong to the sobbing school of Negrohood. . . . No, I do not
weep at the world—I am too busy sharpening my oyster knife."[40]
Hurston's literary virtuosity in capturing the oral dimensions of
black folk culture was widely applauded. Nevertheless, many
black intellectuals complained in the 1930s that her rejection of
a radicalized social realism left too little room in her art for the
indictment of segregation and white racism as barriers to black
opportunity. Hurston lost the support of the black literary estab-
lishment. The full scope of her achievement was recognized only
posthumously after her "rediscovery" in the 1970s.

   Hurston criticized those who sought to formalize black music
according to what she considered an inevitably Eurocentric conceit
of cosmopolitan development. She countered that the folkloric
and ethnographic study of black vernacular culture was itself at a
crude stage and that the "New Negro" concert spiritual was "some
more passing for white."[41] Her protectiveness about folk culture
was, perhaps, an element of a more personal campaign of mournful recuperation and ancestral commemoration; Hurston's work,
as a mournful song of the daughter, placed a limit on her willingness to appreciate a process she termed the hybridic "exchange
and re-exchange of ideas between groups."[42] The literary critic
Hazel Carby has argued that Hurston's ethnographies and novels
idealized a particular folk subculture as the repository of authentic African American culture. Hurston may have reconstituted
her memories and her rural ethnographies into an ahistorical ref-

uge from pressing issues of migration, urban industrialization, and proletarianization. Idealized images of folk cultures as refuges from modernity threaten to harden, of course, into static visions of "otherness." Carby argues that "On the one hand, [Hurston] could argue that forms of folk culture were constantly reworked and remade when she stated that 'the folk tales' like 'the spirituals are being made and forgotten every day.' But, on the other hand, Hurston did not take seriously the possibility that African American culture was being transformed as African American peoples migrated from rural to urban areas."[43] Nevertheless, Hurston's public refusal of Du Bois's "sorrow song" model and Locke's "New Negro" agenda also highlighted the regional, class, and masculinist limitations of her interlocutors. Indeed, despite her claim that there was "no great sorrow dammed up in my soul," many readers have located powerful countercurrents of mournful commemoration in Hurston's writing, including her masterpiece, the novel *Their Eyes Were Watching God* (1937). Hurston's autobiography, *Dust Tracks on a Road* (1942), includes a piercing description of her mother's death and the confession that "I was old before my time with grief of loss, of failure, and of remorse."[44] Hurston's writings have become constant companions in many recent reflections on memory and the folk inheritance, especially in the work of black feminist artists and critics. Her readers have been keen to uncover alternate vernacular paths for mourning the dead and coming to terms with private and public losses.

Hurston's insights struck the black intelligentsia of her own day as unassimilable to dialectical formulations about black progress, but they might now lend valuable sources of energy and possibility to that same dialectic. A rapprochement with the politically progressive, indeed utopian, strains of the Du Boisian tradition may no longer be out of the question. Hurston argued that black folk culture, including its religious dimensions, amounted to more than a raw resource for cosmopolitan refinement or a "premodern" specter or unassimilable remainder from the past. The sublimation of sorrow and joy and the elucidation of memory have, of course, taken on innumerable styles in black diasporic music. Among these sites of cultural memory, the "sorrow song" tradition does not glorify the "open wounds" of collective and personal memory. The tradition seeks instead to cultivate and pass on a practice of compassion rich enough to illuminate the most guarded places of memory and soften the most bitter moments of loss. It is a practice of mourning and restitution that retains deep connections to

long-standing traditions within the black diaspora. Whether
through a cosmopolitan work of concert art, a blues-tinged jazz
ballad, an elegant soul anthem, or a "down-home" spiritual, the
"everlasting song" remains a highly energized tool of memory.

Notes

1. bell hooks, *A Woman's Mourning Song* (New York: Harlem River Press, 1993), 3.
2. Phillipe Ariès, *The Hour of Our Death* (New York: Knopf, 1981). See also Pierre Nora's essay, "Between Memory and History: Les Lieux de Memoire," in *History and Memory in African-American Culture*, ed. Genevieve Fabre and Robert O'Meally (New York: Oxford University Press, 1994), 284–300.
3. Sigmund Freud, "Mourning and Melancholia," in *The Standard Edition of the Complete Psychological Works of Sigmund Freud*, ed. James Strachey (London: Hogarth Press, 1953–74), 14:243.
4. For Holiday's distance from the gospel tradition, see Leon Forrest, "A Solo Long-Song: For Lady Day," in *The Furious Voice for Freedom* (Wakefield RI: Asphodel Press, 1994), 344–95. On black "self-recovery," see bell hooks, *Sisters of the Yam: Black Women and Self-Recovery* (Boston: South End Press, 1993).
5. Forrest, "Solo Long-Song," 377.
6. bell hooks, *Sisters of the Yam* (Boston: South End Press, 1993), 100–101, 102.
7. This essay has been strongly influenced by the analyses of music and cultural memory in Paul Gilroy, *The Black Atlantic: Modernity and Double Consciousness* (Cambridge: Harvard University Press, 1993).
8. Du Bois quoted in David Levering Lewis, *W. E. B. Du Bois: Biography of a Race, 1868–1919* (New York: Henry Holt, 1993), 77.
9. Walter Benjamin, "Theses on the Philosophy of History," in *Illuminations*, ed. Hannah Arendt, trans. Harry Zohn (New York: Schocken Books, 1969), 255.
10. W. E. B. Du Bois, *The Souls of Black Folk* (New York: Vintage, 1990), 180.
11. Houston A. Baker Jr., *Blues, Ideology, and Afro-American Literature* (Chicago: University of Chicago Press, 1984), 194, 196.
12. Du Bois, *Souls of Black Folk*, 182.
13. Ibid., 182, 185. For Du Bois's views on religion, see Wilson Jeremiah Moses, *Afrotopia: The Roots of African American Popular History* (Cambridge: Cambridge University Press, 1998), 136–68.
14. Du Bois, *Souls of Black Folk*, 188.
15. Freud, "Mourning and Melancholia," 253.
16. For another perspective on Du Bois and mourning, see Claudia Tate, *Psychoanalysis and Black Novels: Desire and the Protocols of Race* (New York: Oxford University Press, 1998), esp. 47–85.
17. See Roger Abrahams, "Phantoms of Romantic Nationalism in Folkloristics," *Journal of American Folklore* 106, issue 419 (winter 1993), 3–37.
18. See Slavoj Žižek, *For They Know Not What They Do* (London: Verso, 1991), 20.
19. Du Bois, *Souls of Black Folk*, 8–9. For a contrasting interpretation of Du Bois and dialectical thought, see Shamoon Zamir, *Dark Voices: W. E. B. Du Bois and American Thought, 1888–1903* (Chicago: University of Chicago Press, 1995).
20. Mitchell Robert Breitwieser, *American Puritanism and the Defense of Mourning: Religion, Grief, and Ethnology in Mary White Rowlandson's Captivity Narrative* (Madison: University of Wisconsin Press, 1990), 42.

21. Cornel West, *The American Evasion of Philosophy* (Madison: University of Wisconsin Press, 1989), 143.
22. For a fuller discussion of the spirituals debate, see Paul A. Anderson, *Deep River: Music and Memory in Harlem Renaissance Thought* (Duke University Press, forthcoming).
23. James Weldon Johnson, *Along This Way* (New York: Penguin Books, 1990), 203.
24. Jean Toomer, *Cane*, ed. Darwin T. Turner (New York: W. W. Norton, 1988), 14.
25. For the elegiac mode in modern poetry, see Jahan Ramazani, *Poetry of Mourning: The Modern Elegy from Hardy to Heaney* (Chicago: University of Chicago Press, 1994).
26. Freud, "Mourning and Melancholia," 246.
27. Jean Toomer, "On Being an American," from "Outline of an Autobiography" (ca. 1931–32), in *The Wayward and the Seeking: A Collection of Writings by Jean Toomer*, ed. Darwin T. Turner (Washington DC: Howard University Press, 1980), 123.
28. Ibid., 129.
29. James Clifford, *The Predicament of Culture: Twentieth-Century Ethnography, Literature, and Art* (Cambridge: Harvard University Press, 1988), 244, 241.
30. James Clifford, "Of Other Peoples: Beyond the 'Salvage' Paradigm," in *Discussions in Contemporary Culture*, ed. Hal Foster (Seattle: Bay Press, 1987), 121.
31. Jean Toomer to Waldo Frank, [n.d., late 1922 or early 1923], in *A Jean Toomer Reader: Selected Unpublished Writings*, ed. Frederick L. Rusch (New York: Oxford University Press, 1991), 24.
32. Although the folk Negro lamented in *Cane* had "all but passed away," Toomer nevertheless felt that "when I come up to Seventh Street and Theatre, a wholly new life confronts me. A life, I am afraid, that Sherwood Anderson would not get his beauty from. From it is jazzed, strident, modern. Seventh Street is the song of crude new life. Of a new people. Negro? Only in the *boldness* of its expression. In its healthy freedom. American." Toomer quoted in Michael North, *The Dialect of Modernism: Race, Language, and Twentieth-Century Literature* (New York: Oxford University Press, 1994), 167.
33. Henry Louis Gates Jr., "The Same Difference: Reading Jean Toomer, 1923–1982," in *Figures in Black: Words, Signs, and the "Racial Self"* (New York: Oxford University Press, 1994), 167.
34. Alain Locke, "The Negro Spirituals," in *The New Negro*, ed. Alain Locke (New York: Atheneum, 1968), 201.
35. Alain Locke, *The Negro and His Music* (Port Washington NY: Kennikat Press, 1968), 19.
36. For a critique of "New Negro" music leaders, see Michael Harris, *The Rise of Gospel Blues: The Music of Thomas Andrew Dorsey in the Urban Church* (New York: Oxford University Press, 1992). For a defense, see Jon Michael Spencer, *The New Negroes and Their Music: The Success of the Harlem Renaissance* (Knoxville: University of Tennessee Press, 1997).
37. Zora Neale Hurston, "Spirituals and Neo-Spirituals," in *Negro: An Anthology*, ed. Hugh Ford (New York: Frederick Ungar, 1970), 223, 224.
38. Ibid., 225, 224.
39. Ibid., 224.
40. Zora Neale Hurston, "How It Feels to Be Colored Me" [1928], *I Love Myself When I Am Laughing . . . And Then Again When I Am Looking Mean and Impressive: A Zora Neale Hurston Reader*, ed. Alice Walker (New York: Feminist Press, 1979), 153.

41. Zora Neale Hurston, "Concert" [c. 1942], unpublished appendix to *Dust Tracks on a Road*, in *Zora Neale Hurston: Folklore, Memoirs, and Other Writings*, ed. Cheryl A. Wall (New York: Library of America, 1995), 805.
42. Zora Neale Hurston, "Characteristics of Negro Expression," in *Negro: An Anthology*, ed. Hugh Ford, 28.
43. Hazel V. Carby, "The Politics of Fiction, Anthropology, and the Folk: Zora Neale Hurston," in *New Essays on Their Eyes Were Watching God*, ed. Michael Awkward (Cambridge: Cambridge University Press, 1990), 75, 76.
44. Zora Neale Hurston, *Dust Tracks on a Road* (New York: Harper Perennial, 1991), 64. For a brilliant reading of unconscious and preconscious desire and the work of mourning in Hurston's novels, especially *Seraph on the Suwanee* (1948), see Claudia Tate, *Psychoanalysis and Black Novels* (New York: Oxford University Press, 1998), 148–77. Tate argues that Hurston took up folklore collecting as a way to "work through the trauma of her mother's death" and that this "professional devotion would be more than a vocation; it would be a means of mourning and reparation" (160). I agree but emphasize in this essay how Hurston's critique of the "school of sobbing Negrohood" was a repudiation of the "New Negro" logic of mourning and cultural evolution propagated by Du Bois and Locke.

Further Reading

Breitwieser, Mitchell Robert. *American Puritanism and the Defense of Mourning: Religion, Grief, and Ethnology in Mary White Rowlandson's Captivity Narrative.* Madison: University of Wisconsin Press, 1990.
    A textually sensitive and theoretically audacious reading of a classic early American text that features a powerful interrogation of psychoanalytic models of mourning and melancholia and their applicability to cultural analysis.
Cavell, Stanley. *This New Yet Unapproachable America.* Albuquerque: Living Batch Press, 1989.
    A brief but philosophically powerful meditation on the theme of epistemological skepticism and responses made to it in the work of Wittgenstein, Heidegger, and Emerson that deftly argues for the place of Freud's "Mourning and Melancholia" in the tradition of modern philosophy.
Santner, Eric. *Stranded Objects: Mourning, Memory, and Film in Postwar Germany.* Ithaca: Cornell University Press, 1990.
    Along with a set of elegant psychoanalytically informed interrogations of representations of the Holocaust in German film, this book offers a deep challenge to some basic assumptions in postmodern thought and, particularly, the deconstructivist interpretive models of Paul de Man and Jacques Derrida.
Schiesari, Juliana. *The Gendering of Melancholia: Feminism, Psychoanalysis, and the Symbolics of Loss in Renaissance Literature.* Ithaca: Cornell University Press, 1992.
    A useful overview and powerful feminist critique of patriarchal thinking within psychoanalytic depictions of mourning and melancholia that confronts and finds wanting the work of Freud, Kristeva, Lacan, and others.

II

ARCHITECTURE

LEVI SMITH

WINDOW OR MIRROR

THE VIETNAM VETERANS MEMORIAL AND
THE AMBIGUITY OF REMEMBRANCE

ON 9 MAY 1997, in a revealing if diplomatic comment, the new American ambassador to Vietnam (the first to visit that country since the war ended) and a former POW, said, after landing in Hanoi, that he had not made up his mind whether the war was a mistake or not. Despite the lack of any official agreement on the meaning of the war twenty-two years after it ended, Pete Peterson's presence in Hanoi was clear evidence that the painful divisions the war caused among Americans have apparently been overcome.

Although this process of healing from the first war America lost has taken place through many vehicles, including domestic and international politics and through the cultural productions of the popular media as well as literature and the fine arts, it is generally agreed that the Vietnam Veterans Memorial on the Mall in Washington has played a central role in helping Americans to come to terms with the past.[1] How, despite the lack of any general agreement on the war's meaning, has the memorial managed to be so effective?

It is apparent that the memorial's success is grounded first and foremost in its inclusive presentation of the names of the dead. This feature defines the memory of the war as that of the Americans who gave their lives in it. Through its listing of all the dead, the memorial emphasizes the individual rather than any transcendent national symbol. The administration of the memorial has extended this focus on the individual to all who visit it. Visitors have been encouraged to touch the memorial, to take rubbings of names from it, and to leave objects before the Wall, which are preserved in a national archive.[2]

Underlying this individual focus, and at the center of this interactivity, rests a profoundly ambiguous object—the Wall. A number of its elements combine to create this ambiguity. The wall's form presents a perspectival conundrum—it appears to grow larger as it recedes from the viewer. It points to both the Washington Monument and the Lincoln Memorial, referring to both a "good" war, the American Revolution, and to a tragic one, the Civil War. It is located on the Mall but inverts many of the characteristics of the other memorials there. The names are listed in chronological order but are arranged in a circle, beginning and ending in the center. Its most effective and influential ambiguous element, however, is the high polish of its black granite surface that allows it to appear as a window or as a mirror.

In an important essay on the memorial published in 1986, the philosopher Charles Griswold argued that the Vietnam Veterans Memorial is unique in contextualizing the deaths it records not through the traditional iconography of heroism, service, or sacrifice but by reflecting, in its polished black granite, the image of the beholder over the names of the dead and by "pointing" with its walls to the Washington Monument and the Lincoln Memorial.[3] He characterized the memorial as "fundamentally interrogative." For Griswold, the central element of this interrogative process is the memorial's polished surface: "In looking at the names one cannot help seeing oneself looking at them. On a bright day one also sees the reflection of the Washington or Lincoln Memorials along with one's own reflection. The dead and the living thus meet, and the living are forced to ask whether those names should be on that wall, and whether others should die in similar causes." In the next sentence, however, Griswold identified the beholder and reader as one who did not serve: "Nineteen sixty-nine, perhaps one of your college years: as you studied books, these people were dying one after the other."[4] Is his description of the perception of the memorial true for all who experience it?

In this essay I describe the discovery of the metaphorical significance of the polished surface and its use as it developed over the first ten years of the memorial's existence. I argue that the two interpretations of the polished surface—as a window leading to the past or as a mirror bringing the past, represented by the names, into the present—embody two distinct responses to the memorial, two distinct stages of mourning, and two distinct groups of mourners. Over the course of the first ten years of the memorial's existence, the representation in the media of the polished surface follows a particular evolution—from window to mirror and on to representations that stress the multiplicity of the mirror's reflections. I argue that this evolving interpretation in the media of the polished surface reveals the progress of cultural mourning of the Vietnam War. Finally, I discuss two subsequent memorials, the Vietnam Veterans Memorial in New York City and the Civil Rights Memorial in Montgomery, Alabama, designed by Maya Lin and dedicated in 1989. I suggest that the reception of the Washington Vietnam Veterans Memorial crucially influenced both these memorials' representations of the transparent surface as a medium for intensifying the beholder's encounter with the remembered past.

The Invention of the Symbolism of
the Polished Surface

In the past, death in war has commonly been set in the context of either religion or patriotism. The Vietnam Veterans Memorial is unusual in shunning these traditional elements of contextualization. It did so by design. In fact, the organizers of the competition to build the memorial had specifically cautioned designers against any representation of the purpose or meaning of the war.[5] They feared that any such statement would be likely to arouse opposition to the design and thwart the building of the memorial.[6]

Instead of a representation of the war, the memorial was meant to be a monument to all the Americans who served in the war. The idea of building a memorial to the veterans was originally that of a former private first class, Jan Scruggs, whose only stipulation was that the memorial feature the names of all who had died in the war. Although local and regional war memorials often list the names of the dead, it is highly unusual for a national memorial to do so. Designers were encouraged to make the listing of the names and the distinguished site on the Mall the focus of their designs. Maya Lin's design was chosen by the jury of professionals because it so simply and elegantly fulfilled these requirements.

When Lin's design was announced, many found its funerary emphasis appropriate to the reality of the death of those who had given their lives in the war; they also found it a profound symbol of the tragedy of the war. However, among those who regarded the war as a "noble cause," a few found the memorial insulting.[7] Thomas Carhart, a decorated veteran of Vietnam and a leader of the opposition to the design, specifically rejected the funerary focus of the memorial, declaring: "This is not a memorial to grieve or mourn. This is a memorial to honor those who served."[8] A group of politically powerful conservatives and veterans demanded that the memorial be changed.[9] A compromise was reached over the course of a year in which an inscription was added to the memorial, and a flag and a sculpture of three infantrymen were placed near it. Almost a decade later a final addition—a sculptural group of nurses aiding a wounded soldier—was placed at the east end of the area of the memorial.

The interpretation of the memorial's reflective surface as a central symbolic element contextualizing the names of the dead was first advanced by Maya Lin and her supporters in order to counter the assertion that Lin's design was too exclusively funereal, and that it did insufficient honor to the Vietnam veterans.[10] The polished surface was first interpreted metaphorically a year and a half after Lin's design had been chosen, and only two months before the memorial was dedicated. On 20 September 1982, Frederick Hart officially presented the model of his sculpture of three infantrymen to the public. His characterization of Lin's design at this press conference seems to have spurred her supporters to consider the symbolic effect of the Wall's dark, polished surface. Hart said his sculpture was intended to "effect an interplay between image and metaphor," and he went on to describe the Wall in terms that refigure it as an ocean, the traditional symbol of unfathomability: "I see the Wall as a kind of ocean, a sea of sacrifice that is overwhelming, and nearly incomprehensible in its sweep of names. I place these figures on the shore of that sea, gazing upon it, standing vigil before it, reflecting the human face of it, the human heart."[11] It is in this context, of the Wall interpreted as a dark sea and of Hart's figures as "reflecting the human face of it," that the mirror-like surface of the Wall is first advanced as a profound symbolic element of the memorial.

The next day, in an emotional article in the *Washington Post*, the reflective surface became the medium for an apotheosis of the inscribed names, triumphing over Hart's embodiment of them. For James J. Kilpatrick, the conservative columnist who had long supported the drive to build a memorial, the names' presence in the reflective surface transcended their figural embodiment.[12] He wrote: "On this sunny Friday morning, the black walls mirrored the clouds of a summer's ending and reflected the leaves of an autumn's beginning, and the names—the names!—were etched enduringly upon the sky."[13]

Less than a month later, in an article in the October 1982 edition of the *Journal of the American Institute of Architects,* Maya Lin responded directly to Hart's contention that his sculpture "reflected the human face of the memorial," for the first time specifically describing the symbolic effect of the reflective wall on visitors: "as each person enters the memorial, seeing his face reflected amongst the names, can the human element escape him? Surely seeing himself and the surroundings reflected within the memorial is a more moving and personal experience than any one artist's figurative or allegorical interpretation could engender."[14]

The following month, on Veterans Day 1982, the symbolism of the mirrored surface was promoted by speakers at the official dedication of the memorial. The Wall's reflectivity was described as an agent of the memorial's conciliatory role in a prayer written by John Wheeler, one of the leaders of the drive to build the memorial, and delivered by Chaplain Max D. Sullivan of the U.S. Army. The prayer emphasized the memorial's reflectivity by means of the repeated phrase: "Standing before this monument, we see reflected in a dark mirror dimly . . . the past. . . . a chance to let go of suffering. . . . (and) a time for honoring."[15] The National Commander of the Veterans of Foreign Wars interpreted the memorial's polished surface more generally as an inducement to reflection: "Generations to come will walk before these gleaming walls and, like them, will reflect. They will consider the memories of those who died. They will consider the legacy of the living veterans. And they will take from this memorial a promise to be ever true to their American heritage."[16]

The Wall as Window

Though Lin and others connected with the Vietnam Veterans Memorial Fund promoted the Wall's reflectivity as an important agent and symbol of its conciliatory role, between 1982 and 1984 most descriptions in the popular media located the memorial's power in individuals' emotional confrontations with the reality of death and loss symbolized by the names. In most early accounts that mention the Wall's polished surface, the movement is inward, toward the past, the names and the death of those they commemorate. The polished surface is implicitly interpreted less as a mirror than a window. When one veteran, Thom Famularo, wrote of his experience visiting the memorial for the first time, he did not mention reflections at all. Instead the "large rock carved with names," the "wall of black granite" leads him back into the war and the day when another took the bullets he felt were destined for him.[17]

In Laura Palmer's book *Shrapnel in the Heart,* a collection of twenty-seven short interviews with people who left letters or objects at the Wall between 1985 and 1986, there are few mentions of the Wall's reflective surface. In one account, a woman who went to the memorial to pay homage to a close high school friend described how she only noticed her reflection later, when she saw the developed photographs she had taken at the Wall.[18] This is indicative of the woman's focus, both literal and emotional, on the friend's name.[19]

William Broyles, a Vietnam veteran and editor at *Newsweek,* wrote in late 1982 of his experience at the memorial. As Broyles stood before the names he saw his own reflection. He wrote, "It fell across the names like a ghost." Seeing his reflection made him wonder why he was there instead of them. Beneath that feeling of wonder, he described, "a deep relief tinged with guilt: my name isn't on the Wall."[20] For Broyles, the polished surface does not lead outward from the memorial but acts to place him in the field of the dead, where he ponders his survival in contrast to those who died. The guilt he feels toward his sense of relief suggests one source of the resistance that veterans in particular may feel to reading the reflection in any broader sense.

But the resistance that active mourners feel to seeing the reflections is also grounded in the physical experience of viewing the Wall. The interpretation of the polished surface as a window or a mirror contains an implicit choice of attention—the beholder is focused either on the names "beyond" the gloss of the Wall or on the reflections and not on the names. Because of this, seeing the memorial as a mirror could be interpreted as involving an implicit turning away from the names. For mourners of specific individuals this could be interpreted as an act of infidelity to the memory the names represent. Because of this, mourners may be reluctant to see the reflections. If they are noticed, then the observer must choose whether to interpret them symbolically. This decision represents a further distancing of the observer from the names. In fact, any metaphorical interpretation of the memorial could also be interpreted as a turning away from its primary focus—the names.

By December 1984 Broyles, who criticized Lin's design for its lack of any overt official meaning in the earlier article, had revised his opinion of it, describing the memorial as a site of healing and release from the past.[21] Broyles stressed that what the veterans had missed the most was the camaraderie they had experienced in the war. Drawn together before the memorial, they found each other again. Broyles interprets the memorial's success in terms of its promotion of a community of mourners who aid each other in coming to terms with their grief. His guilt at surviving is alleviated by the companionship of others who shared the experience of the war.

Whereas Broyles indicated that he had come to terms with his memories of the war largely through the companionship that the memorial made possible, other veterans resisted reconciliation. By visiting the memorial at night these veterans set themselves apart from visitors less closely tied to the war. A common experience of veterans traumatized by the war and suffering from post-traumatic stress disorder is nightmares in which they relive the traumatic events of the war. By visiting the memorial at night they find comfort in the presence of their comrades, not so much the living, however, as those listed on the Wall. As the author of an article in *Washington Magazine* on the phenomenon noted: "The dead seem closer at night." At night the memorial's blackness becomes absolute. The engraved names are accented by the small floodlights at its base. At the same time, the Wall's reflectivity is radically reduced.[22]

It is apparent from these examples that visitors whose memories of the war are most immediate and painful and who mourn the loss of specific individuals often ignore or resist broader interpretations of the polished surface's reflectivity. These narratives suggest a stage of mourning in which the glazed surface of the Wall is interpreted as a window to the past. When reflections are acknowledged they are those of individuals rather than of the Mall and its monuments. These reflected individuals, drawn together before the names, are recognized as forming a community in which mourners find sanction for their sorrow and release from the past. For those veterans who remain unappeased, however, the night cloaks the Wall. It cancels the memorial's reflective power while (literally) spotlighting the names of the dead.

The Wall as Mirror

At the other extreme from these mourners are those who emphasized the reflective surface as the memorial's central symbolic attribute. In May 1983 the American Institute of Architects (AIA) gave Maya Lin their award of architectural excellence for her design, calling it "among the strongest designs for a war memorial ever conceived." In an article in the institute's journal celebrating the award, author Robert Campbell found the varied reflections in the Wall "an astonishing integration of almost everything a monument could say about a war." He acknowledged the priority of the inscribed names, writing that it is only a little later that you recognize your own face and other reflections among the names of the dead, "an effect that makes the granite mirror a kind of scrim set between past and present, between living and dead, integrating both on a single dark plane." In contrast to the author of the article mentioned above on the separatism of the memorial's night visitors, who described the Wall's "shimmer" without any mention of reflections, Campbell emphasizes the protean effect of the reflections' greater obscurity at dusk. In the evening, he wrote, the memorial "reaches out beyond itself to engage and transform its surrounding world."[23]

The effects Campbell attributes to the mirrored surface, of "integration," "engagement," and "transformation," are suggestive. They can be interpreted as those of the aesthetic masterwork, but they are also those of the process and goals of political action and of psychotherapy. In their common acceptance of "transformation" they emphasize change rather than the affirmation of tradition.

But, as we have seen, the reflective surface can also be interpreted as conveying more conservative ideals. At the official ceremony on Veterans Day 1984, marking the dedication of Frederick Hart's sculpture and the transferal of the Vietnam Veterans Memorial to government ownership, President Reagan skillfully used references to the Wall's reflections of the Mall and of visitors in his speech to deliver an official interpretation of the deaths of the American soldiers. He emphasized the Wall's reflectivity, noting: "The memorial reflects as a mirror reflects, so that when you find the name you're searching for, you find in it your own reflection. And as you touch it, from certain angles, you're touching, too, the reflection of the Washington Monument or the chair in which great Abe Lincoln sits." Then he offered an official interpretation of the meaning of the reflections, declaring that "Those who fought in Vietnam are a part of us, part of our history. They reflected the best in us. . . . it's good that we (can honor them) in the reflected glow of the enduring symbols of our country."[24]

Whereas the president's interpretation of the mirrored surface contextualizes the deaths of those the memorial commemorates, linking them with national ideals, the art community, following the example of the writer in the architectural journal, stressed the integrative effect of the Wall as mirror. This integration of the living and the dead and of the present with the past may imply a healing of the divisions the war caused or made manifest, but this is not spelled out in art critics' discussions of the memorial.

Although accounts in the popular press, often written by veterans or focusing on them, tended to take the form of individual narratives of suffering and loss, accounts in the art press moved from descriptions of the formal attributes of the memorial through metaphorical readings of them to a celebration of the designer's genius and the memorial's originality. For these critics, the memorial offers its most profound meaning in the aesthetic glorification of the memory of those it commemorates. The actual experiences of mourners before the Wall, emphasized in accounts in the mass media, are largely ignored in the art press. None of the accounts emphasizes a personal connection with the memorial or the names inscribed on it. The injunction in professional critical and academic circles against the personal and anecdotal, combined with most art writers' isolation from the experience of being in the war, leads to a sharp separation between these descriptions of the memorial and those, most often by veterans, in the popular media.

The Fractured Surface of Public Memory

Beginning in February 1985 and climaxing in the middle of April of that year, representations and descriptions of the memorial played a central role in the media's observances of the tenth anniversary of the end of the war. On that occasion both *Newsweek* and *Time* represented the memory of the war through images of the Wall.[25] The cover of the 15 April *Newsweek* featured a close-up, back view, from the shoulders up, of a camouflage-dressed vet pressing a triangular folded flag (the type given to the next of kin at a military funeral) against the Wall.[26] Though the *New York Times Magazine* and *National Geographic* also ran covers featuring the memorial, only *Time* emphasized the reflective surface of the Wall in its cover image, superimposing, like a reflection, a photograph of the last helicopter leaving the roof of the Saigon embassy over a close-up of the names on the Wall.

Inside the magazine, images and captions further suggested the Wall's embodiment of the past in its dark, polished surface. The title page of the article in *Time* featured a famous photograph of the wounded marines of Hue on a track vehicle. On the following page, another photograph shows a veteran in jungle fatigues, his hand on the Wall, staring at a name. The image covers three-quarters of the two-page spread, and on the right, in white on a black column, is a quote from Michael Herr's well-known war memoir *Dispatches*, which emphasizes the chaotic reality of war: "Everything I see is blown through with smoke, everything is on fire everywhere. It doesn't matter that memory distorts; every image, every sound comes back out of smoke and the smell of things burning."[27] The quote's emphasis on smoke and seeing, associated with the image of the veteran looking at the Wall, suggests a reading of the Wall's blackness and polish as a sort of petrified smoke through which the past, embodied in the previous page's famous photograph, can now only dimly be seen. In the quote, Herr acknowledges both the vividness and the inevitable distortion of his memories.

At the time of the anniversary, few commentators emphasized the memorial's reflections of the Mall and the Washington Monument as media for considering the historical particularities of the war and its relation to national ideals. Critics also tended to reject official interpretations, stressing the problematic and unstable nature of symbolic or analogic characterizations of the war.[28] In fact, most commentators admitted the impossibility of settling on any single meaning (and thus memory) of it.[29] Typical is the conclusion of David Fromkin and James Chace, writing in *Foreign Affairs:* "If we could all look at that terrible experience through the same pair of eyes, it could teach us much. But we cannot, so it cannot. That may be the final tragedy of the Vietnam war."[30]

Echoing this acceptance of the variousness of the memory of the war, a new interpretation of the polished surface appears at this time that stresses its multiplicity, fragmentariness, and illusory quality. After a section detailing the encouragement of exaggerated body counts and lying, and the split of language between "officialese" and the soldiers' slang, the author of an article in *Newsweek* described the memorial as a redemptive statement of truth: "The Viet Nam Memorial is, in a sense, the most purely true thing that can be said about the American war in Viet Nam. It has the tragic grace of the incontestably lost and therefore the incontestably true—the names of those who died in such a context of multiple illusions."[31] Although this quotation refers specifically to the government's obfuscatory language, it is possible to read it as suggesting that the reflective surface of the memorial is also "a context of multiple illusions." In the *Nation* magazine, the philosopher Arthur Danto stressed the illusory quality of the reflections. He compared the memorial to Plato's cave, writing that "the living are in (the memorial) only as appearances. Only the names of the dead, on the surface, are real."[32]

In 1986, Charles Griswold's essay on the memorial, mentioned earlier, appeared.[33] In it he emphasized that rather than representing any single interpretation of the war, the memorial, through its list of names, its form, its orientation on the Mall, and, centrally, its reflective surface, leads the beholder to question the memory of the past. Although in Reagan's prescriptive interpretation the memorial reflected the ideals of the nation, in Griswold's essay it is the memorial's reflection of the beholder among the names and within the context of the Mall that compels him or her to question the past.

Two years later, in a remarkable essay on the memorial published in the critical journal *Genre,* Gordon O. Taylor offered a variation of Griswold's thesis, arguing that the Wall and the sculpture are an enticement to attention.[34] Whereas Griswold stressed the Mall's central role in offering a context for the deaths recorded on the Wall, Taylor explored the phenomenological complexity of the experience of reading the engraved names in their glittering field of reflection. The implications of the polished surface's fragmentariness and multiplicity, first remarked upon at the time of the tenth anniversary of the war's end, reach their full development in this academic essay.

Whereas Griswold, along with many other critics, found Frederick Hart's sculpture incidental to the memorial's meaning, Taylor argues that the statues perform a function similar to the Wall. For Taylor, the sculptures appear as symbols not of meaning but of the desire to *find* it. The central meaning of the figures is contained in their gaze, one that echoes the gaze of all who visit the memorial. That gaze represents the effort of reading the Wall.

Unlike Griswold, who found the reflections a contextualizing element of the memorial, Taylor interprets the memorial as a book possessed of pages whose glistening surface makes its words mysterious. The effort of reading the Wall, of penetrating this mystery, involves a complex process of struggling for meaning. The Wall is "unyielding of its secret while compelling an effort to understand."[35] In the same way, Taylor finds that the numerous, at times conflicting, accounts by veterans of the war comprise a dark mass that contains the truth while resisting any easy interpretation. Taylor uses the analogy of "reading between the lines" to suggest the sort of interpretive process that must be undertaken to come to terms with the war. What he finds between the lines is fluctuant and multifarious. This "dark space" is "a region of heart and mind," made actual in the metaphorically water-like space of the Wall: "As they approach the surface—fragments of truth coalescing as they come . . . they refract and are refracted by the chiseled text which contains them all, through the glare-ice sheen of the granite in which that text swims."[36]

Taylor concludes by observing that the unwritten history of the war remains "between the lines" inscribed on the wall: "In a narrative of names both cryptic and clear—Vietnamese names, invisible and unknowable, together with the names of Americans unknown, between the lines, among those claimed as our own— thus is written and still to be inscribed an uncreated American memory of Vietnam."[37] For Taylor, the memorial's glittering surface, which contains both the names and the beholder, both the past and the present, is a perfect symbol of the essential indeterminateness and ambiguity of memory. By 1985 in the popular press, and by 1988 in the academic press, the two interpretations of the polished surface, as window and as mirror, had been joined by a third that stressed the ambiguous effect created by the presence of both.

From Window to Fractured Mirror:
The Memorial in Film

We can follow the evolving interpretation of the polished surface through representations of the memorial in three mainstream films released between 1987 and 1991. The memorial first appeared in a fictional film in 1987 in the opening scene of *Hamburger Hill*. In a re-creation of the disastrous 1969 battle for a strategically insignificant hill, the film begins with a running shot of the memorial on a bleak day. Backed by ominous, anxious music composed by Phillip Glass, the camera dollies along the wall, showing a blur of names against the fluctuating reflection of the Washington Monument and trees. Flickers of movement appear seemingly through the surface of the wall; the sound of gunfire, explosions, and men shouting drowns out the music; and the image of the Wall fades into soldiers scrambling for cover, carrying their wounded through high grass.

The use of the Wall in *Hamburger Hill* brilliantly translates to film the mourning veterans' perception of the memorial. The names

may begin as those of individuals, but they blur into a recollection
of the war. Reflections are an impediment to be overcome by seeing into the Wall and the history it records through the names
inscribed on it. In its run along the Wall, the opening sequence
also records it as a place of passage, both physical and temporal.

Norman Jewison's film version of Bobbie Ann Mason's novel *In
Country*, released in 1989, concludes with an extended scene set
at the Memorial.[38] A suffering vet, his caring niece, and her grandmother search for and find the name of their dead relative, touch
the Wall, take a photograph of the name, and leave treasured objects
before it. The Wall's polished surface is represented as a limpid
reflection of the faces of the family members as they search for the
name and then stand before it. At the end of the film the three
family members are seemingly freed of the weight of the past. In
the film's last shot they walk away from the memorial toward the
Washington Monument, a reunited family happily discussing
breakfast. While *Hamburger Hill* represented the memorial as a
window to the past, *In Country*, set in the present, stresses the
common use of the memorial. Director Norman Jewison even
imitated the actions of visitors to the memorial, visiting it (on 27
September 1989) to leave a copy of the film at the Wall.

The ambiguous and fractured quality of the polished surface is
emphasized in the concluding episode of *China Beach*, a popular
television drama that followed the day-to-day adventures of a
group of nurses and doctors stationed at the 95th Evacuation Hospital located next to "China Beach," a recreational facility connected with the U.S. base at Da Nang. *China Beach* premiered in
the spring of 1988 and in July 1991 broadcast its concluding episode as a special two-hour program. The action takes place in the
near past, long after the war is over and everyone has returned to
civilian life. The last few episodes led from the war to this point.
The protagonists have done well, but nurse McMurphy, the focus
of the series, has not resolved her feelings about the past. The final
episode is framed with McMurphy's crisis, brought to a focus in
her guilt and sorrow at not remembering the name of a dying soldier she comforted on her last day in Vietnam.

The protagonists come together for a reunion and spontaneously
decide to visit the memorial in Washington. They arrive at dawn.
We see them park their cars at the Mall and walk across the lawn
toward the memorial. As they approach the Wall, we see their
reflections splintered, shivering, and broken in the Wall's panels
in a scene shot with a telephoto lens at an extreme angle.[39] As

their distorted reflections flicker on the Wall, we hear a soulful song about letting go of the past. Close-ups show the friends' faces racked with sorrow. The song conflates the process of saying good-bye to a loved one with taking leave of old memories. As the song ends, the protagonists hug each other and leave the memorial.

This could have served as the conclusion for the series, but the producers added a second visit to the memorial. The friends have all said their good-byes and left when McMurphy returns alone with her daughter to the Wall. As she holds the toddler in her arms and shows her the Wall, she says in a voice-over that she finally remembered the soldier's name, and that though they could not save everyone, she realizes that what is important is that they tried. In the last shot, she is shown walking with her daughter up the path along the memorial toward the Washington Monument into a light that could be either dawn or dusk.

The final episode of *China Beach* encourages us to identify with the most general interpretation of the memorial—a symbol of an era now past—and thus with the generational act of "letting go" of past attachments—saying goodbye—which, of course, is what the last show is actually doing. At the same time, the show presents a very specific interpretation of the memorial as a thera-peutic tool for curing the troubled vet. In both interpretations, the memorial's reflectivity plays a crucial part. The fractured, sliv-ered reflections of the individuals in the first scene suggest the multiplicity, the equivalence, and yet the irreconcilability of their experiences. When McMurphy returns with her daughter, the calm mirror of the Wall, which reflects them and their surroundings, suggests McMurphy's recognition and acceptance of her past and present, and of her place in life. When, at the end of the scene, she walks away from the memorial toward the Washington Monument (a scene very similar to the conclusion of the film version of *In Country*), there is the suggestion that her experience, and those of other Vietnam vets, is now placed in relation to the nation's ori-gins and endurance and is transcended by her role as a parent.

The decision of the producers of *China Beach* to conclude the series in the summer of 1991, a few months after the success of the Gulf War, marks the conclusion of an era of remembrance of the Vietnam War. In the wake of the Gulf War, public and media interest in the Vietnam War noticeably declined. Business and political leaders began to press for an end to the thirty-year-old embargo of Vietnam and for the normalization of relations—a movement that ultimately led to Ambassador Peterson's presence in Hanoi. As these developments have progressed, the Vietnam Veterans Memorial has played a less central role in the nation's memory of the war.

The Medium of Memory

In this essay I have attempted to show how the metaphorical interpretation of the polished surface emerged and developed over the course of the first ten years of the memorial's existence. I have argued that its development echoed the progress of the individual mourner as he or she moved from painful confrontation with loss to a reconciliation with the present. Further, I have suggested that the changing interpretation of the polished surface reflects the nation's efforts to come to terms with the divisive memory of the war. In conclusion, I would like to briefly describe two later memorials that explore the metaphor of the glaze as the medium of memory.

In 1985 New York City dedicated its own memorial to Vietnam veterans. The design, by architects Peter Wormser and William Fellows, is adapted from one that they submitted to the original Vietnam Veterans Memorial competition. The memorial consists of a sixty-six-foot-long wall made of glass bricks that are etched with excerpts from the letters and diaries of Vietnam Veterans. There are passageways cut in the Wall so that one can walk through it. In this memorial, memory (or the past) is represented as a translucent medium like amber in which the individual recollections of soldiers appear. This is akin to the experience of Lin's Wall as a window through which one looks into the dark past—and yet it is significantly different. The past is not dark, as in Lin's design; it is a glowing, gelid medium in which the words and experiences of veterans are preserved. The beholder can walk into and through this medium. The memorial emphasizes the individual memories and experiences of those who fought over more general interpretation of the war. The interrogativity that haunts the ambiguous darkness and reflectivity of Lin's design is confined to a few of the veterans' quotations, which question the meaning of the war.

A very different elaboration of the glossy surface as the medium of memory is found in Maya Lin's subsequent design for the Civil Rights Memorial, commissioned by the Southern Poverty Law Center in Montgomery, Alabama, and dedicated there in 1989. In this memorial the glaze—the medium of memory—becomes palpable. The design features a granite table twelve feet in diameter, inscribed with the names of forty freedom fighters as well as landmark events of the Civil Rights movement. Water flows from a circular opening in the center of the disk to cover the inscriptions with a flowing film. The visitor is encouraged to touch the names through the water. Behind this table, a black granite wall nearly nine feet high and thirty-nine feet long, also covered by a veil of water, is inscribed with a biblical quotation that Martin Luther King used in one of his speeches: "(We will not be satisfied) . . . until justice rolls down like waters and righteousness like a mighty stream." This quotation, which Lin read in a book about the Civil Rights movement, was the inspiration for her design.[40]

In the flowing surface that covers the Civil Rights Memorial, Lin found a way to combine two aspects of the Vietnam Veterans Memorial that emerged during its reception—the metaphorical interpretation of the polished surface and the propensity of visitors to touch the names. The beholder reaches through the film of water to touch the names, facts, and dates, an action that produces a reaction from the memorial, as ripples spread across its surface. I have described the final interpretation of the polished surface of the Vietnam Veterans Memorial as symbolic of the multiplicity of possible viewpoints on the past, emphasizing the location of memory in the individual beholder. The flowing surface of the Civil Rights Memorial, reacting to each touch of the beholder, goes still further, implying not only that memory is individual but that each beholder affects memory by his or her own presence and relation to it. Continuously welling from the center, the moving sheen of water also embodies memory as a process rather than a static entity.

Recently I spoke with a man in his twenties, too young to have known the war, who described his visit to the Vietnam Veterans Memorial. He found it very moving. What chiefly struck him were the names; he mentioned that he had not noticed any reflections in the polished surface of the Wall. In constructing this essay I have emphasized the interpretation of the glazed surface of the Wall as an important element of the memorial, contextualizing the names of the dead. I have suggested that the ability to really see the reflections and to interpret them symbolically represents a stage in the separation of the mourner from the object of grief. But attention to and symbolic interpretation of the reflections may also represent a flight away from the reality of the individual deaths that the names represent. As I noted at the beginning of this essay, Charles Griswold is one of the few academic or art critics who specifies the reader of his text and of the Wall's reflections: "Nineteen sixty-nine, perhaps one of your college years: as you studied books, these people were dying one after the other."[41]

I am drawn to believe that my own interest in the interpretation of the glazed surface, which comes at the expense of perhaps focusing more specifically on the names, "reflects" my own experience of the war. I came of draft age in 1970, had a draft number of 20, and was saved by a student deferment. I helped organize an antiwar committee at my high school the year before, and I protested the war. None of my childhood or early adult acquaintances served, let alone died, in Vietnam. So, in focusing so intently on the polished surface, am I also turning away from the names? For the young man I just mentioned, the complex relation that the "Vietnam generation" has to the war and to the Wall does not exist. For him, it is the awesome spread of death, as it covers the four hundred feet of the memorial, that moves him. Perhaps, for later viewers, the polished surface may serve only to beautify the memorial, or perhaps it will someday again become charged with meaning, as Americans attempt to come to terms with another tragedy.

Notes

1. This essay is drawn from my dissertation on the memorial, "Objects of Memory: The Vietnam Veterans Memorial and the Memory of the War," which was submitted to the Department of Art History at the University of Chicago in October 1997. In the first of two sections, I trace the cultural process of coming to terms with the war from the time of its downturn in 1968 to the decision to build the memorial eleven years later. The second section examines the influence of the memorial on the evolving cultural memory of the war during the first ten years of the memorial's existence.
2. Indicative of the unusual interactivity of the memorial, these innovations were enacted in response to visitors.
3. Charles L. Griswold, "The Vietnam Veterans Memorial and the Washington Mall: Philosophical Thoughts on Political Iconography," *Critical Inquiry* 12 (summer 1986): 699–719.
4. Ibid., 711.
5. The specifications sent to prospective designers cautioned them against making "any political statement" concerning the war in their designs. Asked to clarify this, the design committee, in a list of questions and answers sent out to contestants, further defined "political statement" as "any comment on the rightness, wrongness, or motivation of U.S. policy in entering, conducting, or withdrawing from the war." See "Question and Answer Sheet," 10 February 1981, Records of the Vietnam Veterans Memorial Fund, container no. 63, Manuscript Division, Library of Congress.
6. The Vietnam Veterans Memorial Fund committee's fears that antiwar critics might block the creation of the memorial are mentioned in Jan Scruggs and Joel Swerdlow, *To Heal a Nation* (New York: Harper and Row, 1985), 13.

7. During his campaign for the presidency, Ronald Reagan famously characterized the Vietnam War as a "noble cause" in his August 1980 address to the
annual convention of the Veterans of Foreign Wars in Chicago.

8. Transcript of Thomas Carhart's testimony before the Committee on the
Fine Arts, 13 October 1982, Records of the Vietnam Veterans Memorial
Fund, container no. 29, Manuscript Division, Library of Congress.

9. Led by Vietnam veterans Thomas Carhart and James Webb, the opposition
to the memorial was largely funded by Texas billionaire H. Ross Perot (who
had earlier provided much of the funding for the memorial competition) and
directed in Congress by Representative Henry Hyde of Illinois.

10. In the statement that accompanied her design and that was an important
factor in influencing the jurors' decision, Maya Lin made no mention of the
polished surface as symbolically significant. Rather, she stressed the chronological and circular order of the names and the Wall's "pointing" to the
Lincoln Memorial and the Washington Monument. In a 1985 article in
Time magazine, John Wheeler, a leader of the Vietnam Veterans Memorial
Fund, stated that no one anticipated the effect the polished surface would
have. See K. Andersen, "Hush Timmy—This Is like a Church," *Time* 125
(15 April 1985): 61. The first description of the mirroring effect of the polished surface occurred shortly after the opposition to Lin's design had organized itself in Congress under the leadership of Rep. Henry Hyde of Illinois.
In a long article on Maya Lin in the 3 January 1982 *Washington Post*, the
author, noting that many architects and art historians had praised the memorial's design, stated: "In its polished granite they see beauty." The author
then quoted Lin as saying: "It's a mirror, you can see yourself in it. . . . I can't
wait to see it. It makes two worlds, it doubles the size of the park." See Phil
McCombs, "Maya Lin and the Great Call of China," *Washington Post*, 3
January 1982, F11. Although Lin excitedly described its reflective effect and
noted that it "makes two worlds," she did not link this affect to a symbolic
meaning. Rather, the polished surface's effect is described in aesthetic
terms as contributing to the beauty of the memorial.

11. Benjamin Forgey, "Hart's Statue Unveiled," *Washington Post*, 21 September 1982, B4.

12. Kilpatrick states in the article that his visit to the Wall (then two-thirds
completed) was at Scruggs's invitation.

13. James J. Kilpatrick, "The Names," *Washington Post*, 21 September 1982,
A19.

14. "Proposed Viet Sculpture Shown as Architects Fight Additions," *Journal of
the American Institute of Architects* 71 (October 1982): 22, 27.

15. Transcript of the Vietnam Veterans Memorial Dedication Ceremony, *Con-
gressional Record*, vol. 128, no. 139 (2 December 1982): 2.

16. Transcript of the VVM Dedication, 2.

17. Thom Famularo, "The Wall: A Vietnam Vet's Monumental Reflections,"
Gallery, October 1985, 61–64, 112–13. Though published in 1985, the article concerns a 1984 visit to the memorial.

18. Laura Palmer, *Shrapnel in the Heart* (New York: Random House, 1987), 12.

19. This incident also suggests the important role photography plays in strength-
ening the reflective effect of the Wall. It is in fact through photographic repro-
duction that the Wall's reflections can take on their most stable and overt
symbolism. In photographs, the flux of the reflections disappears, and they
become fixed and enduring. While it is impossible for the beholder to focus
on both the names and the reflections, the photograph, by reducing both to
a single plane, makes them simultaneously visible.

20. William Broyles, "Remembering a War We Want to Forget," *Newsweek* 100
(22 November 1982): 82–83.

21. William Broyles, "Why Men Love War," *Esquire* 102, no. 5 (December 1984): 55–65.
22. Toby Thompson, "'Washingtoniana': Night Watch," *Washingtonian Magazine*, November 1988, 176. In the article Thompson describes the heightened effect of the names: "They descend in ranks, 58,156 of America's dead or missing, toward the vertex of the black chevron. . . . The dead seem closer at night. The wall shimmers behind campfire spots that light the names with a special radiance."
23. Robert Campbell, "An Emotive Place Apart," *Journal of the American Institute of Architects* 72 (May 1983): 150.
24. All quotations in this text are from the official transcript of Ronald Reagan's speech of 11 November 1984, Records of the Vietnam Veterans Memorial Fund, container no. 51, Manuscript Division, Library of Congress.
25. Close-up photographs of the Wall in which individual names could be read appeared on the covers of commemorative issues of *Time, Newsweek, New York Times Magazine*, and *National Geographic*, as well as on the cover of *To Heal a Nation*, the history of the memorial co-written by Jan Scruggs and published that year. The latter three chose images that juxtaposed a red carnation with the names. These images reinforced the commemoration's focus on the individual American costs of the war.
26. The emphatic focus on the veteran of this image (and of the text) may reflect the influence of the magazine's editor, William Broyles, himself a Vietnam veteran.
27. Photographs, "Vietnam: The War That Went Wrong, The Lessons It Taught," *Time* 125, no. 15 (15 April 1985): 16–17. Herr, quoted on 18–19.
28. Joseph Lelyveld, for example, wrote disapprovingly that "Ten years later we are talking about Vietnam again, but often as an analogy." See Joseph Lelyveld, "The Enduring Legacy," *New York Times Magazine*, 31 March 1985, 29–44. An article in *America* took Lelyveld's point as the title of an editorial, "A War of Analogies," to argue that anyone "who considers political realities rather than morality-play fantasies" knows that the idea that Nicaragua would turn the Caribbean "into a Communist lake" is fantasy. See "A War of Analogies," *America* 152 (11 May 1985): 382. Frances Fitzgerald argued that the U.S. reaction to the war has been "solipsistic" in framing the veterans' problems as psychological and personal and in the perception of America having suffered "a failure of will." She went on to say that "The war has not prompted a realistic, reasonable debate about what America's foreign-policy goals are: rather it has prompted violent stirrings of emotion over ridiculous symbols." She cites as a perfect example the invasion of Grenada. Fitzgerald's comments are found in a "Harpers Symposium" article: "What Are the Consequences of Vietnam?" *Harpers* 270 (April 1985): 35–38. In a *Washington Post* op-ed piece, R. Emmett Tyrrell Jr. links "all the critics' weird conjuring" about the meaning of Vietnam to "an attempt to make traditional American isolationism appear sophisticated, as a session with one's shrink appears sophisticated." See R. Emmett Tyrrell Jr., "Nixon Is Right on Vietnam," *Washington Post*, 15 April 1985, A 11.
29. For example, in the *Humanist*, J. Allston James, a veteran of the war, stressed that "there were as many Vietnam wars as vets who fought them." See J. Allston James, "Lessons in Search of a Student," *Humanist* 45 (January/February 1985): 24–25. Joseph Lelyveld extended Allston's observation to include the American people, writing that "In the American mind there are, after all, 2, 3, many Vietnams." See Lelyveld, "Enduring Legacy," 42.
30. David Fromkin and James Chace, "What Are the Lessons of Vietnam?" *Foreign Affairs* 63 (spring 1985): 746.
31. Lance Morrow, "A Bloody Rite of Passage," *Time* 125 (15 April 1985): 26.

32. Arthur Danto, "The Vietnam Veterans Memorial," *Nation* 241 (31 August 1985): 153.
33. Griswold, "Vietnam Veterans Memorial and the Washington Mall."
34. Gordon O. Taylor, "Past as Prologue," *Genre*, 21, no. 4 (winter 1988): 579–84.
35. Ibid., 597.
36. Ibid., 582.
37. Ibid., 583.
38. The scenes of *In Country* that involved close-ups at the Wall were shot at a 60 percent mockup of the memorial constructed in Kentucky. In a review of *In Country*, Jay Scott noted that Park Service regulations that forbid protests at the Wall had been extended to cover filming there. Cameras and actors could not both be present at the Wall. Shots of actors walking along it had to be filmed with a telephoto lens from a distance. Dialogue could not be recorded at the memorial. See Jay Scott, "Mirror, Mirror . . . ," *Film Comment*, 25 (September/October 1989): 11–14.
39. While *In Country* had to make do with a mockup, the *China Beach* crew appears to have made a virtue of necessity with its long-distance shots.
40. This inspiration for Lin is mentioned in Linda Kramer, "Maya Lin Lets Healing Waters Flow over Her Civil Rights Memorial," *People Weekly* 32 (20 November 1989): 80.
41. Griswold, "Vietnam Veterans Memorial," 91.

Further Reading

Bodnar, John. *Remaking America: Public Memory, Commemoration, and Patriotism in the Twentieth Century.* Princeton: Princeton University Press, 1992.
> An excellent study of the forms public memory has taken in America and its uses in this century. Bodnar usefully distinguishes between the "official" memories promoted by the government and the "vernacular" memories of individuals. He specifically discusses the Vietnam Veterans Memorial in the prologue.

Curl, James Stevens. *A Celebration of Death.* New York: Charles Scribners Sons, 1980.
> A thorough study of funerary monuments.

Gass, William. "Monumentality/Mentality." *Oppositions* 25 (fall 1982): 127–44.
> An interesting meditation of the nature of monuments and memory in the modern age.

Griswold, Charles L. "The VVM and the Washington Mall: Philosophical Thoughts on Political Iconography." *Critical Inquiry* 12 (summer 1986): 699–719.
> In the most influential essay on the Vietnam Veterans Memorial, Griswold also brilliantly analyzes the symbolism of the Washington Mall and its monuments.

Huyssen, Andreas. *Twilight Memories.* New York: Routledge, 1995.
> A productive discussion of public memory in the age of postmodernism.

Mosse, George L. *Fallen Soldiers.* Oxford: Oxford University Press, 1990.
> An excellent study of the evolution of war memorials during the First and Second World Wars.

Mumford, Lewis. "Death of a Monument." In *Circle: International Survey of Constructive Art,* ed. J. L. Martin, Ben Nicholson, and Naum Gabo. London: Faber and Faber, 1937.
    An influential essay on the modern era's rejection of memorials and monuments.
Scruggs, Jan C., and Joel L. Swerdlow. *To Heal a Nation.* New York: Harper and Row, 1985.
    A gripping narrative on the conception and creation of the Vietnam Veterans Memorial by its founder.
Whittick, Arnold. *War Memorials.* London: Country Life, 1946.
    A good general study of war memorials.

JAMES E. YOUNG

AGAINST REDEMPTION

THE ARTS OF COUNTERMEMORY
IN GERMANY TODAY

I

LIKE OTHER cultural and aesthetic forms in Europe and America, the monument—in both idea and practice—has undergone a radical transformation over the course of the twentieth century. As intersection between public art and political memory, the monument has necessarily reflected the aesthetic and political revolutions, as well as the wider crises of representation, following all of this century's major upheavals—including both First and Second World Wars, the Vietnam War, the rise and fall of Communist regimes in the former Soviet Union and its eastern European satellites. In every case, the monument reflects both its sociohistorical and aesthetic context: artists working in eras of cubism, expressionism, socialist realism, earthworks, minimalism, or conceptual art remain answerable to both the needs of art and official history. The result has been a metamorphosis of the monument from the heroic, self-aggrandizing figurative icons of the late nineteenth century celebrating national ideals and triumphs to the anti-heroic, often ironic and self-effacing conceptual installations marking the national ambivalence and uncertainty of late-twentieth-century postmodernism.

In fact, Andreas Huyssen has even suggested that in a contemporary age of mass memory production and consumption, there seems to be an inverse proportion between the memorialization of the past and its contemplation and study.[1] It is as if once we assign monumental form to memory, we have to some degree divested ourselves of the obligation to remember. In the eyes of modern critics and artists, the traditional monument's essential stiffness and grandiose pretensions to permanence thus doom it to an archaic, premodern status. Even worse, by insisting that its meaning is as fixed as its place in the landscape, the monument seems oblivious to the essential mutability in all cultural arti-facts, the ways the significance in all art evolves over time. In this way, monuments have long sought to provide a naturalizing locus for memory, in which a state's triumphs and martyrs, its ideals and founding myths, are cast as naturally true as the landscape in which they stand. These are the monument's sustaining illusions, the principles of its seeming longevity and power. But, in fact, as several generations of artists—modern and postmodern alike—have made scathingly clear, neither the monument nor its mean-ing is really everlasting. Both a monument and its significance are constructed in particular times and places, contingent on the polit-ical, historical, and aesthetic realities of the moment.

On the one hand, it is true that unlike World War I, the Holo-caust has resulted in no new literary forms, no startling artistic breakthroughs; for all intents and purposes, it has been assimilated into many of the modernist innovations already generated by the perceived rupture in culture occasioned by the Great War. On the other hand, what has certainly changed is the redemptory prom-ise that traditionally underlay innovation and "newness" in mod-ern art and culture: where anti-realist and fragmentation motifs were seen as redemptory of art's purpose after the Great War pre-cisely because they refused to affirm the conditions and values that made such terror possible, art and literature after the Holo-caust are pointedly anti-redemptory of both themselves and the catastrophe they represent.

Indeed, of all the dilemmas facing post-Holocaust writers and artists, perhaps none is more difficult, or more paralyzing, than the potential for redemption in any representation of the Holocaust. Some, like Theodor Adorno, have warned against the ways in which poetry and art after Auschwitz risk redeeming events with aes-thetic beauty or mimetic pleasure.[2] Others, like Saul Friedländer, have asked whether the very act of history-writing itself poten-tially redeems the Holocaust with the kinds of meaning and significance reflexively generated in all narrative. Though as a historian, Friedländer also questions the adequacy of ironic and experimental responses to the Holocaust, insofar as their trans-gressiveness seems to undercut any and all meaning, verging on the nihilistic, he also suggests that a postmodern aesthetics might "accentuate the dilemmas" of history-telling.[3] Even by Friedländer's terms, this is not a bad thing: an aesthetics that remarks its own limitations, its inability to provide eternal answers and stable

meaning. Works in this vein acknowledge both the moral obligation to remember and the ethical hazards of doing so in art and
literature. In short, he issues a narrow call for an aesthetics that
devotes itself primarily *to* the dilemmas of representation, an anti-
redemptory history of the Holocaust that resists closure, sustains
uncertainty, and allows us to live without full understanding.

For many artists, the breach itself between events and their art
now demanded some kind of representation: but how to do it without automatically recuperating it? Indeed, the postmodern enterprise is both fueled and paralyzed by the double-edged conundrum
articulated first by Adorno: not only does "cultural criticism
share the blindness of its object," he wrote, "but even the critic's
essential discontent with civilization can be regarded as an extension of that civilization."[4] Just as the avant-garde might be said to
feed on the illusion of its perpetual dying, postmodern memory-
work seems to feed perpetually on the impossibility of its own
task.[5]

Unlike the utopian, revolutionary forms with which modernists hoped to redeem art and literature after World War I, the post-
Holocaust memory artist, in particular, would say, "Not only is
art not the answer, but that after the Holocaust, there can be no
more Final Solutions." Some of this skepticism has been a direct
response to the enormity of the Holocaust—which seemed to
exhaust not only the forms of modernist experimentation and
innovation, but also the traditional meanings still reified in such
innovations. Mostly, however, this skepticism has stemmed from
these artists' contempt for the religious, political, or aesthetic
linking of redemption and destruction that seemed to justify such
terror in the first place. In Germany, in particular, once the land of
what Saul Friedländer has called "redemptory anti-Semitism,"
the possibility that public art might now compensate mass murder
with beauty (or with ugliness), or that memorials might somehow
redeem this past with the instrumentalization of its memory,
continues to haunt a postwar generation of memory-artists.[6]

Nearly fifty years after the defeat of the Nazi regime, contemporary artists in Germany still have difficulty separating the monument there from its fascist past. German memory-artists are
heirs to a double-edged postwar legacy: a deep distrust of monumental forms in light of their systematic exploitation by the Nazis
and a profound desire to distinguish their generation from that of
the killers through memory.[7] In their eyes, the didactic logic of

monuments—their demagogical rigidity and certainty of history —continues to recall too closely traits associated with fascism itself. How else would totalitarian regimes commemorate themselves except through totalitarian art such as the monument? Conversely, how better to celebrate the fall of totalitarian regimes than by celebrating the fall of their monuments? A monument against fascism, therefore, would have to be a monument against itself: against the traditionally didactic function of monuments, against their tendency to displace the past they would have us contemplate, and, finally, against the authoritarian propensity in monumental spaces that reduces viewers to passive spectators.

Moreover, memorial artists in Germany are both plagued and inspired by a series of impossible memorial questions: How does a state incorporate shame into its national memorial landscape? How does a state recite, much less commemorate, the litany of its misdeeds, making them part of its reason for being? Under what memorial aegis, whose rules, does a nation remember its own barbarity? Where is the tradition for memorial mea culpa, when combined remembrance and self-indictment seem so hopelessly at odds? Unlike state-sponsored memorials built by victimized nations and peoples to themselves in Poland, Holland, or Israel, those in Germany are necessarily those of former persecutors remembering their victims. In the face of this necessary breach in the conventional "memorial code," it is little wonder that German national memory of the Holocaust remains so torn and convoluted. Germany's "Jewish question" is now a two-pronged memorial question: How do former persecutors mourn their victims? How does a nation reunite itself on the bedrock memory of its crimes?

One of the most compelling results of Germany's memorial conundrum has been the advent of what I would call its "countermonuments": memorial spaces conceived to challenge the very premise of the monument. At home in an era of earthworks, conceptual art, and self-destructive art, a postwar generation of artists now explores both the necessity of memory and their incapacity to recall events they never experienced directly. For a new generation of German artists, the possibility that memory of events so grave might be reduced to exhibitions of public craftsmanship or cheap pathos remains intolerable. They contemptuously reject the traditional forms and reasons for public memorial art, those spaces that either console viewers or redeem such tragic events, or they indulge in a facile kind of *Wiedergutmachung*, that is, purport to mend the memory of a murdered people. Instead of searing memory into public consciousness, they fear that conventional memorials seal memory off from awareness altogether; instead of embodying memory, they find that memorials may only displace memory. These artists fear rightly that to the extent that we encourage monuments to do our memory-work for us, we become that much more forgetful. They believe, in effect, that the initial impulse to memorialize events like the Holocaust may actually spring from an opposite and equal desire to forget them.

Widely regarded as two of Europe's most provocative artists of "erasure" and self-abnegation, Jochen Gerz and Esther Shalev-Gerz are still best known for their disappearing "Monument against Fascism" in Harburg-Hamburg, dedicated in 1986. It consisted of a twelve-meter-high lead-covered column that was sunk into the ground as people inscribed their names (and much else) onto its surface; after its complete disappearance in 1994, the artists hoped that it would return the burden of memory to those who came looking for it. With audacious simplicity, their countermonument thus flouted a number of memorial conventions: its aim was not to console but to provoke; not to remain fixed but to change; not to be everlasting but to disappear; not to be ignored by its passersby but to demand interaction; not to remain pristine but to invite its own violation; not to accept graciously the burden of memory but to throw it back at the town's feet. How better to remember a now-absent people than by a vanishing monument?[8]

Just as the countermonuments of Jochen Gerz, Horst Hoheisel, and Stih and Schnock, among others, have thrown into sharp relief both Germany's memorial conundrum and the traditional monument's inadequacy in the face of German memory of the Holocaust, architect Daniel Libeskind's design for Berlin's new Jewish Museum similarly challenges architecture's traditional function as a stabilizing and recuperative site for memory. In the pages that follow, I explore Libeskind's extraordinary response to the nearly paralyzing dilemma Berlin faces in trying to reintegrate its lost Jewish past. The aim here is not merely to explain Libeskind's difficult, even outrageous, design, but to show how, as a process, it articulates the dilemma Germany faces whenever it attempts to formalize the self-inflicted void at its center—the void of its lost and murdered Jews.[9]

II

Indeed, just how does a city "house" the memory of a people no longer at "home" there? How does a city like Berlin invite a people like the Jews back into its official past after having driven them so murderously from it? Such questions may suggest their own, uncanny answers: A "Jewish Museum" in the capital city of a nation that not so long ago voided itself of Jews, making them alien strangers in a land they had considered "home," will not by definition be *heimlich* but must be regarded as *unheimlich*—or, as our translation would have it, uncanny. The dilemma facing the designer of such a museum thus becomes: How then to embody this sense of *unheimlichkeit*, or uncanniness, in a medium like architecture, which has its own long tradition of *heimlichkeit*, or homeliness? Moreover, can the construction of a contemporary architecture remain entirely distinct from, even oblivious to, the history it shelters? Is its spatial existence ever really independent of its contents?

In their initial conception of what they then regarded as a Jewish "extension" to the Berlin Museum, city planners hoped to recognize both the role Jews had once played as co-creators of Berlin's history and culture and that the city was fundamentally haunted by its Jewish absence. At the same time, the very notion of an "autonomous" Jewish Museum struck them as problematic: the museum wanted to show the importance and far-reaching effect of Jewish culture on the city's history, to give it the prominence it deserved. But many also feared dividing German from Jewish history, inadvertently recapitulating the Nazis' own segregation of Jewish culture from German. This would have been to reimpose a distinct line between the history and cultures of two people— Germans and Jews—whose fates had been inextricably mingled for centuries in Berlin. From the beginning, planners realized that this would be no mere reintroduction of Jewish memory into Berlin's civic landscape but an excavation of memory already there but long suppressed.

Freud may have described such a phenomenon best: "This uncanny is in reality nothing new or alien, but something which is familiar and old-established in the mind and which has become alienated from it only through the process of repression. . . . The uncanny [is] something which ought to have remained hidden but has come to light."[10] Thus would Berlin's Jewish Museum generate its own sense of a disquieting return, the sudden revelation of a previously something buried past. Indeed, if the very idea of the uncanny arises, as Freud suggests, from the transformation of something that once seemed familiar and homely into something strange and "unhomely," then how better to describe the larger plight of Jewish memory in Germany today? Moreover, if "unhomeliness" for Freud was, as Anthony Vidler suggests, "the fundamental propensity of the familiar to turn on its owners, suddenly to become defamiliarized, derealized, as if in a dream," then how better to describe contemporary Germany's relationship with its own Jewish past?[11] At least part of the uncanniness in such a project stems from the sense that at any moment the "familiar alien" will burst forth, even when it never does, thus leaving one always ill-at-ease, even a little frightened with anticipation—hence, the constant, free-floating anxiety that seems to accompany every act of Jewish memorialization in Germany today.

After Anthony Vidler's magnificent reading of the "architectural uncanny," I would also approach what I am calling an "uncanny memorial architecture" as "a metaphor for a fundamentally unlivable modern condition."[12] Rather than looking for uncanny memory *per se*, or uncanny memorials or architecture, we might, after Vidler, look only for those uncanny qualities in memorial architecture. In fact, what Robin Lydenberg aptly sees in "uncanny narrative" might be applied here to a particular kind of uncanny memorial architecture, as well: the stabilizing function of architecture, by which the familiar is made to appear part of a naturally ordered landscape, will be subverted by the antithetical effects of the unfamiliar.[13] It is a memorial architecture that invites us into its seemingly hospitable environs only to estrange itself from us immediately on entering.

By extension, the memorial uncanny might be regarded as that which is necessarily anti-redemptive. It is that memory of historical events that never domesticates such events, never makes us at home with them, never brings them into the reassuring house of redemptory meaning. It is to leave such events unredeemable yet still memorable, unjustifiable yet still graspable in their causes and effects.

In 1988, the Berlin Senate agreed to approve financing for a Jewish Museum that would remain administratively under the roof of the Berlin Museum but that would have its own, autonomous building. A prestigious international competition was called in December 1988 for a building design that would both "extend" the Berlin Museum and give the Jewish Department its own space. But because this was also a time when city planners were extremely sensitive to the destructive divisiveness of the Berlin Wall itself, which the Berlin Museum had been founded to overcome, they remained wary of any kind of spatial demarcation between the museum and its "Jewish Museum Department"—hence, the unwieldy name with which they hoped to finesse the connection between the two: "Extension of the Berlin Museum with the Jewish Museum Department."

According to planners, the Jewish wing would be both autonomous and integrative, the difficulty being to link a museum of civic history with the altogether uncivil treatment of that city's Jews. The questions such a museum raises are as daunting as they are potentially paralyzing: How to do this in a form that would not suggest reconciliation and continuity? How to reunite Berlin and its Jewish part without suggesting a seamless rapprochement? How to show Jewish history and culture as part of German history without subsuming it altogether? How to show Jewish culture as part of *and* separate from German culture without recirculating all the old canards of "a people apart?"

Rather than skirting these impossible questions, the planners confronted them unflinchingly in an extraordinary conceptual brief for the competition that put such questions at the heart of the design process. According to the text by Rolf Bothe (then director of the Berlin Museum) and Vera Bendt (then director of the Jewish Department of the Berlin Museum), a Jewish museum in Berlin would have to comprise three primary areas of consideration: 1) the Jewish religion, customs, and ritual objects; 2) history of the Jewish community in Germany, its rise and terrible destruction at the hands of the Nazis; and 3) the lives and works of Jews who left their mark on the face and the history of Berlin over the centuries.[14] But in elaborating these areas, the authors of the conceptual brief also challenged potential designers to acknowledge the terrible void that made this museum necessary. If part of the aim here had been the reinscription of Jewish memory and the memory of the Jews' murder into Berlin's otherwise indifferent civic culture, another part would be to reveal the absence in postwar German culture demanding this reinscription.

Most notably, in describing the history of Berlin's Jewish community, the authors made clear that not only were the city's history and Jews' history inseparable from each other, but that nothing (not even this museum) could redeem the expulsion and murder of Berlin's Jews: "a fate whose terrible significance should not be lost through any form of atonement or even through the otherwise effective healing power of time. *Nothing in Berlin's history ever changed the city more than the persecution, expulsion, and murder of its own Jewish citizens. This change worked inwardly, affecting the very heart of the city"* (emphasis added).[15] In thus suggesting that the murder of Berlin's Jews was the single greatest influence on the shape of this city, the planners also seem to imply that the new Jewish extension of the Berlin Museum may even constitute the hidden center of Berlin's own civic culture, a focal point for Berlin's own historical self-understanding.

As the Wall had instantly transformed Berlin into a divided city, a visible reminder of both World War II and the newer cold war between eastern and western Europe, the other great shaper of Berlin's cultural landscape was not so visible but was now evident only by its absence. The centrality of this museum for understanding Berlin's own history was further reinforced in the planners' description of the ways the Jews have left their mark on the face of Berlin history: "The history of the Jews of Berlin is so closely tied up with the history of the city that it is virtually impossible to separate the two; i.e., an autonomous Jewish Museum is necessary but almost inconceivable without the history of Berlin, in the same way as, conversely, a Berlin Museum of urban history would lose all meaning if it did not take its Jewish citizens into consideration."[16] With this in mind, the aim of the museum would be to show that Jewish history is part of and separate from German history, a balancing act demanding almost impossible discretion, diplomacy, and tact.

Guided by this conceptual brief, city planners issued an open invitation to all architects of the Federal Republic of Germany in December 1988. In addition, they invited another twelve architects from outside Germany, among them the American architect Daniel Libeskind, then living in Milan. Born in Lodz in 1946 to the sole survivors of a Polish-Jewish family wiped out in the Holocaust, Libeskind had long wrestled with many of the brief's questions, finding them nearly insoluble at the architectural level. Trained first as a virtuoso keyboardist who came to the United States with violinist Itzhak Perlman in 1960 on an American-Israeli Cultural Foundation Fellowship to study at Juilliard, Libeskind says he gave up music when, in his words, there was no more technique to learn. From here, he turned to architecture and its seemingly inexhaustible reserve of technique. He studied at Cooper Union

in New York under the direct influence and inspiration of Peter
Eisenman and John Hejduk, two of the founders and practitioners
of "deconstructivist architecture." Thus, in his design for a Jewish Museum in Berlin, Libeskind proposed not so much a solution
to the planners' conceptual conundrum as he did its architectural
articulation. The drawings in the series he submitted to the committee in mid-1989 have come to be regarded as masterpieces of
process art as well as architectural design.

Of the 165 designs submitted from around the world for the
competition that closed in June 1989, Daniel Libeskind's struck
the jury as the most brilliant and complex, possibly as unbuild-
able. It was awarded first prize and thereby became the first work
of Libeskind's ever to be commissioned.[17] Where the other final-
ists had concerned themselves primarily with the technical feat of
reconciling this building to its surroundings in a way that met the
building authority's criteria and to establishing a separate but
equal parity between the Berlin Museum and its Jewish extension, Libeskind had devoted himself to the spatial enactment
of a philosophical problem. As Kurt Forster had once described
another design in this vein, this would be "all process rather than
product."[18] And as an example of process-architecture, according
to Libeskind, this building "is always on the verge of Becoming—
no longer suggestive of a final solution."[19] In its series of complex
trajectories, irregular linear structures, fragments, and displacements, this building is also on the verge of unbecoming—a breaking
down of architectural assumptions, conventions, and expectations.

His drawings for the museum thus look more like the sketches
of the museum's ruins, a house whose wings have been scrambled
and reshaped by the jolt of genocide. It is a devastated site that
would now enshrine its broken forms. In this work, Libeskind asks,
If architecture can be representative of historical meaning, can it
also represent unmeaning and the search for meaning? The result
is an extended building broken in several places. The straight
void-line running through the plan violates every space through
which it passes, turning otherwise uniform rooms and halls into
misshapen anomalies, some too small to hold anything, others so
oblique as to estrange anything housed within them. The original
design also included inclining walls, at angles too sharp for hang-
ing exhibitions.

From Libeskind's earliest conceptual brief onward, the essential drama of mutually exclusive aims and irreconcilable means
was given full, unapologetic play. For him, it was the impossible

questions that mattered most: How to give voice to an absent Jewish culture without presuming to speak for it? How to bridge an
open wound without mending it? How to house under a single
roof a panoply of essential oppositions and contradictions?[20] He
thus allowed his drawings to work through the essential paradoxes
at the heart of his project: How to give form to a void without
filling it in? How to give architectural form to the formless and to
challenge the very attempt to house such memory?

Before beginning, Libeskind replaced the very name of the project
—"Extension of the Berlin Museum with the Jewish Museum
Department"—with his own more poetic rendition, "Between the
Lines." "I call it [Between the Lines] because it is a project about
two lines of thinking, organization, and relationship," Libeskind
says. "One is a straight line, but broken into many fragments; the
other is a tortuous line, but continuing indefinitely. These two
lines develop architecturally and programmatically through a
limited but definite dialogue. They also fall apart, become disen-
gaged, and are seen as separated. In this way, they expose a void
that runs through this museum and through architecture, a discontinuous void."[21] Through a twisting and jagged lightning bolt of a
building, Libeskind has run a straight-cut void, slicing through it
and even extending outside of it: an empty, unused space bisect-
ing the entire building. According to Libeskind, "The new extension is conceived as an emblem where the not visible has made
itself apparent as a void, an invisible. . . . The idea is very simple:
to build the museum around a void that runs through it, a void
that is to be experienced by the public."[22] As he makes clear, this
void is indeed the building's structural rib, its main axis, a central
bearing wall that bears only its own absence.

Indeed, for Libeskind, it is not the building itself that constitutes his architecture but the spaces inside the building, the voids
and absence embodied by empty spaces: that which is constituted
not by the lines of his drawings but those spaces between the
lines. By building voids into the heart of his design, Libeskind
thus highlights the spaces between walls as the primary element
of his architecture. The walls themselves are important only insofar as they lend shape to these spaces and define their borders. It is
the void "between the lines" that Libeskind seeks to capture here,
a void so real, so palpable, and so elemental to Jewish history in
Berlin as to be its focal point after the Holocaust—a negative center of gravity around which Jewish memory now assembles.[23]

After accepting Libeskind's museum design in the summer of 1989, the Berlin Senate allotted some 170 million Deutsche marks (nearly 100 million U.S. dollars) for its construction. This was a huge sum for any German city to spend on one of its museums, even during prosperous times. But with the breaching of the Berlin Wall later that fall and the looming, unimaginable costs of reunification, such a sum became politically and economically unthinkable. All government building plans were put on hold as Berlin and Germany came to grips with its shocking new political topography—no dividing wall between east and west, but a country divided nevertheless between the prosperous and the desperate. Despite calls for the museum's suspension, planners insisted that the Jewish Museum go forward, now altered by the new realities on the ground—both economic and topographical. It is significant perhaps that in the minds of civic leaders, Berlin's reunification could not proceed until the city had begun to be reunited with its missing Jewish past. In any case, despite numerous obstacles, building went ahead.

To trim the museum's costs, city planners ordered the angles of its walls to be straightened, among dozens of other changes, which shaved some 117 million DM off the budget. In addition, a hall intended for outside the main building was absorbed into the ground floor, several of the outer "voids" were themselves voided, and the complex plan for the lower floor was vastly simplified so that it would come into line with the main building. At first, the architect resisted those changes that seemed to neutralize the very difficulty of his design, especially those that removed the museum's estranging properties. Later, however, Libeskind offered a different, more philosophical explanation for what would be necessary changes. What was designed while the Berlin Wall was standing would now be built in a newly reunified city. "As soon as Berlin was unified, I straightened all the walls," Libeskind has written. "I did it because I felt the project was no longer protected by the kind of schizophrenia developed out of the bilateral nature of the city."[24] Elsewhere he stated, "The museum has to stand and open itself in a different way in a united and wall-less city."[25]

The building's radical design is barely apparent as one approaches it from the street. Though its untempered zinc plating is startlingly bright in its metallic sheen, when viewed from the entrance of the Berlin Museum on Lindenstrasse, the new building also strikes one as a proportionately modest neighbor to the older Baroque facade next door. Indeed, over time, the untempered zinc will weather into the same sky-blue shade as the untempered zinc window frames on the Berlin Museum next door. The echo of materials and hue between these buildings is thus subtle but distinct, the only apparent link between them at first sight.

Moreover, Libeskind's museum is lower and narrower than the Berlin Museum, and its zinc-plated facade seems relatively self-effacing next to the ochre hues of its Baroque neighbor. Though outwardly untouched, the stolid Baroque facade of the Berlin Museum itself is now recontextualized in its new setting adjacent the Jewish Museum. For as designed by Libeskind, the connection between the Berlin Museum and Jewish Museum Extension remains subterranean, a remembered nexus that is also no longer visible in the landscape but buried in memory. The Berlin Museum and Jewish Museum are thus "bound together in depth," as Libeskind says. "The existing building is tied to the extension underground, preserving the contradictory autonomy of both on the surface, while binding the two together in depth. Under-Over-Ground Museum. Like Berlin and its Jews, the common burden—this insupportable, immeasurable, unshareable burden—is outlined in the exchanges between two architectures and forms which are not reciprocal: cannot be exchanged for each other."[26]

The exhibition halls themselves are spacious but so irregular in their shapes, cut through by enclosed voids and concrete trusses, that one never gains a sense of continuous passage. "I have introduced the idea of the void as a physical interference with chronology," Libeskind has said. "It is the one element of continuity throughout the complex form of the building. It is 22 meters high and runs the entire length of the building over 140 meters. It is a straight line whose impenetrability forms the central axis. The void is traversed by bridges which connect the various parts of the museum to each other."[27] In fact, six voids cut through the museum on both horizontal and vertical planes. Of these six voids, two are accessible to visitors: these are what Libeskind calls the sixth and fifth voids, which run east and west the full length of the building and are entered by narrow halls off of the main passageways. According to Libeskind's specifications, nothing will ever be mounted on the walls of these voids or be installed on the floors. Only the shapes of visitors in these voids and the sounds they make, or their silences, will be present here.

The fourth and third voids cut through the building at angles that traverse several floors, but these are altogether inaccessible. Occasionally, a window opens into these voids, which are visible but sealed off and thus are completely "unusable space" jutting throughout the structure and outside it. The second and first voids run vertically the height of the building. Of these, the second void reflects the geometry of the building, and the first void is enclosed by a tower: this is the Holocaust void, a negative space created by the Holocaust, an architectural model for absence. This concrete structure itself has no name, Libeskind says, because its subject is not its walls but the space enveloped by them, what is "between the lines." Though connected to the museum by an underground passageway, it appears to rise autonomously outside the walls of the museum and has no doors or windows leading into it from outside. It is lighted only indirectly by natural light that comes through slanting windows up high in the structure, though these openings too are not visible from inside or out.

The spaces inside the museum are to be construed as "open narratives," Libeskind says, "which in their architecture seek to provide the museum-goer with new insights into the collection, and in particular, the relation and significance of the Jewish Department to the Museum as a whole."[28] In other words, instead of merely housing the collection, this building seeks to estrange it from the viewers' own preconceptions. Such walls and oblique angles, he hopes, will defamiliarize the all-too-familiar ritual objects and historical chronologies and cause museumgoers to see into these relations between the Jewish and German departments as if for the first time.

The interior of the building is thus interrupted by smaller, individual structures, shells housing the voids running throughout the structure. They completely alter any sense of continuity or narrative flow and suggest instead architectural, spatial, and thematic gaps in the presentation of Jewish history in Berlin. The absence of Berlin's Jews, as embodied by these voids, is meant to haunt any retrospective presentation of their past here. As such, they have even been described as memorials to the presentation now built into the very structure of the museum.[29]

Moreover, curators of both permanent and temporary exhibitions will be reminded not to use these voids as "natural" boundaries or walls in their exhibition, as markers within their exhibition narratives. Instead, they are to design exhibitions oblivious to these voids, so that when mounted, the exhibition narrative is cut arbitrarily wherever a void happens to intersect it. The walls of the voids facing the exhibition walls will thus remain untouched, unusable, outside healing and suturing narrative.

Implied in any museum's collection is that what you see is all there is to see, all that there ever was. By placing architectural "voids" throughout the museum, Libeskind has tried to puncture this museological illusion. What you see here, he seems to say, is actually only a mask for all that is missing, for the great absence of life that now makes a presentation of these artifacts a necessity. The voids make palpable a sense that much more is missing here than can ever be shown. As Vera Bendt has aptly noted, it was the destruction itself that caused the collection here shown to come into being. Otherwise, these objects would all be part of living, breathing homes—unavailable as museum objects. This is then an aggressively anti-redemptory design, built literally around an absence of meaning in history, an absence of the people who would have given meaning to their history.

III

If modern architecture has embodied the attempt to erase the traces of history from its forms, postmodern architecture like Libeskind's would make the traces of history its infrastructure, the voids of lost civilizations literally part of the building's foundation, now haunted by history, even emblematic of it. The architecture of what Libeskind calls "decomposition" derives its power not from a sense of unity but from what Anthony Vidler has called the "intimation of the fragmentary, the morselated, the broken."[30] Rather than suggesting wholeness and mending, salvation or redemption, such forms represent the breach itself, the ongoing need for *tikkun ha'olam* and its impossibility.

As Reinhart Koselleck has brilliantly intimated, even the notion of history as a "singular collective"—that is, an overarching and singularly meaningful History—is a relatively modern concept.[31] Alois M. Muller has elaborated:

> Until the 18th century the word had been a plural form in German, comprising the various histories which accounted for all that had happened in the world. History as a singular noun had a loftier intent. In [the] future, not only individual minor historical episodes were to be told. History suddenly acquired the duty to comprehend

reality as a continuous whole and to portray the entire history of humankind as a path to freedom and independence. History was no long to be "just" the embodiment of many histories. History as a unity sought to make them comprehensible.[32]

And as Muller also makes quite clear, this project of historical unification had distinctly redemptive, even salvational aims, the kind of history that its tellers hoped would lead to a "better world."

Libeskind's project, by contrast, promises no such relief. His goal is not to provide, as Muller reminds us, a "revelatory monument to the 'good' in history, but to open a shaft for a historical crime perpetrated in the name of history."[33] By resisting continuous, homogeneous history-housing, Libeskind never allows memory of this time to congeal into singular, salvational meaning. His is partly integrationist and partly disintegrationist architecture. His is a project that allows for the attempt at integration as an ongoing, if impossible, project, even as it formalizes disintegration as its architectural motif.

Libeskind would de-unify such history, atomize it, allow its seams to show, plant doubt in any single version, even his own— all toward suggesting an anti-redemptory housing of history, one that expresses what Muller has called a systematic doubt, a lack of certainty in any attempt that makes it all process, never result.

If "estrangement from the world is a moment of art," as Adorno would have it, after Freud, then we might say that the uncanniness of a museum like Libeskind's crystallizes this moment of art.[34] But if the "uncanny is uncanny only because it is secretly all too familiar, which is why it is repressed," as Freud himself would have it, then perhaps no better term describes the condition of a contemporary German culture coming to terms with the self-inflicted void at its center—a terrible void that is at once all too secretly familiar and unrecognizable, a void that at once defines a national identity, even as it threatens to cause such identity to implode.

Notes

1. Andreas Huyssen, "The Monument in a Post-modern Age," in *The Art of Memory: Holocaust Memorials in History,* ed. James E. Young (Munich, 1994), 11.
2. T. W. Adorno, "Engagement," in *Noten zur Literatur* 3 (Frankfurt am Main, 1965), 125–27.

3. Saul Friedländer, *Memory, History, and the Extermination of the Jews of Europe* (Bloomington: Indiana University Press, 1993), 61, 55.

4. Theodor W. Adorno, *Prisms*, trans. Samuel and Shierry Weber (Cambridge: MIT Press, 1981), 27, 19.

5. For a brilliant elaboration on the "ever-dying" of the avant-garde, see Paul Mann, *The Theory-Death of the Avant-Garde* (Bloomington: Indiana University Press, 1991).

6. See Saul Friedländer, *Nazi Germany and the Jews*, vol. 1: *The Years of Persecution* (New York: HarperCollins, 1997), 3.

7. For elaboration of this theme, see Matthias Winzen, "The Need for Public Representation and the Burden of the German Past," *Art Journal* 48 (winter 1989): 309–14.

8. For a detailed discussion of the Harburg countermonument and a number of other countermonuments, see James E. Young, "The Counter-monument: Memory against Itself in Germany Today," *Critical Inquiry* 18 (winter 1992): 267–96. Also see James E. Young, *The Texture of Memory: Holocaust Memorials and Meaning* (New Haven: Yale University Press), 27–48.

9. For the purposes of this essay, I explore only Libeskind's design itself and what I call its "uncanny" properties. In my forthcoming book, *The Holocaust as Vicarious Past: The Arts of Memory in an Anti-Redemptive Age* (New Haven: Yale University Press), I open my discussion of Libeskind's design with the longer history of Berlin's Jewish Museum, dating back to its ill-fated opening in January 1933, two weeks before Hitler was installed as Germany's new chancellor.

10. Sigmund Freud, "The Uncanny," in *The Standard Edition of the Complete Psychological Works of Sigmund Freud* (trans. James Strachey, London: Hogarth Press, 1955), 17:241.

11. Anthony Vidler, *The Architectural Uncanny: Essays in the Modern Unhomely* (Cambridge: MIT Press, 1996), 7.

12. Ibid., x.

13. See Robin Lydenberg's excellent working through of "the narrative uncanny" in "Freud's Uncanny Narratives," *PMLA* 112, no. 5 (October 1997): 1076. Here she also shows how the *unheimlich* (alien and threatening) contains within it its own lexical opposite (*heimlich*—familiar and agreeable). That is, part of the uncanny's power to affect us is just its familiarity, which is all the more disturbing when estranged.

14. See Rolf Bothe and Vera Bendt, "Ein eigenstandiges Jüdisches Museum als Abteilung des Berlin Museums," in *Realisierungs Wettbewerb: Erweiterung Berlin Museum mit Abteilung Jüdisches Museum* (Berlin: Senatsverwaltung für Bau- und Wohnungswesen, 1990), 12.

15. "Nichts in Berlins Geschichte hat die Stadt jemals mehr verandert als die Verfolgung, Verteibung und Ermordung ihrer jüdischen Bürger—dies war eine Veranderung nach Innen, die ins Herz der Stadt traf," in Bothe and Bendt, *Realisierungs Wettbewerb*, 12.

16. Ibid., 159.

17. Though this was Libeskind's first full commission, it was not his first building. Other projects subsequently commissioned have been built in Wiesbaden and Osnabruck, among other places.

18. Forster, quoted in Vidler, *Architectural Uncanny*, 135.

19. Bothe and Bendt, *Realisierungs Wettbewerb*, 169.

20. Ibid., 166.

21. Daniel Libeskind, *Between the Lines: Extension to the Berlin Museum with the Jewish Museum* (Amsterdam: Joods Historisch Museum, 1991), 3.

22. Daniel Libeskind, "Between the Lines," in *Daniel Libeskind: Erweiterung des Berlin Museums mit Abteilung Jüdisches Museum*, ed. Kristin Feireiss (Berlin: Ernst and Sohn, 1992), 63.

23. For further insightful reflection on the role these voids play in Berlin generally and in Libeskind's design in particular, see Andreas Huyssen, "The Voids of Berlin," *Critical Inquiry* 24, no. 1 (fall 1997): 57–81.
24. Daniel Libeskind, *Radix-Matrix: Architecture and Writings* (Munich: Prestel Verlag, 1997), 113.
25. Libeskind, "Between the Lines," 65.
26. Bothe and Bendt, *Realisierungs Wettbewerb,* 169.
27. Libeskind, "Between the Lines," 35.
28. Bothe and Bendt, *Realisierungs Wettbewerb,* 169.
29. Libeskind, *Between the Lines,* 6.
30. Vidler, *Architectural Uncanny,* 70.
31. See Reinhard Koselleck, *Futures Past: On the Semantics of Historical Time* (Cambridge: MIT Press, 1985), 92–93.
32. Alois M. Muller, "Daniel Libeskind's Muses," in Libeskind, *Radix-Matrix,* 117.
33. Ibid., 117.
34. Theodor Adorno, *Aesthetic Theory,* trans. C. Lenhardt (New York: Routledge and Kegan Paul, 1984), 262.

Further Reading

Bothe, Rolf, and Vera Bendt. "Ein eigenstandiges Jüdisches Museum ald Abteilung des Berlin Museums." In *Realisierungs Wettbewerb: Erweiterung Berlin Museum mit Abteilung Jüdisches Museum.* Berlin: Senatsverwaltung für Bau- und Wohnungswesen, 1990.
Here the former directors of the Berlin Museum and its Jewish Museum Department describe the conceptual, integrationist basis for the architectural competition called for the Jewish Museum in Berlin.
Friedländer, Saul. *Nazi Germany and the Jews.* Vol. 1, *The Years of Persecution.* New York: HarperCollins, 1997.
In restoring the accounts of survivors and eyewitnesses to the historical record, Friedländer animates this brilliant first volume of his Holocaust history with the "voices of memory."
Huyssen, Andreas. "The Monument in a Post-modern Age." In *The Art of Memory: Holocaust Memorials in History,* ed. James E. Young. Munich: Prestel Verlag, 1994.
Here Huyssen suggests that in an age of rampant memory production, memory itself may be lost.
———. "The Voids of Berlin." *Critical Inquiry* 24, no. 1 (fall 1997): 57–81.
In this meditation on "the voids of Berlin," Huyssen suggests the void as a central part of the city's new architectural aesthetic.
Libeskind, Daniel. "Between the Lines." In *Daniel Libeskind: Erweiterung des Berlin Museums mit Abteilung Jüdisches Museum,* ed. Kristin Feireiss. Berlin: Ernst and Sohn, 1992.
This is the architect's own conceptual brief on his spectacular design for Berlin's new Jewish Museum.
Vidler, Anthony. *The Architectural Uncanny: Essays in the Modern Unhomely.* Cambridge: MIT Press, 1996.
In this breakthrough book, Anthony Vidler explores in depth the qualities of "uncanny" architecture, the ways such architecture simultaneously houses and estranges the objects and people within.

Young, James E. "The Counter-monument: Memory against Itself in Germany Today." *Critical Inquiry* 18 (winter 1992): 267–96.

   In this essay, the author explores the Holocaust-related monuments by a new generation of German artists dedicated to challenging the monument's traditional redemptory premises.

———. *The Texture of Memory: Holocaust Memorials and Meaning.* New Haven: Yale University Press, 1993.

   In this full-length study of Holocaust memorials, museums, and days of remembrance, the author explores the conceptual, historical, and aesthetic bases of national Holocaust memory in Europe, Israel, and the United States.

III

HISTORY

PATRICK H. HUTTON

OF DEATH AND DESTINY

THE ARIÈS-VOVELLE DEBATE ABOUT
THE HISTORY OF MOURNING

The Place of Mourning in the Historical

Vision of Philippe Ariès

IN THE WINTER of 1943 Philippe Ariès, an aspiring historian coping with the travails of life in Paris under German occupation, made a pilgrimage to Lyon to visit with the remnant of the royalist *Action française* that had gathered in exile there. An enthusiastic participant in the movement while a student at the Sorbonne in the 1930s, Ariès was looking for some validation from his former associates of his fragile hopes for the movement's renewal under the Vichy regime that had taken on the responsibility of governing a defeated nation. The war years had been miserable not only for their privations but also their deceptions. Ariès had just resigned as an instructor at a Vichy-sponsored training school, where he had felt uncomfortable with the collaborationist stance of its director. But the visit to Lyon did little to lift his spirits. The *Action française* had retreated into narrow-minded and self-defeating sectarianism. If anything, he was obliged to acknowledge that the royalist cause was dying and incapable of resuscitation.[1]

On his train ride back to Paris, he reflected on the difficult route he had traveled since his days as a student, when Paris had been his enchanted garden, and his intellectual paths therein had been clearly marked and easy to follow. He had pursued his studies in history and geography with enthusiasm and surrounded himself with friends who shared his idealized vision of old France as the best source for national renewal in the present age. As a journalist for the student newspaper of the *Action française* before the war, he had been an apologist for Charles Maurras, who still exercised a certain mystique over the generation of right-wing intellectuals that was then coming of age. Like many other bright and idealistic youth, Ariès was captivated by Maurras's high-minded erudition, his classical literary tastes, and his uncompromising opposition to the politics of the Republic. He remembered himself as happy in that setting, confident in his convictions, secure in his royalist world in the midst of Paris's intellectual and student life.[2]

That way of life had come to an abrupt end with the coming of the Second World War and the fall of France. At the outset the German Occupation seemed only an unpleasant moratorium that the Vichy regime would bring to an acceptable conclusion. But as its leaders became more beholden to their Nazi overlords, he was obliged to concede Vichy's moral bankruptcy and the illusions of his political apprenticeship in the *Action française.* The train ride from Lyon to Paris, therefore, served as a sobering moment of recognition. His youthful royalist ardor had burned into ashes. But the phoenix of his ambitions would rise again, for this first experience with mourning his losses would inspire him to undertake a historical inquiry into the mores of the traditional world from which he had come. The history of mentalities that he would pioneer was conceived amidst the disappointments of the war years.[3]

By the mid-1970s Ariès (1914–84) would become one of France's preeminent historians of death and mourning. By then he had also opened a new domain of research in the history of childhood and family life. Some of his success may be attributed to his use of the new methods of the celebrated *Annales* school of historical writing. But I argue that his efforts to come to terms with losses in his own life also determined the choices he made as a historian along the way. History became his consolation for a politics that was no longer viable and a way of life that was passing. His historical writing became his means of reconciling himself with the eclipse of a traditional culture that he had loved. More to the point of this essay, his history of attitudes toward death was to be his culminating contribution to this new kind of cultural history, a fitting conclusion to his meditation on a relationship between mourning and destiny that had preoccupied him since the vanishing of his modest hopes for the renewal of the values of old France under Vichy.

Toward the end of the war years, Ariès found his way into two new historical projects: the first demographic, the second historiographical. His excursion into historical demography may have begun as early as 1943 and culminated in his *Histoire des populations françaises* (1948). Here he was trying to come to terms with what he perceived to be the unproductive mourning of his colleagues on the right for the fall of France in 1940. Vichy had been conceived in an atmosphere of mourning, most of it self-defeating. It drew heavily on a fatalism readily expressed by right-wing intellectuals during that era. For many of them, France's rapid military collapse stemmed not only from the inadequate statesmanship of the leaders of the Third Republic, but also and more poignantly from the moral decadence of that regime and even from the biological degeneration of the French people. Notable is the argument of Ariès's mentor, Daniel Halévy, whose assessment in his memoir on the fall, *Trois epreuves* (1940), is erudite and discerning but typical of the sense of resignation with which he accepted its conditions.[4] Ariès admits to having initially shared these sentiments.[5]

The biological fatalism from which such resignation sprang was most fully articulated by Alexis Carrel, a renowned physician whose *L'Homme, cet inconnu* (1935) was a best-seller and a highly influential apology for eugenics. Carrel had spent most of his adult life as a researcher at the Rockefeller University in New York, but he returned to France in 1940 to help leaders of Vichy find constructive solutions for the rehabilitation of the French people in light of their devastating defeat. He, too, worried about the biological decline of the French race, and he proposed a bold program for its "regeneration." Given the recent developments in the life sciences of techniques to prolong the lives of the aged and remedy the deficiencies of the infirm, he speculated, humankind was also in a position to reconstruct its own genetic condition along more positive lines. Carrel envisioned ways to improve the human stock generally and even to fashion a potential elite.[6] For him, the latter need had taken on a certain urgency in light of France's defeat, and he offered his services to Vichy officials with that in mind. The first task, he argued, was to understand the history of France's demographic decline and to use that knowledge as a basis for the rehabilitation of the younger generation. In 1941, with Vichy's subvention, he founded the Fondation Carrel for population studies. In the end, Carrel's program in eugenics was vitiated by its uncomfortably close association with Nazi biological engineering. Cited in the purge following the Liberation, he died shortly thereafter. But his foundation for population studies, divested of its eugenics program, survived in only slightly altered form under a new name and new direction.[7]

Carrel's efforts to institutionalize the study of demography are important for our purposes because it was to this research that Ariès turned near the end of the war. It is uncertain whether he had any dealings with Carrel, but he did establish intellectual contact with the foundation's new director, Alfred Sauvy, shortly after the war and contributed articles relating to his research to its journal.[8] Ariès, too, was seeking an explanation for France's long-range demographic decline. At the training school at which he had briefly taught, he had listened to endless discourse about the biological degeneration of the French race.[9] Increasingly skeptical of this argument as his own research progressed, he advanced an alternative interpretation in which he contended that culture, not biology, is the key to understanding demographic trends in modern France. This insight set the future course of his scholarship, as he sought to explain the rise in expectations about life's opportunities that we have since come to identify with modernity. Beginning in the seventeenth century, he explained, married couples became more sensitive to the burdens and the risks of endless childbearing. Recognizing that they had choices, they made private but conscious decisions to practice birth control as a way of improving the quality of their own lives and those of their children. Such efforts to limit unwanted pregnancies, Ariès suggested, served as a rudimentary beginning to family planning and as evidence of humankind's newfound willingness to take responsibility for its own future. Ironically, it was not a lack of will, as Vichy apologists claimed, but this willful revolution in attitudes, quietly conceived in privacy, that had contributed so significantly to the leveling of the French population in the modern age.

Ariès's history of the French population, therefore, took seriously Carrel's notion about using the techniques of life to human advantage but grounded these in cultural practices that had long since been adopted, not in a eugenics program yet to be enacted. In his first major demographic study, *Histoire des populations françaises*, he explained how the emergence of these new attitudes paralleled the rise of the modern life sciences and reinforced their efficacy. Rather than accept decrepitude and early death fatalistically, humankind in the early modern era had taken control of its own body on these interrelated planes. The revolution in attitudes about birth control he labeled new "techniques of life." Correspondingly, he discussed the advances in medicine that were prolonging life and enhancing its quality as the "new techniques of death."[10] Together they gave rise to what we have come to characterize as the culture of modernity.

Ariès, of course, was no simple convert to its ways. He retained his affection for the mores of old France. His preference was for some balance between continuity and change, between the inertial power of the wisdom of the past and the practical appeal of innovation in the present. While acknowledging the decisive influence of a new, experimental science, he was intent upon maintaining respect for an inveterate, traditional culture. That is why he turned to the study of the family as his major research project during the 1950s.[11] The family was the ideal site for studying the influence of modern attitudes upon a traditional culture, for the family played a dual role. On the one hand, it reorganized familial relationships so as to foster the ambitions of its children. On the other, it remained a private asylum for traditional values that were eroding in the public world at large. Herein he showed how the notion of human destiny was being reconceived in terms of private aspirations.[12]

Ariès's second route into history after the war was an excursion into historiography. As an exercise in mourning, it was prompted by his efforts to come to terms with the waning appeal of the royalist historiography that had framed his conception of history from childhood through his university years. Fondly reminiscing about his early encounter with history, he sought to situate loss within heritage and that in turn within the dynamics of life as it is lived in the present age. Such autobiographical reminiscence enabled him to understand how parochial his first appreciation of history had been, while making it possible for him to recontextualize it within a history broadly reconceived to take cognizance of the culture of everyday life through the ages.

To launch this project Ariès composed a series of essays in the immediate aftermath of the war, which he then collated and published as a book, *Le Temps de l'histoire* (1954). *Le Temps* was a history of history, perhaps the first of its genre. Therein he unraveled the strands out of which modern French history had been woven. He located these deep in collective memories, recorded first in royal genealogies, ecclesiastical and local histories, and other memoirs of the past, and then amalgamated into the grand chronicle of the seventeenth-century royal historiographers. This conflated grand narrative, he argued, became the history over which the political right and left contended through the nineteenth and early twentieth centuries. Paradoxically, he pointed out, it had been honed into a narrow political framework that had whittled away the cultural and social pageant of the past, which nonetheless lived on inconspicuously in popular tradition. This tradition, experienced subjectively as a fading collective memory of the mores of old France, he proposed, ought now to become the object of the historians' attention as a way to understand the past in its multiple dimensions. This new history of mentalities would seek to expose memories that were on the verge of disappearing from living tradition, and so it would assume responsibility for preserving them in the present age.[13]

Ariès's *Le Temps* was prescient in its anticipation of the deconstructionist tenor of historiography today. In this project, he sought to unburden history of its fatalism, as he had demography in his *Histoire des populations françaises*. Herein he distinguished the history we have written from the past in which we have lived. The history we have written, he proposed, is a highly self-conscious reconstruction; the history that we have lived, by contrast, survives in a collective unconscious of unreflective attitudes fashioned out of the practical experience of coping with life as we deal with it every day. Like Hippolyte Taine, who had first popularized the idea in the nineteenth century, Ariès construed the past as a living force, far broader in its possible meanings than our histories can encompass. In this sense, the act of writing history is one of mourning in which we give what limited meaning we can to a past that otherwise slips away in memory's fading revisions.[14]

Ariès on the History of Death and Mourning

In the 1960s Ariès embarked on a massive project of coming to terms with mourning itself. After a decade of research, he sketched a summary of his findings in his *Western Attitudes toward Death* (1974), first presented as a series of lectures at the Woodrow Wilson Center in Washington, D.C.[15] He divided this history of attitudes toward death and mourning into four stages, each easing imperceptibly into the next. In its underlying conception, it was a study of the way in which a tradition is modified while conveying an impression of timelessness. This impression is reinforced, he contended, by the fact that these stages function synchronically as well as diachronically. Each stage is a model, and each model endures into the following ages, so that they coexist in the present even if the earlier models tend to be overshadowed by the more recent ones. As Ariès characterized it, his scheme plays out "like the tiles of a roof" in a descent from the grieving practices of the Middle Ages, conceived as a golden age of mourning. He identifies these four stages as follows:

1. *The tamed death of the High Middle Ages.*[16] Ariès depicts death as an intrusive presence in a world socialized to accept it as integral to life at virtually any age. He alludes to the "promiscuity of the living and the dead," symbolized by the burial of the dead in churches and churchyards frequented everyday by the living. Death was always sad, but mourning was easy because death was readily accepted by the living and the dying as a destiny collectively shared.

2. *One's own death in the age of the Renaissance.* Ariès notes a newfound anxiety over "one's own" death beginning in the fifteenth century. It marks the rising importance of the notion of an individual destiny played out in life and so postponing the final reckoning with death. The effect was to project death into the future and thereby to diffuse its anticipation throughout life. Just as children were trained to prepare for adulthood, so adults were obliged to prepare for the passage from life to death, still seen as the ultimate test that would determine their eternal destinies. Life as lived now was reconceived in light of life as it would be lived in its final hours, which lent a disquieting intensity to meditation on it. Mourning was becoming more difficult.

3. *The death of the other in the Romantic age.* Here Ariès notes the privatization of death and the interiorization of mourning by the late eighteenth century. The more intense rites of mourning in this era, Ariès claims, reflected the new intimacy of private life with its deepening of personal affections. Accepting the death of loved ones became more painful and so required commemorative props. The age of "thy death," therefore, is also the age of more elaborate funerals and commemorative grave statuary. Still, death, alternately conceived as erotic and morbid, had become exotic and so was kept at a greater distance. Cemeteries were relocated at a remove from city centers as parks conducive to grieving over loved ones from time to time. Mourning was being segregated.

4. *Forbidden death in the contemporary age.* So Ariès characterized the plight of atomized individuals in a mass society in the present age. Death has been banished from life reconceived in terms of short-run earthly satisfactions. Its contemplation has become intolerable, as death is perceived to be an embarrassing intrusion into otherwise happy lives. The dying often meet their fate alone, tethered to medical rigs in impersonal hospitals, in poignant contrast

to the medieval tableau of tamed death at home in the presence of one's family. Mourning has become impossible.

Considered in its ensemble, Ariès's interpretation of historically changing attitudes toward death is intimately tied to his conception of changing attitudes toward human destiny. He plots the disintegration of the harmony of life and death in the face of the disappearance of the naive confidence of medieval man in an otherworldly salvation. It was a process in which the acceptance of death was first postponed in the act of preparing for it, then deflected by identifying it with other people or larger causes, and finally banished altogether by denying it any place in public discussion of social life. As human aspirations for life became individuated and in time domesticated, the imagined confrontation with death became more anonymous and less predictable and therefore a destiny more difficult to accept. Rising expectations about life's possibilities, Ariès suggests, were accompanied by rising anxieties about coming to terms with death's realities.

The moral of Ariès's story is that mourning is not simply about coming to terms with losses and endings. The interesting turn in his interpretation concerns the invention of personal mourning in the modern era, which intensified its meaning and inspired a need for personal commemoration. His history, therefore, is also about the compensations and continuities of the traditions into which losses are received. In studying mourning as a mentalities problem, he explained, we note changing attitudes and practices. These are never unambiguous, for change involves trade-offs, not simple progress or decline. History teaches us the wisdom of looking for these negotiations in mores close to life as it is experienced in its most elemental forms—in the way ordinary people face life and death in practical, not abstract, terms. The modern doctrine of linear progress, Ariès charged, is an illusion, and today we pay a price for it in our inability to reckon with our own personal demise. The more we ask of life, the more difficult it becomes to accept its losses and endings. The destiny to which we have aspired in the modern age implies an impossible perfection. The destiny at which we have arrived, therefore, is an inability to mourn a past that can never meet our expectations.[17]

Ariès's assessment of the trend toward "forbidden death" in the contemporary age might be regarded as a particularly pessimistic diagnosis of the human condition in the present age. But it would be more apt to say that it reflects his suspicion of happy endings under any circumstances. These presuppositions of his views

were drawn out by his running debate during the 1970s with the
Marxist historian Michel Vovelle, whose work provided a counterpoint to his own.

Michel Vovelle and Mourning the Demise of the
Revolutionary Tradition

It is interesting that Michel Vovelle (b. 1933) should have become
Ariès's scholarly rival. Vovelle, too, aspired to write a comprehen-
sive history of mourning in the Western world, but he came out of
a left-wing political tradition that was reckoning with its own
losses. Whereas Ariès was a royalist, Vovelle was a Jacobin, with
intellectual commitments to a Marxist vision of history and at
least a nominal attachment to the Communist Party. Some twenty
years Ariès's junior, Vovelle came of age in the postwar era. He
was touched by the Vichy experience to the degree that he was
caught up in the idealism of the postwar Communism that was a
response to it. Like other youth with sympathies for the left, he
was taken with the heroism of the party in the Resistance.
Vovelle and his political companions were of the first generation
to read the young Marx, whose struggle for liberation from bourgeois oppression lent meaning to their own against Nazism and
other tyrannies.[18]

In contrast with Ariès's erratic career as a student, Vovelle's
story was one of ongoing academic success. He graduated from
the Ecole normale supérieure at Saint Cloud and then went on for
doctoral work with Ernest Labrousse at the Sorbonne. Labrousse
was the key figure in directing the research of the aspiring left-
wing historians who came of age in the 1950s and in integrating
them into the work of the great tradition of historical writing
about the French Revolution, from Jean Jaurès via Albert Mathiez
and Georges Lefebvre to Albert Soboul. This history was not doctrinaire but rather appreciative of Marxism for the insights it permitted into the goals of the popular revolution, considered against
the backdrop of the boom and bust of preindustrial economic
cycles. Labrousse was famous for his thesis about the conjuncture
between economic privation and political discontent as the
source of the radical "revolution from below" in 1789 and beyond.
His work and his mentoring shaped the conceptions of many of
the best historians of this generation, Vovelle among them.[19]

Vovelle approached Labrousse with a proposal to study the Paris

Commune of 1871. But Labrousse redirected his protégé to a study of the social structure of the city of Chartres in the late eighteenth century, through which, he opined, Vovelle might contribute a passage to the "grand fresco of social history" being painted according to his mentor's design. Such was Labrousse's authority that Vovelle dutifully complied, but he was savvy enough to see that the historiography of the French Revolution had grown sterile in continually revisiting a well-worn thesis about the social foundations of the "revolution from below." In his later writings about the Revolution, he continued to invoke the plot line given in the Jacobin-Marxist interpretation of modern French history.[20] In looking for avenues for new research, however, he turned to cultural history as an unexplored domain. His political allegiances had been shaken by the Soviet repression of the uprising in Hungary in 1956, and he had become interested in obstacles to change in the struggle to create the good society. Mentalities, which he construed as habits of mind tenaciously resistant to innovation, was a topic that promised to shed light on this neglected aspect of modern history.[21]

Vovelle's crossing from social to cultural history was not uncommon among his generation of left-wing historians. Even Labrousse gave his approval by baptizing mentalities a "third level" of sophistication in quantitative research. Vovelle himself explained it as a search for a more complex dialectic of history, one that integrated the multiple dimensions of the past. Cultural issues, he cautioned, must be considered in relation to the social tensions and economic processes in which they are grounded. In this his methodological thinking was close to that of the Marxist philosophers Lucien Goldmann and Louis Althusser, both of whom he admired.[22]

But in turning to mentalities, Vovelle, like Ariès, had a particular past to mourn, and it lent poignancy to the history of mourning on which he soon embarked and eventually to his exchange with Ariès over its interpretation. Although not as visible as the decline of the royalist tradition, the revolutionary tradition was losing its practical appeal, and Vovelle was trying to come to terms with that. By the late 1960s, a younger generation of left-wing historians wanted to address contemporary issues in new ways, rather than reaffirm past visions of the future. As an ideological beacon out of the past for guiding contemporary politics toward unrealized goals, the French Revolution was growing dim. Of what value was it for a society that no longer believed in the Communist revolution, they asked? Or for one that sensed the waning appeal of its proposed destiny for modern history generally?

In seeking answers to these questions, many of these historians on the left were engaged in the same kind of soul-searching as had Ariès a generation earlier concerning the nature of their political commitment in relation to the history they would write. Like Ariès, they, too, found an intellectual refuge in cultural history. Most would repudiate their ideological past in doing so.[23] Vovelle was an exception. He retained his affection for the Jacobin vision of a sansculotte democracy and for the rationalist rigor of Marxist analysis practiced by its great left-wing historians.[24] There was in his convictions an element of loyalty to the revolutionary tradition as well. In a rare autobiographical aside, he noted that he, a child of school teachers and a descendant of humble artisans, had been permitted to take advantage of his opportunities for upward social mobility but did not want to lose sight of the egalitarian ideal of the popular culture that was his heritage.[25] Maintaining a buoyant optimism about a Marxist historiography that most of his colleagues had abandoned, he confidently tried to reconcile the old social history with the new cultural history.[26]

Vovelle on the History of
Death and Mourning

Vovelle first developed his argument on the history of death and mourning in regional studies of Provence.[27] But he also published *Mourir autrefois* (1974), a précis of his broader argument analogous to Ariès's *Essai sur l'histoire de la mort*, written at about the same time.[28] His Marxist vision of history is implicit in his argument, as he identifies changes in attitudes toward mourning with rational consciousness-raising across the span of Western civilization. Coming to terms with death in Western society over the long run, he contends, has been a matter of de-mythologizing it, of ridding it of the illusions of the sacred in which it has been enshrouded.

Rather than devoting his primary attention to plotting the long-range patterns of commonly held attitudes, however, Vovelle focuses on transitional periods of crisis in which tensions over opposing attitudes toward death presented themselves. Here he holds fast to Labrousse's model of showing the breakdown of long-term structures in short-term crises of conjuncture. It is in these decisive moments of recognition, he explains, that the historical meaning of long-term social conflict is revealed. In its way, Vovelle's account of these crises over the representation of death signifies the struggles and triumph of the bourgeoisie over the aristocracy in the passage from traditional to modern society. Still, none of this is stated directly. In this history, class conflict is no longer boldly delineated in the way it had been in classic Marxist historiography. In Vovelle's rendering, the Marxist terminology of social struggle passes into tacit understanding, as he directs our attention to the cultural contexts of consciousness-raising. The task, he argues, is to grasp the dialectic of cultural conflict for what it reveals about a long-range historical process.[29] In dying, as in living, he concludes, our destiny lies in a dialectical process of becoming conscious of our predicament and of addressing it in a rational way.

Although broadly conceived, Vovelle's history of mourning tends to privilege the boundary between the Baroque culture of the seventeenth century and the Enlightened culture of the eighteenth century as a crucial divide. It was a time of rupture between old attitudes in which death was seen in a morbid way as the ultimate punishment for our sins and new views in which it came to be accepted as a natural phenomenon. Baroque attitudes, he explains, were an exaggerated expression of a religious mentality in its passionate death throes. Like the supernova of a dying star, the Baroque death ritual tended to be intensely emotional and given to brilliant display.[30] Enlightenment attitudes, by contrast, evinced a decorum and acceptance of death as part of the natural order. Proof of this change in sensibility, Vovelle explains, is to be found in waning references to hellfire and damnation in the learned discourse of theologians and more tellingly in the wills and testimonies of ordinary people. Even purgatory faded into oblivion.[31] Quiet meditation replaced pomp and circumstance in the protocols of mourning during this era.

At the same time, Vovelle maintains, this is not a simple tale of traversing a great divide between the religious traditions of the old regime and the secular ones of the modern age. The passage presupposes a more complex dialectic in that each of these traditions has its own inner tensions. Within Baroque culture, for example, there are opposing viewpoints about the merits of ostentatious display versus austere simplicity in commemorative rituals. Correspondingly, on the Enlightenment side one notes tensions between deists and materialists, the former preferring to link grieving to rarefied conceptions of immortality, the latter wishing to dismiss such abstractions altogether. Such tensions have their historical antecedents in the conflict between clericalists and humanists at the end of the Middle Ages. The discord in that era turned on efforts to purge Christian mourning of its pagan vestiges of belief in the miraculous. Resistance to that change produced an exaggerated anxiety about death, evinced in macabre descriptions of its realities. In the modern age the romantic obsession with death recalls the grotesque depictions of the late Middle Ages and reveals new forms of resistance to the larger trend. The neo-romantic mourning of the late nineteenth century is an even fainter echo of this same process.[32]

Vovelle's interpretation suggests an oscillation between periods of acceptance and periods of anxiety over death. But his history converges on the central drama of de-mythologizing death in the eighteenth century, an emblem of the social crisis of the aristocracy that culminated in the French Revolution. The tensions attending these changing attitudes toward death linger into the modern era, confirming the difficulties of the hard-won struggle of the bourgeoisie to overcome remaining resistances to the general trend toward a rational acceptance of the natural order.[33]

The Ariès-Vovelle Debate as a
Rendezvous with Destiny

Like Ariès, Vovelle was loyal to a political tradition whose fortunes were waning, and he tried to integrate his respect for it into his understanding of changing interpretations of its meaning.[34] Ariès's encounter with Vovelle, therefore, was not only about scholarship but also about the fortunes of the political right and left in the present age. Their debate evoked the enduring substance of a political quarrel that on its surface had lost its force but that in its cultural depths laid claim to opposing conceptions of human destiny. Their debate lasted nearly a decade, from a conference at Strasbourg in 1974 to one at Saint-Maximin in 1982, shortly before Ariès's death. They published conference proceedings of their exchange along the way.[35] Ariès's big book, *L'Homme devant la mort*, appeared in 1977, Vovelle's *La Mort en l'Occident* in 1983, and their final texts were based upon revisions undertaken in light of this exchange. Both worked with wills and testaments, and both were sensitive to the uses of iconography as historical evidence. Their empirical findings were not that far apart, and they

plotted the long-range changes in attitudes toward mourning in
much the same way. Rather, they differed in their respective interpretations of the human destiny such a history revealed.

In these culminating studies, the broad outlines of their respective theses remained largely intact, but their debate highlighted
three issues in which they made some reassessments:

   1. The question of historical periodization. Vovelle was puz-
zled by Ariès's indifference to Baroque death rituals, given their
importance for understanding Christianity as a factor in attitudes
toward death and mourning. For Vovelle, the age of the Baroque
had been the crucial moment of his history, for it signified a rising
anxiety over the loosening authority of Christianity as a cultural
force in the modern world. Hence its rites and rituals, especially
those attending mourning, became more emotion-laden and exaggerated.[36] Ariès had not paid particular attention to the period, or
for that matter the religious issue it raised, in his 1974 study because he did not see this era as decisive in the longer-range transition from a focus on the self ("one's own death") to an emphasis
on the other ("thy death"). For him, the crisis was not about an
old-time religion but a newborn individualism. More important,
he claimed, was the effort dating from the Renaissance to diffuse
personal awareness of death across life. As affection among family
members was deepened and the obligation to grieve for loved ones
passed into tacit understanding, some formal aspects of mourning
lost their raison d'être and were abandoned. It was not a matter of
giving up traditional ways of mourning but rather of incorporat-
ing them into the private sphere, where they retained their intensity. For Ariès, the techniques of life and death continued to go
hand in hand. In "thy death," mourning displayed the affection
and intimacy characteristic of romantic love.[37]

   2. The question of mentalities. Vovelle also accused Ariès of
having taken the history of mentalities in a new direction, one that
severed its "ideological" links to social and economic realities. He
argued that mentalities, as originally conceived by Lucien Febvre
and renewed by Robert Mandrou and even by his own mentor,
Ernest Labrousse, put the accent on forces that retard change. For
Vovelle, mentalities are the habits of mind that bear the inertial
power of the past. As such, they are the counterpoint to ideologies
in the dialectical equation, for they operate in constant tension
with the innovative ideas that inspire creative change. Their interaction reveals the nature of social tensions at play. Ariès, Vovelle
charged, was spiritualizing the history of mentalities, recasting it

in such a way that it acquired an autonomy divorced from social and economic realities. In light of this, he revisited more critically Ariès's working notion of a "collective unconscious," which he now construed as a disembodied spiritualism, impossible to locate and a temptation to mystification.[38]

For Ariès, the notion of a "collective unconscious" constituted a realm of tacit understanding whose subtleties he had not analyzed closely before. Now he was obliged to wrestle with the substance of the term, for it was crucial to his thesis. At their last formal encounter, that at the conference at Saint-Maximin, Ariès acknowledged the quasi-religious significance he had invested in the term, but he contended that his early usage of it had in fact been quite concrete, an attempt to get at the visceral realities of life that had inspired the revolution in attitudes about birth control in the seventeenth century. In the intervening discussion of death, he observed, this source of his notion may have been obscured and easily misconstrued as disembodied fantasies of the sort that Vovelle had identified with the morbidity of the late Middle Ages and the spiritualism of the Romantic era. As a concession to Vovelle, Ariès now sought to divest the term of spiritualist connotations by renaming it the "collective non-conscious," which he characterized as the living memory that sustains evolving traditions. It embodies popular wisdom that has been integrated into the common sense of life experience.[39]

3. *The question of destiny.* Ariès had a question to pose to Vovelle as well, one that went to the heart of what he believed to be the Marxists' need for happy endings. In a critique of Vovelle's forthcoming book, he noted the inconclusiveness of Vovelle's findings in terms of the larger issue of history's patterns. Ironically, he suggested, there is no moral to Vovelle's story of the sort the Marxist vision of history had originally anticipated. The dénouement that the social and cultural crisis of the eighteenth century supposedly foretold remains not only unrealized but unrecognized. Instead, the historical pattern that emerges in Vovelle's history is one of crescendo/decrescendo, culminating in the Enlightenment's secularization of attitudes toward death and then playing out in struggles of diminishing intensity into the present age. Implicitly, Ariès was chiding Vovelle for having bracketed the Marxist vision of destiny. Vovelle's history, he suggested, for all the crises of attitudes it highlights, points not toward some ultimate crisis of the sort that Marx had prophesied but only toward the remodeling of ongoing social tensions in the modern age. While Vovelle insisted

on the generative role of conflict in historical change, the Marxist
notion of a culminating crisis is rendered problematic in his account of tensions of dwindling importance in the approach to the
present age.[40]

In his book published in the following year, Vovelle demurred
before a full-scale reply. But he did reaffirm his faith in the spirit
in which he had embarked on the project some twenty years before: the prospect of a better future through consciousness-raising.
"Our investment in death," he reflected, "is not so much derived
from our hope for life as it is from our hope for well-being [*bon-
heur*], which is more complex and saturated with meaning." In
breaking the silence that has surrounded the topic of death for
nearly a century, he noted, we historians in the late twentieth
century may not have fully deciphered its meaning. But we have
at least become aware of the way it is rooted "in the depths
[*l'épaisseur*] of time."[41]

As for Ariès, he had couched his question in light of his own
reassessment of the relationship between death and destiny in the
modern age. A few years before, he had written an article on pattern and meaning in the civilizing process, in which he denied
that civilizations rise and fall. All our causes are transient, he
explained, and they change with circumstances. In the modern
age we may have the sense that we can shape our private lives
with more assurance that ever before, but ultimately we cannot
control our destiny, whose historical meaning is not to be found
in demonstrated progress but rather in ongoing reconfigurations
of the human quest for fulfillment. Death is a reality. But the destiny it implies is a human imagining, conceived in light of the
faith we hold in the future. Its pursuit may have become more self-
conscious, but it is conducted with the acceptance of our limits
and our place within our living traditions. In this respect, our reference point is not the future but the present.[42]

So culminated the respectful, even friendly, debate that Ariès and
Vovelle had conducted. They were linked at least in their fidelity
to their respective traditions, for each remained true to the spirit
of his youthful ideological allegiance, while transposing his convictions to the more erudite plane of the history of mentalities. As
cultural historians, they carried on what had been the more visibly political quarrels of their ideological predecessors. That it
should have been conducted so politely suggests that the traditions they honored were dying. In their exchange they mourned
the passing of the revolutionary tradition over which royalists and

republicans had struggled since the eighteenth century. In that sense, their dialogue about death was a requiem for the modern age that was passing. In their modest expectations for the future, they gave expression to what some philosophers would soon characterize as the end of history. From this perspective, the Ariès-Vovelle debate on death and mourning in the 1970s prefigured a wider one about the destiny of France as a nation in the 1980s.[43]

Tombs without Sepulchers: From Mourning to Memory in the New History of Commemoration

Ariès died in 1984. In the same year Vovelle was named to the famous chair in the history of the French Revolution at the Sorbonne. Soon thereafter he was chosen to coordinate the preparations for the bicentennial of that event. It was a prestigious job, but it turned out to be a troubled one.[44] Almost immediately, he was obliged to confront the historians' waning enthusiasm for this commemorative enterprise and a problematizing of the meaning of the revolutionary tradition that it had inspired. The assault on the Revolution as heritage came from within the academy—indeed, from one of its own historians. I am referring to François Furet, whose revisionist argument subverted the justification of a celebration modeled on that of the centennial, staged as an apotheosis of the revolutionary tradition.[45] Furet, too, had been trained in the Jacobin-Marxist tradition of historiography, though he had since repudiated it. His critique, therefore, was all the more vehement. He captured the historians' attention with his provocative claim that the French Revolution as a model for political inspiration had outlived its usefulness. He argued that the notion of destiny had been an invention of the Jacobins, enshrined by historians sympathetic to its egalitarian vision.[46] Playfully, he raised the question of whether the Revolution should be celebrated at all, for it had lost its commemorative role as a guide for action in the present age.[47]

The quarrel about the staging of the bicentennial thus stimulated a new debate about the meaning of the heritage of the French Revolution. For the first time in a hundred years, the Revolution was again an object of historiographical contention. Vovelle's planning for the bicentennial, therefore, was conducted under this shadow, for Furet had challenged its supposed role as an emblem of a shared national identity. Under the circumstances, Vovelle's words did not carry the incontrovertible authority of the sort once exercised by his eminent predecessors, and he soon found himself managing a quarrelsome politics of splintering factional identities. No longer was the Revolution an event to be mourned. Once a touchstone of moral intention for the nation, it had become the prey of the culture wars of present politics.[48]

The issue about destiny raised in the Ariès-Vovelle debate was thus transposed into a different historiographical context. The focus, however, remained the philosophical issue about historical time first raised by Ariès in *Le Temps de l'histoire* some forty years before: specifically, the dissolution of a way of understanding history as moving toward a dénouement. It was in that work that he had first called for a reconceptualizing of historical time in order to focus on the present, not the future, and so to pay greater attention to differences between past and present.[49] Vovelle may have continued to judge the meaning of history in light of his commitment to the revolutionary tradition, but he, too, had abandoned any simple sense of a sustained direction in historical change of the sort in which his illustrious predecessors had believed.[50] History might continue to proceed through the dialectical resolution of conflicts, he maintained, but for those of the present age he clearly had diminished expectations.

Focusing on the present age, moreover, carried important implications for understanding the relationship between history and memory, or as Ariès had put it, between history and History. As collective identity reverted to places of memory, the grand narrative whose construction Ariès had plotted in *Le Temps* unraveled into multiple story lines located at sites without temporal, conceptual, or logical connections. As the grand narrative dissolved, history was reconceived spatially as a congeries of topical problems. In an interesting coincidence, 1984, the year of Ariès's death, also marked the appearance of the first volume of Pierre Nora's *Lieux de mémoire*, an ambitious collaborative study of the French national identity. It signified a historical stance on mourning in a larger, collective sense, a mourning of national rather than personal identities of the sort about which Ariès and Vovelle had written. Proceeding genealogically from the present, this inquiry reframed the past spatially around discrete sites of memory whose numbers multiplied in the deepening recessional into the past. So conceived, French history had no beginning or end. In such circumstances, Nora queried, how might mourning, in the modern age so closely tied to notions of destiny, henceforth be understood?[51]

In pioneering this line of inquiry into mourning, Ariès, too, had been obliged early on to establish a critical distance from his personal experience. But he did carry with him a personal perspective, of which he gave careful readers a glimpse in a passage buried within the text of his culminating study, *L'Homme devant la mort*. The passage concerns the death of his mother, thinly disguised as the legend of the death of Mélisande, a mythological queen.[52] She accepted her death with such modesty that her passing was barely perceived by the loved ones who attended her. Her son was distraught that he had not had time to say good-bye adequately. But he later came to see that such modesty in the face of death is a virtue. Mélisande's death was testimony of the natural dignity of the dying, in keeping with the diminished conception of destiny in the present age.[53]

This image of the modest death of the mother also tells us something of the modest perspective on mourning at which the son had arrived in the course of his life and work. In the Middle Ages, he observed, "death was the awareness by each person of a Destiny" to which he surrendered without qualms. He acknowledged that in our technological culture it is no longer possible "to regain the naive confidence in Destiny that had for so long been shown by simple men when dying."[54] In the present age, he concluded, "death must simply become the discreet but dignified passing of a gentle person from a caring society that is not torn, nor even upset by the idea of a biological transition without significance, without pain or suffering, and ultimately without fear."[55]

In taking on the topic of mourning, Ariès was justifying his own minimalist historical perspective on the way in which destiny may be conceived in our times. In doing so, he showed us how the spectrum of permissible mourning contracted over time while the need remained essentially the same. His encounter with Vovelle brought out the conflicts punctuating this history and revealed how mourning in its many styles has been our constant way of reconciling ourselves to time's passages.

Notes

1. Philippe Ariès, *Un Historien du dimanche,* ed. Michel Winock (Paris: Editions du Seuil, 1982), 81.
2. Patrick Hutton, "The Politics of the Young Philippe Ariès," *French Historical Studies* 21 (1998): 475–95.
3. To his unhappiness over the fate of royalism was added his grief over the death of his brother Jacques in a military campaign of the French army in the last days of the war. Ariès later confided in a friend that this loss brought

home all the others and inspired him to launch his historical inquiry into the collapse of the culture of old France. Philippe Brissaud, interview by author, Paris, 19 April 1996.

4. Daniel Halévy, *Trois Epreuves: 1814, 1871, 1940* (Paris: Plon, 1941), 127–73.

5. Ariès, *Historien du dimanche*, 74–76.

6. Alexis Carrel, *Man, the Unknown* (1935; reprint, New York: Halcyon House, 1938), 273–322. See also Alain Drouard, *Alexis Carrel (1873–1944); De la mémoire à l'histoire* (Paris: Editions L'Harmattan, 1995), 165–98.

7. Alain Drouard, *Une Inconnue des sciences sociales; La Fondation Alexis Carrel, 1941–1945* (Paris: Editions de la Maison des sciences de l'homme, 1992), 271–78.

8. Ariès's early essays on demography, originally published in *Population*— "Attitudes devant la vie et devant la mort du XVIIe au XIXe siècle" (1949), "Sur les origines de la contraception en France" (1953), and "Contribution à l'histoire des pratiques contraceptives: Chaucer et Mme de Sévigné" (1954) —are reproduced in Philippe Ariès, *Essais de mémoire*, ed. Roger Chartier (Paris: Editions du Seuil, 1993), 309–28.

9. Philippe Ariès, "Le Secret" (1978), in *Essais de mémoire*, 46–49.

10. Philippe Ariès, *Histoire des populations françaises et de leurs attitudes devant la vie depuis le XVIIIe siècle* (1948; reprint, Paris: Editions du Seuil, 1971), 344–412.

11. The key article illuminating Ariès's move from demography in the late 1940s to mentalities in the 1960s is his "Interpretation pour une histoire des mentalités" in *La Prévention des naissances dans la famille*, ed. Hélène Bergues (Paris: Presses universitaires de France, 1960), 311–27.

12. Ariès, *Histoire des populations*, 322–43; Philippe Ariès, *L'Enfant et la vie familiale sous l'ancien régime* (1960; reprint, Paris: Editions du Seuil, 1973), 176–86, 306–16.

13. Philippe Ariès, *Le Temps de l'histoire* (Monaco: Editions du Rocher, 1954), 9–12, 25–60, 313–25.

14. Ibid., 22–24, 300–311. See also Ariès's late-in-life reflection, "Le Temps de l'histoire" (1983), in *Essais de mémoire*, 45–58.

15. Philippe Ariès, *Western Attitudes toward Death* (Baltimore: Johns Hopkins University Press, 1974). A French version, augmented with related essays, was published as *Essais sur l'histoire de la mort en Occident du Moyen Age à nos jours* (Paris: Editions du Seuil, 1975).

16. Ariès had an early fascination with this conception of tamed death. In one of his newspaper articles while a student at the Sorbonne before the war, he cited the tableau of such an edifying deathbed scene from Fyodor Dostoyevski's *The Brothers Karamazov*. Philippe Ariès, "La Terre promise," *Etudiant français*, 10 January 1938, p. 3. His interest at the time may have been peaked by witnessing the ceremonies attending the death of his grandparents in the 1930s. See his reference in Ariès, *L'Homme devant la mort* (Paris: Editions du Seuil, 1977), 2:282.

17. On Ariès's critique of the illusion of progress in contemporary culture, see esp. his "Une Interprétation tendancieuse de l'histoire des mentalités," *Anthinéa* 3, no. 2 (February 1973): 7–10; and "Confessions d'un anarchiste de droite," *Contrepoint*, no. 16 (1974): 87–99.

18. Michel Vovelle, *Les Aventures de la raison: Entretiens avec Richard Figuier* (Paris: Pierre Belfond, 1989), 11–12; Georg Lichtheim, *Marxism and the French Left* (New York: Columbia University Press, 1966), 69–111.

19. Vovelle, *Les Aventures*, 11–14. For Vovelle's appreciation of Labrousse's role, see his article, "La mémoire d'Ernest Labrousse," in *Annales historiques de la Révolution française* (hereafter *AHRF*), no. 276 (April–June 1989): 99–107. See also Labrousse's interesting personal commentary in an interview

with Christophe Charle, "Entretiens avec Ernest Labrousse," *Actes de la recherche en sciences sociales*, no. 32–33 (April–June 1980): 111–25.

20. Michel Vovelle, "Pourquoi nous sommes encore Robespierristes," *AHRF*, no. 274 (October–December 1988): 498–506; Vovelle, "La Galerie des ancêtres" (1988), in *Combats pour la Révolution française*, by Michel Vovelle (Paris: Editions La Découverte, 1993), 13–23.

21. Vovelle, *Les Aventures*, 19–22; Vovelle, "Histoire des mentalités, histoire des résistances, ou les prisons de longue durée" (1980), in *Idéologies et mentalités*, by Michel Vovelle (Paris: La Découverte, 1985), 236–61.

22. Vovelle is thus a good example of the way intellectuals who remained loyal to the Marxist vision redirected their work from social and economic subjects to cultural and religious topics. His intellectual progress thus parallels that of the philosophers Henri Lefebvre, Lucien Goldmann, and Louis Althusser. Vovelle, *Les Aventures*, 14–15, 18–22, 27.

23. Two such prominent historians were Emmanuel Le Roy Ladurie, author of the best-selling *Montaillou* (1976), and François Furet, acclaimed for his revisionist history of the French Revolution. See Ladurie, *Paris-Montpellier* (Paris: Gallimard, 1982), and Furet, *Histoire de la Révolution et la révolution dans l'histoire* (Paris: Editions de l'Ecole des hautes études en sciences sociales, 1994), personal accounts of their repudiation of their youthful Marxism.

24. Michel Vovelle, "L'Historiographie de la Révolution française à la veille du bicentenaire," *AHRF*, no. 272 (April–June 1988): 113–26, and no. 273 (July–September 1988): 307–15.

25. That is why Vovelle identified to some degree with the rise of Joseph Sec, whose biography he recounted in *L'Irrésistible Ascension de Joseph Sec, bourgeois d'Aix* (Aix-en-Provence: Edisud, 1975). As Vovelle explained: "Here was a man who rose on the basis of talent yet never denied his origins. He remained a good Jacobin, uncorrupted by his social ascent." *Les Aventures*, 40.

26. Michel Vovelle, "Idéologies et mentalités: Une clarification nécessaire" (1980), in *Idéologies et mentalités*, 5–17; Vovelle, "Jalons pour une histoire des mentalités sous la Révolution," in *La Mentalité révolutionnaire*, by Michel Vovelle (Paris: Editions sociales, 1985), 9–16.

27. Michel Vovelle, *Piété baroque et déchristianisation en Provence au XVIIIe siècle* (1973; reprint, Paris: Editions du Seuil, 1978); Michel Vovelle and Gaby Vovelle, *Vision de la mort et de l'au-delà en Provence* (Paris: Colin, 1970).

28. Michel Vovelle, *Mourir autrefois: Attitudes collectives devant la mort aux XVIIe et XVIIIe siècles* (Paris: Gallimard/Julliard, 1974).

29. To understand the dialectic of changing attitudes toward death and mourning, Vovelle explained, the historian must integrate three perspectives: death as measured *(la mort subie)*, in which he includes quantitative data of wills and testaments; death as perceived *(la mort vécu)*, by which he means eyewitness accounts; and death as discourse *(discours sur la mort)*, the edifying essays of theologians and other intellectuals. Disparate sources, they nonetheless enable the historian to plot a navigational fix on the crises that reveal the meaning of long-range change. Vovelle, *La Mort en l'Occident de 1300 à nos jours* (Paris: Gallimard, 1983), 7–12. See also his essay on method, "L'Histoire et la longue durée," in *La Nouvelle Histoire*, ed. Jacques Le Goff (1978; reprint, Paris: Editions Complexe, 1988), 96–104.

30. Vovelle, *Mourir autrefois*, 81–137.

31. Ibid., 183–204.

32. Ibid., 39–53, 141–48, 231–32.

33. Ibid., 233–34; Vovelle, *La Mort en l'Occident*, 33, 651–70.

34. Vovelle's rejection of Soboul's doctrinaire Marxism as a conceptual framework for understanding the Revolution is analogous to Ariès's rejection of Maurras's stance for understanding royalism. See Vovelle, "Albert Soboul, Historien de la société," *AHRF*, no. 250 (October–December 1982): 547–53.
35. The proceedings of the debate between Ariès and Vovelle at Strasbourg are found in the *Archives de sciences sociales des réligions* 39 (1975): 7–29; the proceedings for the conference at Saint-Maximin appear in *La Mort aujourd'hui* (Les Cahiers de Saint-Maximin), ed. Roger Chartier (Marseille: Editions Rivages, 1982).
36. Michel Vovelle, "Les Attitudes devant la mort, front actuel de l'histoire des mentalités," *Archives de sciences sociales des réligions* 39 (1975): 23–24.
37. Ariès, *L'Homme devant la mort,* 2:9–26.
38. Michel Vovelle, "Y a-t-il un inconscient collectif?" *Pensée,* no. 205 (May–June 1979): 125–36.
39. Philippe Ariès, "Inconscient collectif et idées claires," *Anthinéa,* no. 8 (August–September 1975): 3–4; Philippe Ariès, "Table ronde sur la communication de Roger Chartier," in *La Mort aujourd'hui,* 127–30.
40. Philippe Ariès, "Du livre (à paraître) de Michel Vovelle: 'La mort en Occident,'" in *La Mort aujourd'hui,* 159–68.
41. Vovelle, *La Mort en l'Occident,* 25–26. See also his historiographical reflection, "Sur la mort" (1978), in *Idéologies et mentalités,* 101–19.
42. Philippe Ariès, "Vie et mort des civilisations," in *La Mort, un terme ou un commencement?* ed. Christian Chabanis (Paris: Fayard, 1982), 103–18; Philippe Ariès, "La Sensibilité au changement dans la problématique de l'historiographie contemporaine," in *Certitudes et incertitudes de l'histoire,* ed. Gilbert Gadoffre (Paris: Presses universitaires de France, 1987), 169–75.
43. On the Ariès-Vovelle debate, see also Pierre Chaunu, *L'Historien en cet instant* (Paris: Hachette, 1985), 224–42.
44. On Vovelle's role on the bicentennial committee, see the detailed account by Steven Laurence Kaplan, *Farewell, Revolution: The Historians' Feud, France, 1789–1989* (Ithaca: Cornell University Press, 1995), 144–92.
45. On the centennial, see Pascal Ory, "La Preuve par 89," in *Les Lieux de mémoire,* ed. Pierre Nora (Paris: Gallimard, 1984–92), 1:523–60; Steven D. Kale, "The Countercentenary of 1889," *Historical Reflections* 23 (1997): 1–28.
46. François Furet, *Penser la Révolution française* (Paris: Gallimard, 1976).
47. François Furet, "Faut-il célébrer le bicentenaire de la Révolution française?" *Histoire* 52 (1983): 71–77.
48. Kaplan, *Farewell, Revolution,* 12–24. See also Vovelle's reply to Furet, "La Révolution est-elle terminée?" (1979), in *Combats pour la Révolution française,* 87–94.
49. Philippe Ariès, "Confessions d'un anarchiste de droite," 87–99; Philippe Ariès, "La Ressemblance" (1980), in *Essais de mémoire,* 59–67. See also François Hartog, "Temps et histoire: 'Comment écrire l'histoire de France?'" *Annales: Historie, Sciences Sociales* 50 (1995): 1219–36.
50. Michel Vovelle, "Réflexions sur l'interprétation révisionniste de la Révolution française" (1990), in *Combats pour la Révolution française,* 99–100.
51. Nora has since been criticized for having adopted a mournful approach to French history. See Steven Englund, "The Ghost of Nation Past," *Journal of Modern History* 64 (1992): 299–320. In fact, Nora was studying why the French past was no longer mourned as it had been in the rivalry of royalists and republicans over the fate of the revolutionary tradition. If anything is to be mourned, he suggests, it is the ways of modern historiography, marked by the death of the grand narrative. Pierre Nora, "Comment écrire l'histoire de France," in *Lieux de mémoire,* 3:11-32.

52. The legend was dramatized by Maurice Maeterlinck in a play (1892) and by Claude Debussy in an opera (1902).

53. Ariès, *L'Homme devant la mort,* 2:282. Ariès borrowed the image from Vladimir Jankélévitch, *La Mort* (Paris: Flammarion, 1977), 246, 282.

54. Ariès, "Les Attitudes devant la mort," 73, 75.

55. Ariès, *L'Homme devant la mort,* 2:324.

Further Reading

Ariès, Philippe. *L'Homme devant la mort.* Paris: Editions du Seuil, 1977. Republished in English translation as *The Hour of Our Death.* Trans. Helen Weaver. New York: Oxford University Press, 1981.
His major work on the history of attitudes toward death and mourning in the Western tradition.

————. *Western Attitudes toward Death: From the Middle Ages to the Present.* Trans. Patricia M. Ranum. Baltimore: Johns Hopkins University Press, 1974.
A pilot project for Ariès's larger study on death and mourning, based on lectures he delivered at Johns Hopkins University in April 1973. These lectures, together with related essays, were subsequently republished in French as *Essais sur l'histoire de la mort en Occident du Moyen Age à nos jours.* Paris: Editions du Seuil, 1975.

Chaunu, Pierre. *La Mort à Paris: XVIe, XVIIe et XVIIIe siècles.* Paris: Fayard, 1978.
A major contribution to the field by an historian identified with the *Annales* tradition.

Chartier, Roger, ed. *La Mort aujourd'hui.* Marseille: Editions Rivages, 1982.
Proceedings of a conference at Saint-Maximin (France) on death and mourning, including the last dialogue between Philippe Ariès and Michel Vovelle on the subject.

Marris, Peter. *Loss and Change.* Rev. ed. London: Routledge and Kegan Paul, 1986.
A clear and thoughtful anthropological study.

Morin, Edgar. *L'Homme et la mort.* Rev. ed. Paris: Editions du Seuil, 1970.
Important early contribution to studies of attitudes toward death and mourning.

Nora, Pierre, ed. *Les Lieux de mémoire.* 3 vols. Paris: Gallimard, 1984–92. Republished in part in English translation as *Realms of Memory: Rethinking the French Past.* Trans Arthur Goldhammer. New York: Columbia University Press, 1996.
A major collaborative study on the French national memory, including essays by many of France's leading historians.

Vovelle, Michel. *La Mort en l'Occident de 1300 à nos jours.* Paris: Gallimard, 1983.
His culminating study on death and mourning.

————. *Mourir autrefois: Attitudes collectives devant la mort aux XVIIe et XVIIIe siècles.* Paris: Gallimard, 1974.
A concise overview of his thesis on the history of death and mourning, illustrated with passages drawn from primary sources.

————. *Piété baroque et déchristianisation en Provence au XVIIIe siècle.*
    1973; reprint, Paris: Editions du Seuil, 1978.
        Presented first as a thesis at the Université de Lyon, this research project
    on a region of France launched his important investigations into the history
    of changing attitudes toward death and mourning.
Whaley, Joachim, ed. *Mirrors of Mortality: Studies in the Social History
    of Death.* New York: St. Martin's Press, 1981.
        An anthology of essays by English scholars dealing with a variety of top-
    ics in the history of attitudes toward death and mourning.

DORIS L. BERGEN

MOURNING, MASS DEATH, AND THE GRAY ZONE

THE ETHNIC GERMANS OF EASTERN EUROPE AND THE SECOND WORLD WAR

THE PHOTOGRAPH of the SS man in full uniform came as some-thing of a shock. It was 1989, and I was looking at family pictures with an elderly woman who had recently arrived in West Germany from what then was still the Soviet Union. The woman was an ethnic German, a *Volksdeutsche*, to use the terminology of earlier decades of this century, one of the millions of people living out-side the borders of Germany in the 1930s and 1940s who never-theless identified themselves culturally as Germans (but not as Jews).[1] In 1939 there were *Volksdeutsche* in the Baltic states, Czechoslovakia, Poland, Ukraine, Romania, Hungary, Yugosla-via, and elsewhere. Nazi racial policy designated the *Volksdeut-schen* carriers of "Aryan blood" and made them, at least in theory, beneficiaries of the expulsion and murder of Slavs and Jews.[2]

That some ethnic Germans had cooperated with the German invaders of central and eastern Europe during World War II was not new to me; well-known Jewish memoirs tell of *Volksdeutschen* who stole Jewish property, betrayed their neighbors, or served as guards at concentration camps.[3] I also knew that many ethnic Germans had suffered terribly in the years after the war, driven from their homes, banned to Siberia, branded traitors by their neighbors and governments.[4] The woman next to me, for exam-ple, had spent years doing hard labor in a Siberian forest; her father had starved to death there in 1946. But she and her family were Mennonites, members of what I knew as a pacifist, Christian group with a long history of persecution for nonconformism and a commitment to being "in" but not "of" the world. So what was an SS man doing in her photograph album?

The man in the picture was her brother Georg, the woman told me. Later I discovered that in fact his parents had called him Isaak, a name that turned out to be "too Jewish" for a certified member of the so-called master race. She cried when she told me that Isaak/Georg "fell" in France before the end of the war. She showed even stronger emotion, however, when we came to another photograph. This one, of recent Soviet provenance, featured an elderly man with his wife and grown children. The man was her cousin, the woman said, but unlike the rest of her relatives, who over the years had been admitted into the Federal Republic of Germany, he was forced to remain behind because he had been in the SS. It was sad, unjust, and so wrong, she told me, her voice shaking with anger and grief, to separate someone from his family that way, just because he had "done his duty" in a German uniform.[5]

That woman and her photographs introduce some difficult issues about ethnic Germans and the World War II past. Those issues in turn raise questions about mourning and its possibility for people who live through times of exceptional suffering and atrocity. Freud defined mourning, in contrast to the narcissistic and self-destructive process of melancholia, as an honest engagement of loss, however slow and painful; through mourning one comes to recognize that the object of love no longer exists and to comprehend that nevertheless one can and will go on without it.[6] Clearly those ethnic Germans who experienced the war have a great deal to mourn: loss of their idealized image of the German "motherland"; explosion of their faith in Adolf Hitler and his promises of German superiority; involvement or implication in the crimes of the Third Reich by themselves or members of their families and communities; deprivation of their homes and homelands after the war; persecution, suffering, and death of loved ones and neighbors during the war itself, its aftermath, and the subsequent years under Communism.

Yet how can such massive, complex work of mourning occur, and not only on an individual level but collectively as well?[7] In what ways do relationships of power, from national politics to gender, complicate or obstruct mourning? Is empathetic mourning possible in the face of mass death and in the context of what Primo Levi, a survivor of Auschwitz, called the "gray zone," that area of "ambiguity which radiates out from regimes based on terror and obsequiousness?"[8] In other words, is there a kind of mourning that not only grieves for one's own losses but also acknowledges the suffering of others, suffering occasioned by crimes to which one was a witness and perhaps even a perpetrator? Finally, what role might the historian play in mourning a past as terrible as World War II and the Holocaust?

This essay explores those questions by focusing on issues of mourning in relation to the ethnic Germans of eastern Europe after World War II. The first section, "Psychology, Historiography, and Mourning the Nazi Era," situates this discussion in a historiographical context: it surveys how insights from psychology, including Freud's concept of mourning, have affected the study of the Holocaust and the Second World War in Europe. The second section of the essay, "'Inability to Mourn' or the Impossibility of Mourning?" examines failure to mourn and obstructions to mourning among the *Volksdeutschen*, with reference to Alexander and Margarete Mitscherlich's influential analysis of postwar Germany, *The Inability to Mourn: Principles of Collective Behavior.*[9] The third section, "The Historian and the Challenge of Mourning," addresses the historian as mourner. All three sections reflect a dilemma of mourning: on the one hand, they demonstrate the importance, indeed the urgency, of collective mourning as a response to the pain of the past. On the other hand, they reveal the difficulty, perhaps the impossibility, of the kind of group process of mourning that seems to be called for in the case of the *Volksdeutschen* (and other groups of people, elsewhere). Melanie Klein's assessment of mourning as "difficult and dangerous" appears to be an accurate if understated description of the challenges involved.[10]

Psychology, Historiography, and
Mourning the Nazi Era

Psychology and psychoanalysis have probably had more impact on the study of the Nazi era and the Holocaust than they have on any other field of historical inquiry. Bruno Bettelheim published his original study of "infantilism" in Nazi concentration camps immediately after his own incarceration during the 1930s in Dachau and Buchenwald; he later incorporated that analysis into his renowned work, *The Informed Heart.*[11] Already during the war, in the United States press, in public settings, and in the inner circle of President Franklin D. Roosevelt's advisers, psychological diagnoses and models shaped some of the most important discussion of the nature of the Nazi "disease."[12] The 1960s and 1970s revisited such approaches with psychohistories of Adolf Hitler.[13] The 1980s, in contrast, saw psychologists and psychiatrists engage the emerging subjects of Jewish child survivors and the "second" and "third generations"—that is, the children and grandchildren of survivors of the Shoah.[14]

Until the last decade or so, scholars tended to use psychological insights to explore pathologies that they assumed characterized people involved in the trauma of the Holocaust, whether as perpetrators, bystanders, or victims.[15] Studies of perpetrators sought to comprehend what enabled them to commit such heinous crimes against fellow human beings; investigations of victims tried to categorize the scars their suffering left in its wake.[16]

More recently, at least with regard to the victims, psychology seems to have broken out of that pathological orientation to open up new possibilities for scholarship. People like Yale psychiatrist Dori Laub have contributed enormously to the collection and assessment of oral testimony from Holocaust survivors.[17] Their psychologically informed insights in turn have helped historians and literary critics develop new ways to analyze eyewitness accounts.[18] The historian Saul Friedländer's interest in memory has given his writing a depth that resonates across disciplinary lines and continues to inspire scholars of all generations.[19] And whereas attention to private memory has stimulated the collection and use of oral testimony, interest in public memory has opened up another productive field of investigation: the study of Holocaust monuments and memorials.[20]

Few studies of the victims of the Holocaust invoke Freud's concept of mourning explicitly, but many of them communicate an attitude of mourning nonetheless. Often written by Jewish scholars who experienced the war years as refugees or exiles, in hiding or in camps, or by the children or grandchildren of survivors, the most effective works arguably reflect the painful combination of sorrow and distancing that Freud described as mourning.[21] They grieve in the remembering and retelling of Jewish suffering and at the same time use the scholarly tools of objectivity to provide some healing detachment.[22]

Work on the perpetrators has not seen the same changes that in recent years have transformed scholarship on the victims. Certainly interest in those who carried out Nazi mass murder remains high. Daniel Goldhagen and others have pointed out that grasping the "how" and examining the terrible "why" of the Shoah necessitate the study of those who committed the atrocities.[23] Perhaps the very scope and depravity of the crimes have kept scholars who use psychological approaches to the perpetrators focused on pathology. A prime example is Christopher R. Browning's *Ordinary Men,* an investigation of a German killing squad in Poland. Browning draws on the famous Milgram experiment and its conclusions about obedience to authority in order to account for the murderous capabilities demonstrated by seemingly unremarkable men who slaughtered thousands of Jews, including old people, women, and babies.[24]

It is not surprising that oral testimony and emphasis on memory and commemoration have not appealed to scholars of the perpetrators and bystanders in the same way as they have to those who study the targets of genocide.[25] Killers and their accomplices in mass murder have personal as well as legal reasons to keep their recollections to themselves. Their sons, daughters, and grandchildren arguably have even less interest in plumbing the depths of those wartime memories.[26] The often-invoked call to remember in order to pay respect to the dead and celebrate life becomes a cynical, brutal violation if applied to the history of those responsible for the misery and murder of so many others.

In this regard the historiography concerning ethnic Germans from eastern Europe differs considerably from that of Germans from Germany. In ethnic German circles personal reports, oral testimonies, and interest in memory abound. Such historical work began among ethnic German "displaced persons" after World War II and continued, primarily in West Germany, throughout the decades of the cold war. In the late 1940s and 1950s, West German historians, sponsored by the government of the Federal Republic, gathered eyewitness accounts from thousands of *Volksdeutschen* who had been forced to leave their homes in the east. Between 1954 and 1961, they published eight volumes of selections.[27] Scholars with ethnic German origins continue to work on the history of their communities. Archives, museums, and organizations of ethnic Germans collect memoirs, interview seniors about their experiences, and preserve photographs and artifacts. Activities of the Siebenbürger Saxons—ethnic Germans from Transylvania in Romania and Hungary, now mostly living in Germany—are an example;[28] similar associations of Germans from Russia, the Baltic states, and elsewhere exist throughout Germany and in North America. Glasnost, the collapse of Communist regimes in eastern Europe after 1989, and the resulting flood of ethnic Germans into Germany gave their enterprises an enormous boost.

In some ways such endeavors resemble efforts by Jewish groups to record and interpret memories of the Shoah. There is, however, a crucial difference: almost without exception ethnic German projects focus on the period after World War II; most begin with the arrival of the Red Army in their home territories in 1944 or 1945.[29] They describe the dispossession, expulsion, and rape that *Volksdeutche* experienced, but not the horrendous violations against Jews, Poles, and others that some of them committed and many of them witnessed during the war. In the subfield of ethnic German studies, the influences of psychology seem largely confined to the period of least ambiguous victimization.

I know of no studies that use Freud's concept of mourning to address ethnic Germans and their relationship to World War II.[30] This essay is intended as the beginning of such an analysis. There are, however, a number of works that discuss mourning in the context of general German dealing with the past. Most of them, influenced by Alexander and Margarete Mitscherlich's by-now classic work, *The Inability to Mourn*, take a critical stance and identify a failure of mourning.[31]

For more than thirty years the Mitscherlichs' analysis has set the tone in discussions of what has become known as *Vergangenheitsbewältigung*—German for "mastering the past." In different ways scholars across the disciplines, from the Germanist Eric L. Santner to the philosopher Susan Neiman and the historian Robert Moeller, confirm the two psychoanalysts' diagnosis of a society characterized by denial, inability to admit its own sense of loss— lost ideals, the lost, loved führer—and flight into the refuges of materialism and an exaggerated, sometimes maudlin sense of its own victimization.[32]

Some of the Mitscherlichs' insights—particularly those on denial and the victimization defense—are easily applicable to the ethnic Germans. In significant ways, however, the Mitscherlichs' analysis needs to be extended when used to understand mourning among the *Volksdeutschen* of eastern Europe. Here critiques by the historians Charles S. Maier, Dominick LaCapra, and Michael Geyer are particularly helpful.

Maier introduces the notion of a "surfeit of memory."[33] Contrary to the Mitscherlichs' assessment, Maier maintains that one cannot describe West Germany in the decades after the Second World War as silent about the Nazi past. Instead, selective memories and histories draw attention to Germans' suffering and recast the past in terms of their own claims to victimization. Maier's insight fits at least as well to characterize ethnic Germans from the east. Instead of total silence, one finds within their circles nostalgia about the past and an abundance of vivid if edited memories that at times have threatened to upset the stability of central Europe.[34]

Like the Mitscherlichs' study, LaCapra's work on the Shoah and its historians reflects intense engagement with Freud. Mourning and more generally working-through are central concepts for LaCapra, too.[35] But LaCapra asks a question that the Mitscherlichs left aside: in the case of perpetrator and bystander groups after World War II, what is the proper object of mourning? If Hitler, as the Mitscherlichs suggested, was the "lost loved object" to be mourned, would not mourning in fact obscure the suffering and murder of Jewish victims rather than enabling an honest engagement with the past? "It seems necessary," LaCapra writes, "not only to recognize the lost object in order to allow for processes of mourning to be engaged, . . . but perhaps to criticize the inclination to remain invested in—as well as the very need to mourn—unworthy objects." LaCapra's observation has special pertinence for the ethnic Germans. Their wartime losses include lost privilege and dominance as the "chosen people" of Nazi racial hierarchies in the east; mourning such objects would be far from "ethicopolitically desirable and effective in reducing anxiety," to borrow LaCapra's careful language.[36]

Geyer's objection to the Mitscherlichs' analysis also has particular relevance to the *Volksdeutschen*. The Mitscherlichs' study, he contends, "obscured the experience and the traumatic consequences of mass death."[37] For Germans, according to Geyer, World War II was the culmination of a "long and unbroken continuity of the experience of death." Instead of sorrow and mourning, he claims, the reaction to such mass death is "an exclusion and a quarantine of the dead and of the experience of death among the survivors." Geyer characterizes the resulting detachment as never fully stable, requiring constant effort to keep the wound closed, "in no way, then, a forgetting or a silence, but a convulsive closing of the injuries as a result of the experience of mass death."[38] During the first half of this century, *Volksdeutsche* in eastern Europe faced the same years of killing and death as did Germans within Germany, but in addition to the World Wars many of them lived through the "mass deaths" of the Russian Revolution, civil war, famine, and Stalinist purges both before and after World War II. The Mitscherlichs' call to mourning does not recognize the tortured, bloody, gray zone of mass death, an area inhabited by many *Volks-deutschen* in eastern Europe for at least two generations.[39]

"Inability to Mourn" or the Impossibility
of Mourning?

The Mitscherlichs defined mourning as "the psychic process by which the individual copes with a loss." They saw difficulties in generalizing the concept to a large group, because "here the immense range of living circumstances and character differences adds new and unknown factors."[40] Nevertheless, they concluded that in postwar Germany as a whole, four widespread defense mechanisms blocked mourning of the Nazi past: "denial, isolation, transformation into the opposite, and above all, . . . withdrawal of interest and affect."[41] In significant ways those four tendencies also characterize attitudes of many ethnic Germans from eastern Europe after World War II.

The word *denial* features prominently in the Mitscherlichs' text, in which it is defined as a "defense mechanism related to disturbing perceptions of external reality." The forms it took among postwar Germans include denial of defeat by the Soviet Union, an enemy most Germans considered inferior to themselves, and denial or reinterpretation of all events in which "Germans were guiltily implicated."[42]

One need not be a psychoanalyst to see that the term *denial* fits many ethnic Germans, too. Most of their postwar recollections simply omit mention of the large numbers of them who participated in the paramilitary *Selbstschutz* organizations, the SS, or the Wehrmacht, the German armed forces.[43] In conversations, interviews, and memoirs, men who served in those capacities habitually describe their work as limited to translation or routine guard duties, even though a staggering array of contemporary sources documents their direct involvement in atrocities against civilians.[44] Scholars and eyewitnesses from within ethnic German communities who draw attention to such evidence find themselves marginalized and censured by their fellows.[45]

Denial among ethnic Germans takes many forms, from disavowing information about the goals of National Socialism to denying contact with Jews or knowledge of their murder during the war. Evidence to the contrary, however, appears in contemporary sources and in statements of ethnic Germans who for various reasons do not take part in denial. For example, one *Volksdeutsche*, a woman from Ukraine, told an interviewer shortly after the war that of course she knew about the killing of Jews; many Jews lived nearby, she pointed out, and a member of her own community had a Jewish husband. German SS men poisoned that woman's child before the mother's eyes, she said.[46] Such an honest answer would be much less likely in the months and years to follow, once the shame of defeat after so much arrogance and the guilt of knowledge, perhaps even participation, in the terrible deeds of the Third Reich had time to develop.[47] Moreover, the passage of time allowed responses to uncomfortable questions—like those about Jews—to be standardized.

Isolation is the second defense mechanism that the Mitscherlichs identified. They described postwar West German society as stuck in a kind of "creative stultification" resulting from, among other things, Germany's "affective isolation" from the rest of the world.[48] Outsiders, after all, ask painful questions and threaten the protective wall of denial. One can certainly observe considerable isolation among ethnic Germans living in Germany today. They tend to live in groups, as in the almost completely ethnic German city of Espelkamp in Westphalia. Often they communicate with each other in languages other than German and feel alienated from the larger German society.[49] Some Germans from Russia have even proposed forming their own political party in order to lobby more effectively for what they consider their unique interests.[50]

In the case of the ethnic Germans, it is difficult to determine to what degree isolation has been imposed from without rather than chosen from within. Those ethnic Germans who remained in eastern Europe after World War II under Communist regimes faced abuses ranging from dispossession, incarceration, and forced relocation to petty discrimination at school or in the workplace. It is hardly surprising that suspicion of people deemed outsiders might result. Even in 1998, in the security of their German homes, ethnic Germans became visibly nervous when I produced my tape recorder—for them a reminder of innumerable interrogations at the hands of the KGB.

Among the most powerful accounts of ethnic German isolation are the novels of Herta Müller. Müller grew up as part of the German minority in Romania; since 1987 she has lived in Germany. Paradoxically, by describing the profound alienation of Romania's ethnic Germans, Müller's books help open their community to inspection—and to introspection. "My father was a member of the

SS," Müller said in a 1989 interview; "I know what I'm talking about."[51]

The Mitscherlichs call the third defense mechanism "transformation into the opposite." Attempts to shake off guilt, they indicate, erase the victims and turn attention to one's own suffering.[52] Many observers of the postwar Germanies have noted this tendency to cast recent history in terms of German victimhood rather than confront the complex realities of initiative and agency.[53] According to the Mitscherlichs, such "identification with the innocent victim is very frequently substituted for mourning."[54]

A similar proclivity is apparent among many ethnic Germans. One man I encountered, a memoirist and amateur historian, displays a large map of eastern and central Europe on the wall in his home. Colored pins mark the sites of his suffering under Communism. For him that map is the history of the 1930s and 1940s. In their interviews several ethnic Germans explicitly labeled their postwar experiences a "holocaust." Everyone talks about the Jews, a *Volksdeutscher* from Ukraine told me. "But we suffered just the same. The only difference is that we were not granted a merciful, quick death in the gas chambers."[55]

Both humanistic and scholarly reasons make it difficult not to be outraged by such remarks. But one must keep in mind that ethnic German claims to victimhood are based on very real suffering. Those who lived through the 1920s and 1930s in the Soviet Union experienced the violence and destruction of civil war, collectivization, famine, and purges. Arrests, executions, and exile to Siberia in the years around 1937 took a terrible toll; German invaders in 1941 observed that some ethnic German villages were almost entirely devoid of adult men.[56] During the war, the *Volksdeutschen*'s Nazi benefactors often turned out to be cruelly indifferent to the needs and desires of their supposed clients. And when Hitler's state collapsed, more than ten million refugees from the east fled westward, leaving their homes behind forever. Thus *Volksdeutsche* who describe their twentieth century in terms of victimization need not fabricate stories of anguish and desperation; their experience of mass death was all too real.

Still, ethnic Germans' narratives of pure victimization are selective. In many cases they did have only incomplete, inaccurate information about Nazi Germany. Nevertheless, they say almost nothing about the impact of Nazi propaganda on their attitudes or relations with their neighbors. They leave out the ways that perhaps their own impotence as minorities under repressive systems made them vulnerable to Nazism's "world-redeeming dreams" of greatness.[57] All but the most unusual ethnic German memoirs omit consideration of particular Jewish suffering.[58] And in many cases they privilege women's narratives and downplay men's.

In ethnic German accounts, conventions of gender facilitate the transformation from perpetrators and witnesses into victims. When they talk about wartime events, both male and female *Volksdeutsche* tend to foreground female experiences: giving birth, nursing babies, fear of rape, the treks westward at war's end. There are also a relatively large number of women's memoirs, for example, at the archive of the Siebenbürger Saxons in Gundelsheim, Germany.[59] Such atypical equality of opportunity is no feminist recognition of women's special suffering. Instead, it constitutes an appropriation of women's experiences for political ends, to legitimate claims of male loss and innocence.[60] Ethnic German women's war stories lend themselves more readily than do men's to transformation from the gray area of multiple roles— perpetrator, bystander, injured party—to an imagined zone of unambiguous victimhood.

The fourth defense that the Mitscherlichs address is lack of interest or affect. After the war, they argue, the Federal Republic of Germany "did not succumb to melancholia; instead those who had lost their 'ideal leader,' the representative of a commonly shared ego-ideal, managed to avoid self-devaluation by breaking all affective bridges to the immediate past."[61] But as Maier and Geyer show, such detachment is never complete. And as the Mitscherlichs demonstrate, it requires massive expenditures of psychic energy.

The *Volksdeutschen* also exhibit lack of interest in that past most closely linked with cause for their own guilt. In the decades since the war, ethnic Germans from Romania, the Soviet Union, Hungary, Poland, and elsewhere in central and eastern Europe have produced a torrent of literature. Yet only a tiny portion of that material addresses the years from 1933 to 1945. Most memoirs and scholarly analyses begin at the very end of the war, with the arrival of the Red Army. Typical is the massive collection of eyewitness accounts edited by the German historian Theodor Schieder.[62] Schieder had his own reasons to omit the war years; in October 1939 he authored a memorandum that was a foundational document to the infamous *Generalplan Ost*, the Nazi blueprint for deportation, resettlement, attrition, and murder of the peoples in the east.[63] Even in private conversations, ethnic Germans from eastern Europe showed disengagement with the war years. When asked in interviews to recount their experiences they invariably jumped to the end of the war and focused on their treatment in the years to follow.

Among ethnic Germans, lack of interest motivated by denial seems stronger even than the tendency to stress their own victimization. In examining the archival record, I am often struck by the brutality and contempt that German functionaries showed toward their supposed brothers and sisters in the blood. Bureaucrats who cared more about their careers than their ethnic German charges arbitrarily relocated entire communities; SS racial experts categorized individuals and families as if they were livestock; economic interests exploited ethnic Germans' labor, and military authorities used them as particularly expendable cannon fodder.[64] Nazi planners promised the *Volksdeutschen* farms and properties stolen in Poland and then used those promises to rationalize and accelerate the dispossession and murder of Polish Jews and gentiles.[65] But meanwhile the often eager beneficiaries of these monstrous schemes frequently languished in camps for years, waiting to be assigned homes, guarded by police and barbed wire, reduced to begging to return to the places from which they had come.[66] Ethnic Germans filled Nazi files with letters of complaint, but few mention those discontents in postwar accounts.

The woman with the photographs provides a case in point. In 1943, the Germans evacuated and relocated her family from their home in southern Ukraine. Instead of receiving the promised farm of their own in the Warthegau, they were sent as hired hands to work for a storm trooper inside Germany. The reason, she told me, was a low racial classification. SS race experts, concerned about incidents of "feeblemindedness" in the extended family, deemed the woman, her siblings, and her parents undesirable and untrustworthy. Even a brother in the SS did not help. When pressed, the woman told me something about the storm trooper boss's vicious treatment of her family, especially his abuse of her father. But even that description quickly glided into a more passionate discussion of prejudices experienced years later, back in the Soviet Union.[67] Any lingering in the history of the Nazi era, it seems, creates discomfort among many ethnic Germans.

"Mourning without solidarity," Eric Santner writes, "is the beginning of madness."[68] But solidarity extends in two directions. It would be both unjust and of little use to identify a failure of mourning among ethnic Germans in the postwar period without

pointing to the enormous barriers to a critical collective mourning. The task of the historian is neither to excuse nor to accuse
but to help develop the self-knowledge necessary for thinking
through and working through.[69] And that task requires empathy
"in relation to events the very scale of which makes empathy
impossible."[70]

Ethnic Germans face some of the same obstacles to mourning
as do other perpetrator or bystander groups. For example, Germans
at home in Germany also may have chosen denial and silence
out of fear of the reproaches of the next generation. Nor were
the *Volksdeutschen* alone in the tendency to allow more recent
suffering—their own—to bury earlier experiences, especially if
those earlier memories included considerable moral ambiguity
about their role in the suffering of others. Here ethnic German
responses might have some comparability to those of Polish
Christians who lived the war even more deeply in the gray area, as
perpetrators, beneficiaries, and witnesses, but also sometimes
as victims of mass murder.[71]

The cold war also blocked mourning among ethnic Germans.
As the Mitscherlichs point out, for all Germans after the war,
anti-communism allowed "covert ideological elements of Nazism"
to "coalesce with the ideology of the capitalist West."[72] International politics on both sides of the iron curtain rewarded Germans
for fostering illusions about the past. In the West, Germans could
retain the notion that the real enemy had always been the Soviet
Union; in the East, the self-image of victimization fit neatly into
the official position of Communist workers as the real targets of
fascism.

For ethnic Germans—those in the Federal Republic and those
who remained in eastern Europe—both tendencies were exacer-
bated. Those who fled to Germany or found their way there in the
decades following the war were rewarded for publicizing their suffering or self-styled martyrdom for the German/western cause at
the hands of so-called Asiatic barbarism. Their existence served to
legitimate the anti-communist positions of the Federal Republic
and to underscore an image of the east as a vast prison. Ethnic
Germans in the east who suffered abuses under Communism
could interpret their experiences, not as a call to examine their
wartime conduct, but as evidence of a continuity of persecution.

A group of *Volksdeutschen* from Ukraine told me about a
member of their community whom Soviet authorities after the
war accused of participating in atrocities against Jews. Sentenced

to years of hard labor in northernmost Siberia, he decided to throw himself from the train rather than face that torment. As he stood ready to jump, his friends told me, Jesus appeared to him in a vision and told him to live. Later the man's sentence was reduced, and he returned to his family. For members of his ethnic German community, that man's story was not part of a quest for postwar justice—they dismissed the accusations as false—but another saga in the cruel Soviet harassment of Germans. Likewise, his "rescue" did not constitute an opportunity to engage the wartime past but meant instead a chance to celebrate the triumph of Christian faith over godless Communism.[73]

Tendencies to emphasize German victimization have also served to reward ethnic Germans for their failure to mourn. In a scenario where Germans cast themselves as the real victims of Nazism, specific Jewish suffering becomes a taboo topic, to be replaced by detailed accounts of German misery—bombings, rapes, separation of families. Experiences of ethnic Germans, and in particular of ethnic German women, could be and have been appropriated to this end. Thus the very real suffering of ethnic German women, who faced expulsion, deprivation, and assault in their panicked flight from the Red Army, often without the companionship or protection of their men, has been doubly appropriated: within ethnic German circles to validate professions of innocence and in the wider German context to support claims to victimhood.

Two pieces of visual evidence illustrate such uses of the past. In 1980 a journalist and a historian in West Germany published a collection of photographs of ethnic Germans. Entitled *Flucht und Vertreibung: Deutschland zwischen 1944 und 1947* (Flight and expulsion: Germany between 1944 and 1947), the book featured picture after terrible picture of women: weeping, struggling, exhausted women, young women with babies, old women dressed in black. Images of men are rare; those included are almost all either very old or dead.[74] The book, clearly an expensive production, contained little commentary and no explanations as to the identity of these suffering women or the situations from which they had come. The misery it depicted was very real, but by offering those images without context and labeling them "Germany between 1944 and 1947," its authors implied that the specific fact of ethnic German women's suffering was instead a general truth about German victimization.

In 1955, West German postal authorities sponsored a contest to design a stamp commemorating ten years since the end of the war. Many themes emerged as potential focal points: the economic miracle of West German recovery, European integration, rebuilding of German cities. The winning design showed none of those scenes of accomplishment, nor did it express any regret for the destruction unleashed by Nazi Germany. Instead, it pictured a ragged band of ethnic German expellees, driven from east to west (right to left across the stamp), clutching their pathetic small parcels of belongings and heading into what appeared to be a bitter, cold wind. Here, too, female images dominated; two women, a child, and a baby occupy the center of the picture; two men on the sides frame them.[75] The blank background provides no information as to why these people are fleeing or what their fate might have to do with the war whose conclusion the stamp marked.

The Historian and the Challenge of Mourning

The failure of mourning among ethnic Germans, perhaps the impossibility of mourning death and murder as massive as that of World War II, leaves us with questions about the role of those who chronicle and interpret that past. Is there a posture of mourning appropriate to a historian of the perpetrators and bystanders of atrocities, a stance that reflects not nostalgia, denial, or rationalization but an honest, questioning, open-ended acceptance of responsibility? And is history as an act of mourning possible for the perpetrators themselves, or for those associated with them: their countrymen and collaborators, their children and grandchildren?

I am not sure what the answers are. Perhaps the most important response is to accept the impossibility and undesirability of closure. Here I agree with Michael Geyer's conclusion that "the only possible and conceivable history after the rupture of civilization in World War II, present as yet only in its inceptions, is . . . a multiple and contestatory history."[76] Self-critical, pluralistic histories may be the only kind that can accept the challenge to mourn and recognize the continued urgency of mourning the past beyond the generation directly involved.

In suggesting that the call to mourn extends across the generations, I am not advocating some notion of collective guilt. Rather, I am making the somewhat obvious point that dishonesty and denial in one generation poison relations with the next. I recently learned from an acquaintance in Canada that his uncle, an ethnic German from Ukraine, is under investigation by the federal war crimes office. The man has been charged with concealing his wartime activities as a member of the Waffen SS. My acquaintance, who is in his early forties, bears no responsibility for the actions of his uncle; nevertheless, he is directly affected by them. His relationship to his parents and their generation, his own identity as a German-Canadian, and perhaps most sharply the sense of family history that he will communicate to his children are all at stake. How will he mourn—and what will he mourn? The Jewish and other victims of his uncle's SS unit in the east? The loss of his ideals of family innocence? Or the supposed scapegoating of his uncle by conspiratorial forces? The burden of the previous generation's inability to mourn now rests with him.

The costs of failure to mourn are high. It can result in complete loss of a group's history, something already apparent among the new generation of ethnic Germans living in Germany. The real suffering as well as the crimes of the *Volksdeutschen* get buried in clichés and silences. Anything that might be learned, the empathy that is gained from realizing that no matter who one is, one is connected into families, communities, and nations whose own hands are not clean, the humility that is the beginning of tolerance—all are forfeited in the refusal to mourn.

Even more frightening is the political risk of failure to mourn. Mythologized histories make those who believe in them eminently manipulable. Nazi propagandists realized this point. That is why they accompanied the invasion of Poland in September 1939 with a campaign of lies about the Polish slaughter of tens of thousands of ethnic Germans. Nazi authorities used images of suffering children, weeping women, male corpses, and ravaged female bodies to stir up German support at home for assault on Poland and vicious treatment of Poles, including particularly vile attacks on Jews.[77] At least some of those images were authentic; angry Poles did attack ethnic Germans during the war, although never in the numbers that German propaganda claimed. Nazi authorities, however, had no interest in mourning the dead, only in using them to legitimate more carnage. We need not look far—Yugoslavia and Rwanda will suffice—to see how a public history based on lies provides means to manipulate people into acts that destroy not only their neighbors' lives but their own. Mourning is indeed a dangerous and difficult time, and wartime mourning poses its own possibly insurmountable challenges.[78] The alternatives, however, are much worse.

Historians of mass death face another challenge of mourning: the need to accept their shattered ideals—of human nature, of the ethnic, national, or religious groups with which they identify. Like

Herta Müller, I have an inkling of what this confrontation might involve; the woman with the photographs I described at the start of this essay is related to me. My parents also are ethnic German Mennonites from Ukraine, although they immigrated to Canada in the 1920s. This past is mine as well.

Notes

Thanks to Patrick Hutton, Peter Homans, Thomas A. Kselman, and Peter Novick for comments and criticism. I am grateful for the support of the University of Notre Dame; the Charles H. Revson Foundation and the Center for Advanced Holocaust Studies at the United States Holocaust Memorial Museum in Washington, D.C.; the German Academic Exchange Service (DAAD); and the German Marshall Fund of the United States.

1. For the National Socialist definition see Hans-Heinrich Lammers, "Betrifft: Formulierung der Begriffe 'Deutschtum im Ausland, Auslandsdeutscher und Volksdeutscher,'" 25 January 1938, Bundesarchiv Potsdam, 51.01/ 23905. Translations are my own unless otherwise specified.
2. The most explicit discussion of connections between Nazi policy toward the *Volksdeutschen* and the murder of Jews is Götz Aly, *"Endlösung": Völkerverschiebung und der Mord an den europäischen Juden* (Frankfurt a. M.: S. Fischer Verlag, 1995).
3. For example, *Volksdeutsche* appear as perpetrators in Alexander Donat's *The Holocaust Kingdom: A Memoir* (New York: Holt, Rinehart, and Winston, 1965) and Adina Blady Szwajger's *I Remember Nothing More: The Warsaw Children's Hospital and the Jewish Resistance* (London: Harvill, 1990).
4. There is a vast literature on the postwar experiences of ethnic Germans, in particular their expulsion from parts of central and eastern Europe. For example, see Alfred-Maurice de Zayas, *A Terrible Revenge: The Ethnic Cleansing of the East European Germans, 1944–1950* (New York: St. Martin's Press, 1994).
5. These remarks were made to me by an ethnic German woman in Westphalia during an informal conversation in 1989 and a subsequent interview in 1998. I have altered the names.
6. Sigmund Freud, "Mourning and Melancholia" (1917), in *The Standard Edition of the Complete Psychological Works of Sigmund Freud*, ed. and trans. James Strachey, 24 vols. (London, 1953–74), 14:237–60.
7. As Dominick LaCapra points out, mourning often takes collective forms, as in rituals. The relevant question is not whether mourning can be a group process but whether it can "be effective on the level of massive, 'imagined' communities such as nation-states." LaCapra, "Revisiting the Historians' Debate: Mourning and Genocide," in *History and Memory* 9, no. 1–2 (fall 1997): 80–81.
8. Primo Levi, "The Gray Zone," in *The Drowned and the Saved*, trans. Raymond Rosenthal (New York: Vintage International, 1989), 58. Most of Levi's essay explores moral ambiguity among the Jewish targets of Nazi genocide, but several remarks indicate that he also sees "the gray band" as extending to other groups. I use the concept not to exculpate individual ethnic Germans for atrocities but to point to the overlapping categories of perpetrators, bystanders, victims, and even rescuers, particularly among a group of people whose wartime experience was characterized by both privilege and manipulation.

9. Alexander Mitscherlich and Margarete Mitscherlich, *The Inability to Mourn: Principles of Collective Behavior*, trans. Beverley R. Placzek (New York: Grove Press, 1975).

10. Melanie Klein, "Mourning and Its Relation to Manic-Depressive Stages," in *Contributions to Psycho-Analysis: 1921–1945* (London: Hogarth, 1948), 311–38.

11. Bruno Bettelheim, *The Informed Heart* (Glencoe IL: Free Press, 1960). On Bettelheim, see Terrence Des Pres, *The Survivor: An Anatomy of Life in the Death Camps* (Oxford: Oxford University Press, 1976), excerpted in *Holocaust: Religious and Philosophical Implications*, John K. Roth and Michael Berenbaum, eds. (New York: Paragon House, 1989), 206–7.

12. On wartime psychological literature in the United States, see Michaela Hönicke, "'Why Do Germans So Easily Forfeit Their Freedom?' Psychological Interpretations of National Socialism," part 2, chapter 2 of "'Know Your Enemy': American Interpretations of National Socialism, 1933–1945," unpublished diss., Department of History, University of North Carolina at Chapel Hill, 1998.

13. Best known is Robert G. L. Waite, *The Psychopathic God: Adolf Hitler* (New York: Da Capo, 1977).

14. Examples are Sarah Moskovitz and Robert Krell, "Child Survivors of the Holocaust: Psychological Adaptations to Survival," *Israeli Journal of Psychiatry and Related Sciences* 27 (1990): 81–91; and John J. Sigal and Morton Weinfeld, *Trauma and Rebirth: Intergenerational Effects of the Holocaust* (New York: Praeger, 1989).

15. The one psychologically informed study of bystanders with which I am familiar, the "Good Samaritan" experiment conducted at Princeton, adopts a pathological view as well: social scientists sought to determine what made people fail to assist a stranger in distress. Studies of those who rescued Jews tend to invert pathology. They ask, How do we explain the ability of some people to defy authority and peer pressure, risking their own safety in the attempt to save others? See Samuel P. Oliner and Pearl M. Oliner, *The Altruistic Personality: Rescuers of Jews in Nazi Europe* (New York: Free Press, 1988); Eva Fogelman, *Conscience and Courage: Rescuers of Jews during the Holocaust* (New York: Doubleday, 1994); and Nechama Tec, *When Light Pierced the Darkness: Christian Rescue of Jews in Nazi-Occupied Poland* (New York: Oxford University Press, 1986).

16. For a critical assessment, see K. R. Eissler, "Die Ermordung von wievielen seiner Kinder muß ein Mensch symptomfrei ertragen können, um eine normale Konstitution zu haben?" *Psyche* 5 (1963): 241–91.

17. See Dori Laub and Shoshana Felman, *Testimony: Crises of Witnessing in Literature, Psychoanalysis and History* (New York: Routledge, 1992).

18. For example, Lawrence L. Langer shows the influence of Laub and of psychology in *Holocaust Testimonies: The Ruins of Memory* (New Haven: Yale University Press, 1991); see also Geoffrey H. Hartman, ed., *Holocaust Remembrance: The Shapes of Memory* (Oxford: Basil Blackwell, 1994).

19. Friedländer's work is too vast to summarize in a note. Most significant here are his memoir, Saul Friedländer, *When Memory Comes* (New York, 1979); the essays in Friedländer, *Memory, History, and the Extermination of the Jews of Europe* (Bloomington: Indiana University Press, 1993); and Friedländer, *Nazi Germany and the Jews*, vol. 1: *The Years of Persecution, 1933–1939* (New York: HarperCollins, 1997). On Friedländer, see the special issue of *History and Memory* 9 (no. 1/2, fall 1997), *Passing into History: Nazism and the Holocaust beyond Memory*, ed. Gulie Ne'eman Arad (Bloomington: Indiana University Press, 1997).

20. Here James E. Young broke new ground with *The Texture of Memory: Holocaust Memorials and Meaning* (New Haven: Yale University Press, 1993).

21. Freud's description of the "work of mourning" also captures aspects of the work done by historians of the Shoah: "Each single one of the memories and expectations in which the libido is bound to the object is brought up and hypercathected, and detachment of the libido is accomplished in respect of it." Freud, "Mourning and Melancholia," 245.
22. Friedländer provides the best examples, both of an explicit acknowledgment of this aspect of the historian of the Holocaust's work and of the actual writing of such a history. See Saul Friedländer, "Trauma, Transference, and 'Working Through' in Writing the History of the Shoah," *History and Memory* 4, no. 1 (spring/summer 1992); and Friedländer, *Nazi Germany and the Jews*, vol. 1: *The Years of Persecution, 1933–1939*.
23. Daniel Jonah Goldhagen, *Hitler's Willing Executioners: Ordinary Germans and the Holocaust* (New York: Alfred A. Knopf, 1996); also Raul Hilberg, *The Destruction of the European Jews*, 3 vols. (New York: Holmes and Meier, 1985).
24. Christopher R. Browning, *Ordinary Men: Reserve Police Battalion 101 and the Final Solution in Poland* (New York: HarperCollins, 1992), 171–89; see also Stanley Milgram, *Obedience to Authority: An Experimental View* (New York, 1974).
25. Of the few attempts to interview Nazis and analyze their accounts, the most successful is Gitta Sereny's *Into That Darkness: An Examination of Conscience* (New York: Vintage Books, 1974). Also note Alison Owings's *Frauen* (New Brunswick NJ: Rutgers University Press, 1993). Both authors are journalists.
26. The Mitscherlichs describe "two distinct psychic processes: the retrospective warding off of real guilt by the older generation and the unwillingness of the younger to get caught up in the guilt problems of their parents." Mitscherlich and Mitscherlich, *Inability to Mourn*, xx. There are exceptions, such as the children of Nazi perpetrators who have joined the organization "One by One," devoted to developing dialogue with children of Jewish survivors. It is telling, however, that during a recent trip by members of the organization from the United States to Germany, the Jewish participants so outnumbered the Germans that meaningful exchange was hardly possible.
27. Theodor Schieder, ed., *Dokumentation der Vertreibung der Deutschen aus Ost-Mitteleuropa*, 8 vols. (Göttingen: Schwartz, 1954–1961).
28. Much of this work with regard to the Siebenbürger Saxons centers around the *Arbeitskreis für Siebenbürgische Landeskunde*, headquartered in Schloß Horneck in Gundelsheim (Neckar). I am grateful to the staff of the library there for their help during my visit in August 1998.
29. Questionnaires sent to ethnic Germans in the late 1940s and 1950s from authorities in the Federal Republic asked them to begin by noting when Soviet troops arrived in their communities. "*Fragebogenberichte zur Dokumentation der Vertreibung der Deutschen aus Ost-Mitteleuropa (Gemeindeschicksalsberichte)*," Bundesarchiv Koblenz, *Ost-Dokumentation* 1. Since I used them, these materials have been relocated to the Federal Archive's Bayreuth branch.
30. There is, however, the hint of such an analysis in Dan Diner's remarks on de Zayas' *Terrible Revenge* in Diner, "On Guilt Discourse and Other Narratives: Epistemological Observations Regarding the Holocaust," *History and Memory* 9, no. 1/2 (fall 1997): 317–18.
31. Examples are *Streit um die neue Wache: Zur Gestaltung einer zentralen Gedenkstätte* (Berlin: Akademie der Künste, 1993); Reinhart Koselleck and Michael Jeismann, eds., *Der politische Totenkult: Kriegerdenkmäler in der Moderne* (Munich: Fink, 1994); and Bernd Faulenbach and Franz-Joseph Jelich, eds., *Reaktionäre Modernität und Völkermord: Probleme des Umgangs mit der NS-Zeit in Museen, Ausstellungen, Gedenkstätten* (Essen: Klartext, 1994).

190 DORIS L. BERGEN

32. Eric L. Santner, *Stranded Objects: Mourning, Memory, and Film in Postwar Germany* (Ithaca: Cornell University Press, 1990); Susan Neiman, *Slow Fire* (New York: Schocken, 1991); Robert Moeller, "War Stories: The Search for a Usable Past in the Federal Republic of Germany," *American Historical Review* 101, no. 4 (Oct. 1996): 1008–48. See also references to the Mitscherlichs in Bernd Weisbrod, "Der 8. Mai in der deutschen Erinnerung," *WerkstattGeschichte* 13 (1996): 72–81, esp. 77.
33. Charles S. Maier, "A Surfeit of Memory? Reflections on History, Melancholy, and Denial," *History and Memory* 5 (1993): 136–51.
34. A recent example involves the 1997 agreement between the Czech Republic and Germany. The German government expressed its regret for the destruction of the Czechoslovak state in 1938 in return for an apology from the Czech government for the expulsion of ethnic Germans after World War II. Most Europeans heralded this exchange as a breakthrough. However, many ethnic Germans from Czechoslovakia accused Helmut Kohl's government of betrayal.
35. See LaCapra, "Revisiting the Historians' Debate"; also Dominick LaCapra's collection of essays, *Representing the Holocaust: History, Theory, Trauma* (Ithaca: Cornell University Press, 1994), esp. 205–23. An earlier version of the piece on the historians' debate appears on pp. 43–67.
36. LaCapra, *Representing the Holocaust*, 214.
37. Michael Geyer, "The Place of the Second World War in German Memory and History," *New German Critique* 71 (spring–summer 1997): 17.
38. Ibid., 10, 17.
39. Ibid., 10.
40. Mitscherlich and Mitscherlich, *Inability to Mourn*, xxv.
41. Ibid., 62–63.
42. Ibid., 27, 7, 16.
43. See, for examples, Victor Schuller, "Meine Heimat: Sternreporter reisen in die Vergangenheit," *Stern*, no. 14 (30 March 1978): 34–56, 154–56; and Ioan Margineau's fictionalized memoir *Todeswaggons*, trans. Wolfgang Fuchs (Hermannstadt: H. G. Tipotrip, 1996).
44. A graphic account of ethnic German atrocities in Poland is Christian Jansen and Arno Weckbecker, *Der "Volksdeutsche Selbstschutz" in Polen 1939/40* (Munich: R. Oldenbourg Verlag, 1992). More polemical but useful on the Romanian *Volksdeutschen* are E. Denndörfer, *Die "Volksdeutschen" als Werkzeuge des deutschen Imperialismus* (Bucharest: Staats-Verlag, 1949); and Margot Hegemann, "Die 'Deutsche Volksgruppe in Rumänien'—Eine Fünfte Kolonne des deutschen Imperialismus in Südosteuropa," *Jahrbuch für Geschichte der UdSSR und der volksdemokratischen Länder Europas* 4 (1960): 371–81. Those uneasy with the Communist perspective can confirm the involvement of individual ethnic Germans in Nazi German brutality in myriad archival sources. See Bergen, "The 'Volksdeutschen' of Eastern Europe, World War II, and the Holocaust: Constructed Ethnicity, Real Genocide," in *Germany and Eastern Europe, 1870–1996: Cultural Identities and Cultural Differences*, ed. Keith Bullivant, Geoffrey Giles, and Walter Pape (Amsterdam: Rodopi, 1999), 70–93.
45. An example is Hans Wolfram Hockl, an ethnic German from Romania and self-described voice of "critical confrontation with our past." See Hockl, *Offene Karte: Dokumente zur Geschichte der Deutschen in Rumänien, 1930–1980* (Linz: self-publication, 1980); and Hockl, *Offenheit hat überzeugt* (Metzingen: ProVobis, 1990); also Johann Hamrich, "Lebenserinnerungen eines Siebenbürger Sachsen eine 'modische Verirrung'?" (Gundelsheim: typescript, 1986); and Stefan Mazgareanu, "Im nationsozialistischen Verbrechen verstrickt," *Zeitschrift für Siebenbürger Landeskunde* 18, no. 2 (1995): 189–91.

46. Interview with Anna Braun, 20 Sept. 1946, Funkenkaserne (displaced persons camp in occupied Germany), in David P. Boder, "Topical Autobiographies of Displaced People," Bound Section 4, chapter 16, 28–29, United States Holocaust Memorial Museum Archive, Washington, DC (hereafter USHMMA).
47. On links between shame and denial, see Mitscherlich and Mitscherlich, *Inability to Mourn*, 61.
48. Ibid., 10–11.
49. A sociological study of ethnic German isolation is Sybille Wölfing, "Wenn alles anders wird: Identitätsgefährdungen und Identitätsstrategien bei Aussiedlern aus Siebenbürgen," Ph.D. diss., Münster, 1995.
50. Information from conversations in summer 1998 with ethnic Germans in Espelkamp and Freiburg/Br.
51. Herta Müller, quoted in Larry Wolff, "Strangers in a Strange Land," *New York Times Book Review*, 1 December 1996, 38. Wolff reviewed Müller's novel *The Land of Green Plums*, trans. Michael Hofmann (New York: Metropolitan Books, 1996).
52. "If somehow, somewhere, one finds an object deserving of sympathy, it usually turns out to be none other than oneself." Mitscherlich and Mitscherlich, *Inability to Mourn*, 25; see also 40–41.
53. An example is Elizabeth Heineman, "The Hour of the Woman: Memories of Germany's 'Crisis Years' and West German National Identity," *American Historical Review* 101, no. 2 (April 1996): 354–95.
54. Mitscherlich and Mitscherlich, *Inability to Mourn*, 45.
55. Interview conducted June 1998 in Espelkamp, Germany.
56. See, for example, the report by Nazi "race expert" Karl Stumpp on travels through occupied Soviet territory, "Bericht Nr. 5 (26.9.–10.10./41) v. Dr. Stumpp," in USHMMA RG 31.002 M, reel 11, no frame numbers.
57. Mitscherlich and Mitscherlich, *Inability to Mourn*, 12.
58. One such exception is Hans Zikeli, "Allianz der Sachsen und Juden in Mediasch 1940 gegen die Aggressionen der 'Eisengardisten': Erinnerungen des letzten deutschen Bürgermeisters der Stadt Mediasch, in Siebenbürgen" (Gundelsheim: typescript, 1994). Zikeli, an ethnic German and Nazi sympathizer, presents as heroism the willingness of local *Volksdeutschen* to provide guard service in exchange for the properties of the town's Jews.
59. Examples are Elfriede Csallner, *Lebenswende* (Munich: self-publication, 1975); Annemarie Müller-Wagner, "Meine Geschichte" (Neuhausen: manuscript, undated [c. 1975]); and Else Stoll, *Die Vertreibung* (Vaterstetten: self-publication, 1997).
60. For another context, see Juliana Schiesari, *The Gendering of Melancholia: Feminism, Psychoanalysis, and the Symbolics of Loss in Renaissance Literature* (Ithaca: Cornell University Press, 1992); most relevant here are pp. 12, 61, and 190.
61. Mitscherlich and Mitscherlich, *Inability to Mourn*, 26.
62. Schieder, ed., *Dokumentation der Vertreibung*.
63. Theodor Schieder (1908–84) became one of the most influential historians of postwar West Germany. See Götz Aly, "Rückwärtsgewandte Propheten: Willige Historiker—Bemerkung in eigener Sache," in *Macht, Geist, Wahn: Kontinuitäten deutschen Denkens* (Berlin: Argon Verlag, 1997), 153–83.
64. German officials deliberately kept the *Volksdeutschen* vulnerable to enhance their manipulability. See Bergen, "The Nazi Concept of 'Volksdeutsche' and the Exacerbation of Antisemitism in Eastern Europe, 1939–1945," *Journal of Contemporary History* 29, no. 4 (October 1994): 569–82.
65. See Aly, *"Endlösung."*
66. For example, see complaints of ethnic Germans from Bosnia who wanted to go back in 1943: "Bericht," signed Schapmeier, Einwandererzentralstelle

Litzmannstadt, to Reichssicherheitshauptamt, 23 June 1943, Bundesarchiv
Berlin Lichterfelde R 69/396, 22.
67. Interview conducted June 1998 in Petershagen, Westphalia.
68. Santner, *Stranded Objects,* 26.
69. "It is obvious," the Mitscherlichs point out, "that the murder of millions of
people cannot be 'mastered.' . . . Rather by 'mastering' we mean a sequence
of steps in self-knowledge. Freud called these 'remembering, repeating,
working through.'" Mitscherlich and Mitscherlich, *Inability to Mourn,* 14.
70. Ibid., 67.
71. For analysis of Polish Christians' and Jews' relations to the past, see Michael
C. Steinlauf, *Bondage to the Dead: Poland and the Memory of the Holocaust* (Syracuse: Syracuse University Press, 1997).
72. Mitscherlich and Mitscherlich, *Inability to Mourn,* 30. It is interesting to
speculate as to whether this claim applied equally to East and West Germans.
73. Conversation with ethnic Germans in Petershagen, Westphalia, June 1998.
74. Frank Grube and Gerhard Richter, *Flucht und Vertreibung: Deutschland
zwischen 1944 und 1947* (Hamburg: Hoffmann und Campe, 1980).
75. Thanks to Margarete Myers Feinstein for drawing this stamp to my attention and sharing her knowledge about it.
76. Geyer, "Place of the Second World War," 39.
77. See the book prepared under supervision of the German Foreign Office and
circulated in several languages: Deutsche Informationsstelle, ed., *Dokumente Polnischer Grausamkeit* (Berlin: Foreign Office, 1940).
78. It is no coincidence that Freud wrote his analysis of mourning and melancholy in 1917, in the midst of war.

Further Reading

Crimp, Douglas. "Mourning and Militancy." *October* 51 (winter 1989):
3–18.
On the need for a male practice of mourning.
Durkheim, Emile. *The Elementary Forms of the Religious Life: A Study
in Religious Sociology.* Trans. Joseph Ward Swain. London: George
Allen and Unwin, n.d.
Section on piacular rites contains interesting discussion of mourning.
Friedländer, Saul. "Trauma, Transference, and 'Working-Through' in
Writing the History of the Shoah." *History and Memory* 4, no. 1
(spring/summer 1992).
Reflections by the most psychologically informed historian of the Holocaust.
LaCapra, Dominick. *Representing the Holocaust: History, Theory, Trau-
ma.* Ithaca: Cornell University Press, 1994.
Last section in particular engages issues of mourning.
———. "Revisiting the Historians' Debate: Mourning and Genocide."
History and Memory 9, no. 1–2 (fall 1997): 80–112.
Most explicit attempt to apply Freudian concepts to the history of the
Shoah.
Mitscherlich, Alexander, and Margarete Mitscherlich. *The Inability to
Mourn: Principles of Collective Behavior.* Trans. Beverley R. Plac-
zek. New York: Grove Press, 1975.
Standard work on postwar Germans' relation to the Nazi past, analyzed
in Freudian terms.

Ne'eman Arad, Gulie, ed. *Passing into History: Nazism and the Holocaust beyond Memory—In Honor of Saul Friedländer on his Sixty-Fifth Birthday.* Bloomington: Indiana University Press, 1997.

    Collection of articles from *History and Memory*, including LaCapra's piece on the historians' debate and other articles by Dan Diner, Omer Bartov, and Sidra Ezrahi, among others. All have been influenced by Friedländer's interest in memory.

Santner, Eric. *Stranded Objects: Mourning, Memory, and Film in Postwar Germany.* Ithaca: Cornell University Press, 1990.

    Insightful discussion of postwar Germany, using concept of mourning as analytical frame.

Schiesari, Juliana. *The Gendering of Melancholia: Feminism, Psychoanalysis, and the Symbolics of Loss in Renaissance Literature.* Ithaca: Cornell University Press, 1992.

    Study of how melancholia became gendered as male in the Renaissance, with depression the more mundane female counterpart.

Young, James E. *The Texture of Memory: Holocaust Memorials and Meaning.* New Haven: Yale University Press, 1993.

    Exploration of memory, architecture, and commemoration.

IV

PSYCHOLOGY

PETER SHABAD

THE MOST INTIMATE OF CREATIONS

SYMPTOMS AS MEMORIALS TO ONE'S LONELY SUFFERING

IF WE ASSUME that the development of character or personality or self never comes to a halt but is continually unfolding, we discern a picture of a dynamically malleable process that is potentially renewable at any given moment. At each incoming moment, sandwiched between past and future, we are free to use and consume newborn moments as fulfillingly as possible before they disappear over the horizon. Through a process of self-revelation we attempt to create an everlasting "moment in the sun," a monument that will be remembered and that will testify to the actuality of our existence. In Ernest Becker's words, each of us is attempting to form out of ourselves an "object of primary value" in the eyes of the cosmos.[1] If each moment were to be encountered as if for the first time, however, the experiences and relationships of the past would lose significance. The literalness of being present in the current moment would then lend an elusively surreal, dreamlike quality to the rest of our lives. Equipped as we are, for better and for worse, with the sweet curse of memory, we have no choice but to extend the usage of "a moment in the sun" figuratively to include the sum of our lives. We seek to create a dramatic moment in the sun, if even as a flickering crest of a wave before it dissolves in the river of time, out of the integrity of our whole lives.

In order to derive dramatic meaning from the entirety of our lives, we create coherence from one moment to the next.[2] In this endeavor, we enlist consciousness to aid us in providing an ongoing narrative as we proceed through our experiences. Romanyshyn (1982) notes that "Reflection re-figures the person in the event world and fact as story."[3] With the first glimmerings of self-reflection, then, an overseeing or narrative function ensures that meaning will be imposed on a continuous flow of experiences so as to make a coherent and meaningful story. Moreover, this narrator—we—not only oversees the creation of a story but also intercedes actively in its making. So much so that we not only create what we find, but we find what we create. That is, we not only *impose* the meaningful shape of narrative on experience, but we also *derive* ever-changing meanings from that narrative. In addition to actively transcribing our experiences, we also reenact those transcriptions in relation with others. A child, elaborating upon his experiences of suffering and then reenacting those now "transcribed" experiences—both intrapsychically and in relations with others—indelibly alters the meaning of those experiences.

For example, throughout my tenure as a father, I have had ample opportunity to observe my two sons endure assorted accidents as they negotiated their respective ways through the obstacles of every-day toddlerhood. On those occasions, when one son would scrape his knee or bump his head, I noticed that it was usually only after a short time delay that he would break into tears and seek me out for comfort. What kinds of meanings were being imposed on the injury as soon as it occurred? What sort of impact does the realization of injury have on the search for a restorative solace?

Consciousness is a powerful homegrown overseer of a story constructed around the dramatic creation and search for a moment in the sun. As subjective agents of our lives, we embellish, minimize, inhibit, and ultimately fashion a meaningful story out of our experiences. In acts of constructiveness or spiteful destructiveness, our lives resemble art pieces in which we are continually re-creating and creatively elaborating the reality that we encounter. Otto Rank made this notion of living as an artistic process of self-creation a centerpiece of his will psychology. Each day brings with it hope for a meaningful "new beginning," an opportunity to create oneself anew.[4] By elevating our experiences through their dramatization into the objectivity of something monumental, we attempt to ensure that the dignity of our experiences be taken seriously, that attention be paid.

The process of dramatization, however, is incomplete in and of itself. The multitude of meanings that can be imposed on prior experience retroactively is so malleably dependent on the shifting actions, moods, purposes, and will of the person in the present that it is easy to doubt the real existence of that experience. At the beck and call of such impermanence—where only doubt is certain —the meaningful continuity of a person's coherent life story degenerates into the meaninglessness of randomness: one interpretation of meaning is as good as another.

We may hunger then *not* to have so much interpretive power over our experience, but for something that has its own "real" existence independent of our subjectivity. In this regard, we seek not so much the freedom to "deconstruct" objective events into so many relative elements of differently experienced perspectives but to elaborate our experience into the memorable status of something real and objective. Our task entails discovering a reality outside of our creative control in order to confirm that our experience is not merely a dreamlike figment of our imagination. Through the validation offered by another person outside of the "sphere of omnipotence," we can emerge from our inner worlds to make the unconscious conscious and the created real, thereby arriving at a sense of realization.[5]

The Uncertainty of Being One's Own Witness

In a commentary to a recent paper I published,[6] Paul Russell recounted the following autobiographical incident:

> Some years ago when the Dutch elm disease was taking its toll, I was driving on a windy day, when a huge dead tree was suddenly blown over just as I, a bit too speedily, was approaching it. It crashed, with a mighty thunderous thud, across the road just in front of me. I immediately honked my horn and put on the brakes. I managed just barely to slow down enough so that bumping into the trunk of the tree did not do much damage to the car or myself. I had to back up and find a detour. As I did so, I thought, ever so briefly, about what would have happened had I been just a fraction of a second farther along. Twenty minutes later, having finally arrived at my destination, I was describing to a friend what had just happened. I found myself, for the first time, feeling faint, dizzy, and sweaty. I had to sit down.[7]

It is significant that Russell's near accident occurred when he was alone. It is only twenty minutes later, when in the presence of a friend, that Russell displayed his symptomatology of feeling "faint, dizzy, and sweaty." When my son injured his knee, he was more fortunate in that there was someone he could turn to for solace and recognition *at the time* that it happened, someone who could bear witness to the "reality" of his suffering.

Perhaps it is this very transformation of experienced suffering into a witnessed reality at the moment it occurs that inoculates experience against traumatization. For if, as Russell proposes, trauma can be known only "after the fact" through its residual trail of post-traumatic communication, it suggests that being alone and not being able to convey one's experience immediately are intrinsic to the transformation of suffering into trauma. Stolorow and Atwood similarly have said that "painful or frightening affect becomes traumatic when the requisite attuned responsiveness that the child needs from the surround . . . is absent."[8] As Russell suggests, a person may need a sense of connectedness in order to have the freedom to feel.

Often, however, when children suffer, they are not aware of what is triggering their emotional pain, let alone able to convey it in words to someone else. When no one is there to offer comfort to suffering children, they "adapt" by learning how to go it alone and rely on their own resources, a stoic self-reliance that all too often seems to be one of the residual effects of growing up. Without another person to validate the "event" of our suffering, we are forced into the awkward, involuted position of bearing witness to our own experience. This places us alone in the proverbial situation of the falling tree: if there is no one to hear a tree falling in the forest, then did it make noise?

Unlike a tree, however, we can enlist our minds as homegrown witnesses to our own experience. At the same time that we take dissociative flight from the trauma endured within our bodies, we use involuted mental activity to watch over ourselves. Thus, we not only have the experience of suffering, but we also have a self-consciousness of our predicament, a self-consciousness charged with the caretaking responsibility of taking up the slack for the witness who was supposed to be there but was not. Now, like a lioness fiercely protective of her injured cub, we may, through the filter of self-consciousness, "feel sorry for ourselves," becoming indignant on our own behalf.

There are problems, however, in this makeshift attempt to become witness to our own suffering. Self-consciousness, born of disillusionment and the flight of dissociative defense, is not grounded in the substantive reality of the body. To the extent that we are not inhabiting ourselves and life is not being lived from within, we do not have a corpus of lived experience to fall back on for a sense of certainty. We know and do not know what should be there; we therefore both know and do not know what is not there, and thus we know and do not know that we have actually experienced a trauma.

Russell uses the metaphor of a camera photographing its own injury to describe our attempt to bear witness to our own experience. He suggests that because "the photographic perceiving and recording apparatus itself is damaged while it is being built . . . the camera cannot photograph its own injury."[9] "Bearing witness" here has to do with bearing the responsibility of remembering and testifying to the actuality of one's suffering. Pervaded with doubts, the mind is an uncertain witness to itself. The burdensome tensions to prove the real existence of our experience eventually become too fatiguing for one person to carry.

Thinking-In and Acting-Out

Aloneness is a subtle destroyer of the sense of the real. Within our self-enclosed solitude we can become caught up in involuted spirals of "thinking-in."[10] The derealizing process of thinking-in works against our quest to prove that our suffering was not only a figment of our imagination, but a real event. Through our mind's eye, doubt is sown and cultivated as we now are less certain that what happened "out there" actually happened. Within the isolation of our own mind, we chase the tail of the real but never quite catch up because we are looking for something that can only be found outside of ourselves. Our lack of success in our quest seduces us into circles of obsessional thinking that are perpetuated indefinitely. One of Freud's early disciples, Wilhelm Stekel, put it this way: "The more the patient loses himself in his world of fantasies, the stronger becomes his doubt which always compares fantasy with reality and is unable to obtain congruity."[11]

After a passionate love affair ends abruptly, each lover is left to gather up the real pieces of the breakup that occurred so much more rapidly than they could realize. To grasp hold of the elusively real story, the lovers' minds may work overtime as they feverishly attempt to catch up to the facts that have passed them by. They think back to their first encounter, to their growing attraction to each other—as if to confirm for themselves that they were drawn together by irresistible excitement. They remind themselves of how they became intimate and declared "I love you" while staring into each other's eyes. Or did they? She seemed to mean what she said, or did she? With hesitant step and delicate feeling, he then begins to tread down the memory path of the breakup. He painstakingly retraces the steps of how good turned to bad, and reenacts scenes of how the full bloom of passion gave way to her complaints about the need for space. His mind then trails off; the burden of bearing witness to his own suffering is too much to bear. No matter how much he goes over it, it does not make sense. He still cannot believe what happened. And so he tries to catch the sequences of events one more time.

To return to the metaphor of the camera photographing its own injury, I would suggest that although the photographic apparatus is damaged, we nevertheless, through the use of self-consciousness, attempt to photograph our own injuries. Our aim of objectifying our experience is made difficult by the fact that we have placed our own narrative stamp of memory on our suffering as soon as it occurred. Because of the nature of the involuted mental equipment, when the photograph is developed, it is dreamlike and blurry. With regard to the uncertainty conveyed by the Winnicottan paradox (Did I create this or did I find it? or Did I do this or was it done to me?), we remain trapped in doubt.[12]

To secure a witness to our experience and prove it was an objective event, we must continually re-create or make the "photograph" of the trauma. In a desperate attempt to develop a clear picture of a real injury, we snap the picture again and again, typically with the same faulty equipment, typically to no avail, and therefore repeatedly. For the traumatized person, then, it may not be easy to discern between trauma as our intended, omnipotently created experience and trauma as an objective event that is independent of our omnipotence. Thus, whereas thinking-in has a derealizing effect on our experience of lonely suffering, so the countervailing urge to resolve doubt and achieve the objective clarity of realization fuels the various forms of "acting-out" of the repetition compulsion.

Corresponding to this fundamental indeterminacy of the cause of trauma (Did I create my own suffering or did I find it?) is a dark underbelly of recrimination that forms an indeterminacy of blame (Do I blame myself for my suffering or do I blame another for doing this to me?). To the extent that we continue to search for a validating witness by re-creating this traumatic scene, we may begin to hate ourselves for reproducing our own torment. Locked in our own self-enclosure, we feel we must "answer to ourselves" for not fulfilling our own wishes narcissistically and for continuing to maintain them in the face of an overwhelmingly frustrating reality. We blame our predicament on wanting something better that cannot be and attempting to distance ourselves from wishes that only lead nowhere.

These wishes, however, are also a bridge back to the imagined idealized scenarios of others who "should have been there" as witness to our experience. Therefore, they also are a disillusioning reminder of the "reality" of lonely suffering that we endured instead. By inhibiting the imaginative elaboration and expression of these wishes for a better alternative, we risk further derealizing our pain of lonely suffering.

Here, the self-preservative defensive functions of thinking-in, of bracing for disappointment by prohibiting the emergence of disillusioned wishes, conflict with the self-expressive urge to bring out remembered proof of our suffering by acting out the elaborations of those denied wishes. In this sense, the polarized doubleness of thinking-in and acting-out is paralleled by the split between prohibition and impulse.

Addictions are a prime example of how we become bound up in cycles of prohibitive thinking-in and impulsive acting-out. We frequently aim ruthless criticism toward ourselves in the aftermath of overeating or engaging in impersonal sex. Although with great shame and self-hatred we may declare *mea culpa*, perhaps but one week later we ensconce ourselves secretly with the refrigerator, with the prostitute, in the gay bar—as if attempting to remain unknown to ourselves.

Where there is impulse, prohibition is sure not to be far behind. The more we become burdened with the conviction that we have omnipotently created our own suffering and the more we are disconnected from the reality of being victimized by another, the more urgently we attempt to convey proof of our victimization. The impulsive "acting-out" of addictiveness is a desperately defiant means of bringing the dignity and meaning of reenacted reality to experiences that have been rendered unreal.

Maybe it is not coincidental that when we are isolated from social reality, the primitive quality of a one-person psychology drive theory of wish and discharge indeed seems to apply. Without the delicately intangible interchange of social discourse available, we urgently and intensely attempt to maintain ourselves by falling back on the tangible solidity of our biological needs. The spirals of this primitive sort of "malignant regression with the aim of gratification" continue endlessly precisely because we remain self-enclosed.[13] As long as we do not find the realization of experience that can be discovered only through the eyes of another, inner battles to maintain a sane grip on the real will linger, unbeknownst to any outside observer.

The Self-Betrayal of Rendering to Oblivion

Russell concludes his commentary by saying: "The repetition compulsion is an illness of loneliness. . . . It is also the individual's only means of reattachment and emotional growth."[14] I would say a person's unique constellation of psychological symptomatology reflects the solitary, unspoken journey of the repetition compulsion to carry out the message of lonely sufferings.

Symptoms not only are compromise formations between wishes for drive discharge and their inhibitions, but they are also a means of combating the paralyzingly derealizing effects of thinking-in on the testimony of memory. When people massively repress their childhood sufferings, when they make their minds a "blank" in order to survive, they often give a voice of dignity to their muteness through their symptomatology. Behind every person lies a yet-to-be unraveled and spoken story of lonely suffering. In this regard, Greenspan describes the symptoms of Holocaust survivors as an attempt to recount or "make a story" from what is "not a story."[15]

Jack is a forty-two-year-old man who presented with symptoms of depression and an inability to experience pleasure. Although he reported having a successful house-painting business, a good marriage, and three college-age children whom he loved dearly, much to his mystified chagrin he could not seem to derive much joy from his life or significant relationships. And although he was tormented by obsessional concerns of the "other shoe dropping" on the peaceful stability of his family life, of something catastrophic occurring to one of his close family members, he spoke with seeming indifference about his own death, "whenever it happens, it happens."

As Jack continued to unfold his story, it became apparent that his attainment of some measure of success in love and work was a testament to human fortitude and resilience. He came from a broken home that was impoverished emotionally and financially. His father was an unreliable, infrequent visitor to a household in which he lived with his alcoholic mother and younger sister. On numerous occasions, he watched his inebriated mother engage in intercourse with assorted men. He saw it as his responsibility to take care of his sister, for the children were two orphans against the storm. He reported that more than once he would walk miles with his sister to more well-to-do neighborhoods and knock on doors asking people to feed his sister. Often he would then receive a meal for himself as well.

He recounted that his depression might have something to do with an incident that occurred when he was thirteen years old. He had gone away to visit his grandmother for three weeks in another state, only to find that there were strangers living in his house when he returned home. His mother had left no forwarding address, and his stamp and model collections were gone forever. He slept on a nearby park bench for a few days until he was picked up by the police. Although he located his mother soon after this episode, some friends of the family took him in and became his unofficial guardians for the duration of his high school years. Without looking back, Jack then proceeded on to adult life.

To survive his childhood sufferings psychically intact, Jack did his best to put his experiences behind him. He became one of the numerous secure, well-to-do suburbanites with nice houses and stable families who long ago he had resented and envied. In attempting to "take the money and run" without so much as a glance backward, however, Jack betrayed a silent loyalty oath he had taken with himself never to forsake his early hardships. Like the Holocaust survivor who was charged with the responsibility of ensuring that the world bear witness and never forget, Jack, too, secretly had sworn to himself to bring out the message of his own private holocaust.

Jack's dilemma was one not unlike that of an obese person who undergoes rapid weight loss and then feels alien and fraudulent in her newly attained body, yet is still unable to look at photographs of her previously heavy self. Jack, never having caught up with himself, was trapped in limbo between two unintegrated identities, between the desire for a better life and his loyalty to a more unhappy one.

It is in this light then that we can understand Jack's symptoms of anhedonic depression as a not-so-gentle reminder to heed his unfortunate beginnings. As possessively envious parents might begrudge their child a better life, Jack, through his anhedonia, spoiled and enviously robbed himself of his own pleasures for the transgression of rendering the memory of his lonely suffering to oblivion. It thus is not coincidental that Jack's symptoms led him to seek psychotherapy and retrieve by "remembering in words" with the therapist as witness those experiences of suffering that heretofore had remained unrevealed.[16]

For people who as children have endured psychological hardship in isolation, it is almost incomprehensible when good fortune knocks on the door many years later. If such individuals were to embrace a contented life, then who would carry the baton of remembering what occurred long ago? If Jack were to live happily ever after, then no one would ever know the travails he had to get through to live securely. These experiences, never relayed to another person, would sink into the meaninglessness of unrealized obscurity. If so, then toward what end did he suffer? For what? What was the point of it all if his experiences never were to be memorialized through the validating eyes of a witness?

It is similar to a boxing match in which one boxer pummels the other one mercilessly, until finally knocking him into submission. The victorious boxer stands over the prone figure for a moment and then leaves the ring with hands raised in triumphant pride. Slowly, the humiliated, defeated boxer struggles to his feet. Now, finally, ready to fight again and win back his dignity, he begins to shadowbox, all the while saying to himself, "I'll show him, he won't get away with that." The problem is that now there are nothing but shadows left to fight, because the winner has long since departed from battle and gone on to new challenges. Thirty years may go by, but haunting afterimages of his humiliation will not let him forget. He never did get satisfaction for his wounded sense of dignity.

The indignity of such victimizations is made infinitely worse if there is no one to witness the event and offer consolation. Another person's compassion implicitly demonstrates to the sufferer that the witness not only has seen what occurred but also has some feeling for what the person has gone through and shares that person's suffering in spirit. The sufferer knows he or she is not alone and does not have to go to great lengths to prove that what happened really happened.

For persons who never have secured a witness to validate their experience, it is both too early and too late to encounter an empathic, generous lover or a comfortable, secure life many years after the fact. Too early, because they are not ready to relinquish the memory of their lonely suffering until it has seen the realized light of day. Too late, because their benevolent fortunes have arrived at the scene of the crime only after the damage has been done.

There are, however, those few individuals who seem to have a sixth sense of knowing what is good for them. Such persons often are able to use their lonely suffering as a starkly contrasting reminder from which to appreciate with immense gratefulness the new life in which they find themselves. Although at times they may feel "it is all too good to be true," a certain practical streak seems to keep them headed in the right direction. Many persons, however, cannot easily give up the resentment and indignation of their lonely suffering until their experience of victimization has been recognized to their satisfaction. If it is too late to bring newly discovered witnesses back in time to the scene of their suffering, it is not too late to bring reenacted proof of that experience into the present.

Rather than embrace the ready-made solution provided by a newly found empathic witness, such persons often are compulsively drawn to individuals who will enable them to reenact and attempt to solve the original problem. Some women who had unreliable, alcoholic fathers, although professing a desire to settle down, are frequently attracted to unreliable, restless men who will not commit to them. If a stable, generous man does enter the life of such a woman, she may find him "boring"—almost as if his stability does not fit who she is and who she has been. Romantic attraction thus can become a vehicle by which problems of the past are reidentified and reenacted to ensure that they not be forgotten. Sometimes, however, this sort of reenactment as memory is manifested primarily as part of a person's character. As we have seen in the case of Jack, the story of lonely suffering is actively maintained and memorialized in symbolically encapsulated form through the repeated symptom of anhedonic depression.

Symptoms as One's Intimate Creations

Symptoms may be viewed as self-created communicative actions intended to build a lasting monument once and for all to one's experience of suffering. This self-revelatory urge to transform one's forgotten experience into the objectivity of a memorable reality strikingly resembles the animating impetus to the artistic process.

If the artistic process consists in creatively elevating one's experience through its dramatization into an objective event, then the neurotic creates an "illness" of symptoms in a dramatic attempt to objectify his or her unwitnessed experience of suffering. Because this illness is an involuted work of "art" with a very

private language, however, its artistic aim of objectification through
self-disclosure remains ever-elusive. For this reason Rank described
the neurotic as an *artiste manquée* (missed artist).[17] In effect, the
neurotic is a missed artist because his or her insulated communicative attempts never find their sought-for audience.

Perhaps the more unheeded the symptomatic message, and the
more doubt-laden the memory of our suffering, the more we must
raise the decibel level of our choked-off communications. Thus,
the self-enclosing pressures of thinking-in are so isolating that
character structure can disintegrate or "break down." Extreme
obsessional defenses frequently are the last bastion of character
maintenance before a nervous collapse. In breaking down or collapsing emotionally, we seek desperately to come out of the circular fixity of chasing our own tails and find an opening to others. In
this sense, an acute psychotic episode may be viewed as a radical
attempt to cure ourselves by initiating an otherwise prohibited
transition out of our self-imposed ruts.

The view of psychological symptoms as self-created for the purpose of conveying and memorializing one's suffering has fundamental implications for the concept of resistance in clinical work.
Although symptoms may be experienced as unwelcome alien
intruders, they are among the most intimate of one's creations. If
things are to proceed well in treatment, everyone—therapist and
patient included—must be happy to be rid of the troublemaking
symptoms. In a modern-day version of ridding ourselves of devils
by burning witches at the stake, there is something counterfeit
about a cure that claims mental health by eradicating symptoms.
Whereas many years ago witches were burned in order to exorcize
their devils, we have now become more sophisticated in disentan-
gling people from their unwanted "devils."

Through behavior modification, we attempt to detach persons
from their devilish symptoms by differentiating between person
and behavior: "It is not you I dislike, it is your behavior." Many
mental health professionals probably cope with much of their
countertransference hatred in this fashion. They attribute their
dislike of a patient to the patient's psychopathology or "illness"
rather than viewing it as an inherent part of the person. In so doing,
however, clinicians rob patients of their personal dignity as adults
who are responsible, to a great degree, for earning like or dislike
from others.

In classical psychoanalysis, although the quest for self-understanding and self-knowledge is a method of investigation, the expectation to behave "appropriately" still is a primary aim of cure. Thus, it is expected that when the laser beam of the analyst's interpretation is directed at the underlying motives of a patient's acting-out or acting-in, that patient will no longer behave problematically. But patients may view their symptoms as something akin to very personal, secret friends of whom they are publicly ashamed but privately proud. It is not unlike a situation in which a parent may say: "I can come down on my child, but let someone else try to do that, and I will defend him to the death." When symptoms are possessed as intimate creations in this way, we cannot be surprised that we encounter resistance until the raison d'être of the symptoms has been fully acknowledged and witnessed by the therapist. From the patient's point of view, when any cure leaves his story of lonely suffering untold, there may be a feeling of selling out for the sake of adaptation.

Many masochistic patients exact a belated "passive aggressive" revenge against their parents by self-destructively devoting their lives to the spiting of parental ideals that never were truly made their own. These patients then entertain fantasies of parents who at long last would bear witness to their suffering and beg for forgiveness of the patient.

A perfectionistic bulimic patient, used to complying with the high achievement standards of her parents, emerged from a hair salon feeling very happy about her new coif. She was relatively satisfied with her weight at the time and felt more attractive than usual. On her way home she received many looks that confirmed her feelings. When she arrived home, her roommate complimented her on the new hairdo. A few minutes later, when she was alone in her room, the patient found herself feeling extremely annoyed and irritable. When all goes well, sometimes it goes too well.

Unheard voices, locked away in the dark oblivion of the unconscious, strive at the most inopportune of times for the dignity of realized expression. Through guerilla-like forays of repeated symptomatology, patients rebel against their own tyranny of repression foisted in the name of compliantly getting along. It is precisely because everyone would be rid of these inconvenient, troublemaking symptoms that patients hold on all the more tenaciously to their "black sheep children," as if in sentimentalized embrace against all those who would do them harm.

A married man reported having unwanted homosexual liaisons

with anonymous men. It was not readily apparent what the patient's sexual orientation was; what was significant, however, is that because of the patient's ruthless self-condemnation, he defiantly sentimentalized his homoerotic feelings in protection against imagined global enemies. As parents might compensate their children for neglecting them by showering the children with reparative gifts, this patient indulged his disavowed wishes with compulsively expressed actions. These symptomatic reenactments implicitly expressed an urgent demand for the unconditional acceptance of those yearnings that he perceived everyone (most importantly himself) had vilified.

It is not unusual for patients to come to their sessions and recount sheepishly, as if apologizing to the therapist, how they "screwed up" by manifesting their own particular type of symptomatology again. At these junctures in treatment, I sometimes suspect that such patients take a secretly perverse pride in persistently maintaining their symptoms in the face of being seduced into changing for the better, with me as therapist posing as the serpent. When therapeutic movement comes too quickly, patients are tempted to break a silent loyalty oath they took with themselves during the loneliest of times, an oath never to forget.

For if these patients' symptoms were to be killed off, the story that they contain would not be told, and the patients' experiences of suffering, starved of a life-giving witness, would shrivel up into the meaninglessness of a hallucinatory episode. Symptoms thus are pregnant with constructive meaning, constructed as they are with the purpose of bringing the dignity of recognition, sometimes many years later, to a person's experiences of lonely suffering. As those experiences finally are revealed in the presence of a credibly empathic witness, they are infused with the meaningful breath of having real life, if even for a briefly conscious moment.

Notes

1. Ernest Becker, *The Denial of Death* (New York: Free Press, 1973).
2. B. Cohler, "Personal Narrative and Life Course," in *Life-Span Development and Behavior,* vol. 4, ed. Paul Baltes and Orville G. Brim Jr. (New York: Academic Press, 1982).
3. R. Romanyshyn, *Psychological Life* (Austin: University of Texas Press, 1982).
4. Otto Rank, *Will Therapy and Truth and Reality* (New York: Alfred A. Knopf, 1936).

5. D. W. Winnicott, "Transitional Objects and Transitional Phenomena," in *Playing and Reality* (1953; reprint, New York: Tavistock/Routledge, 1971), 1–25.

6. Peter Shabad, "Resentment, Indignation, Entitlement: The Transformation of Unconscious Wish into Need," *Psychoanalytic Dialogues* 3, no. 4 (1993): 481–94.

7. Paul Russell, "The Essential Invisibility of Trauma and the Need for Repetition: Commentary on Shabad's 'Resentment, Indignation, and Entitlement,'" *Psychoanalytic Dialogues* 3, no. 4 (1993): 517.

8. R. Stolorow and G. Atwood, *Contexts of Being: The Intersubjective Foundations of Psychological Life* (Hillsdale NJ: Analytic Press, 1992), 53.

9. Russell, "Essential Invisibility," 518.

10. Peter Shabad, "Paradox and the Search for the Real: Reply to Ghent, Russell, and Lachmann," *Psychoanalytic Dialogues* 3, no. 4 (1993): 523–33.

11. Wilhelm Stekel, *Compulsion and Doubt* (1949; reprint, New York: Grosset and Dunlap, 1962), 259.

12. Winnicott, "Transitional Objects," 12.

13. M. Balint, *The Basic Fault* (London: Tavistock, 1968).

14. Russell, "Essential Invisibility," 521.

15. H. Greenspan, "Lives as Texts: Symptoms as Modes of Recounting in the Life Histories of Holocaust Survivors," in *Storied Lives: The Cultural Politics of Self-Understanding*, ed. George C. Rosenwald and Richard L. Ochberg (New Haven: Yale University Press, 1992), 145–64.

16. Sigmund Freud, "Remembering, Repeating, and Working-Through," in *The Standard Edition of the Complete Psychological Works of Sigmund Freud*, trans. and ed. James Strachey (London: Hogarth Press, 1953), 12:145–46.

17. Otto Rank, *Will Therapy.*

Further Reading

Becker, Ernest. *The Denial of Death.* New York: Free Press, 1973.
>   This is a brilliant, Pulitzer Prize–winning book that examines the human fear and denial of death from a psychoanalytic and existential point of view.

———. *Escape from Evil.* New York: Free Press, 1975.
>   A follow-up to *The Denial of Death*, this book examines how the denial of death and the escape from the need to mourn wreak havoc in human society.

Bowlby, John. *The Making and Breaking of Affectional Bonds.* London: Tavistock, 1979.
>   This book is a good, concise summary of Bowlby's thinking, including his important three stages of a child's reaction to separation: protest, despair, and detachment.

Dietrich, David, and Peter Shabad, eds. *The Problem of Loss and Mourning: Psychoanalytic Perspectives.* Madison CT: International Universities Press, 1989.
>   A good overview of the field of loss and mourning from a psychoanalytic point of view. The book includes sections on development, theory, research, clinical practice, and the Holocaust.

Dostoevsky, Fyodor. "The Grand Inquisitor," in *The Brothers Karamazov.* Trans. Constance Garnett. New York: Modern Library, 1937.
>   This chapter from *The Brothers Karamazov*, an essay in its own right, is for me the most profound depiction of the human condition that I have yet read.

Freud, Sigmund. "Mourning and Melancholia" and "Remembering, Repeating and Working-Through." In *The Standard Edition of the Complete Psychological Works of Sigmund Freud.* Trans. and ed. James Strachey. London: Hogarth Press, 1953, 14:243–60 and 12:147–56.
　　These two papers are a crucial, illuminative introduction to a psychoanalytic understanding of mourning and the consequences of not mourning.
Romanyshyn, Robert. *Technology as Symptom and Dream.* London: Routledge, 1989.
　　A very interesting, original examination of the mentality that produces a runaway technology in our culture.

MARIE-CLAIRE LAVABRE

STALIN'S DOUBLE DEATH
MEMORY AND MOURNING
AMONG FRENCH COMMUNIST
PARTY ACTIVISTS

IN HIS "Mourning and Melancholia," Freud defines mourning as a painful state characterized by loss of interest in the outside world, the inability to choose a new love object, and the abandonment of all activity not related to the memory of the deceased. This state differs from melancholy, which also includes the loss of self-esteem. Mourning, Freud wrote, is a "reaction to the loss of a loved one or of an abstraction playing a similar role—the fatherland, liberty, an ideal, and so forth."[1]

This definition opens the way for a discussion of Stalin's "double death"—the death in 1953 of the person or "loved one" himself and the death in 1956 of the ideal he personified. Such a double death raises the question of a double process of mourning. With death comes mourning, but the reaction to the death of a loved one can become a denial of the loss, entailing an idealization of the deceased. We can hypothesize that Stalin's second death, the death of the ideal, dictated a process of mourning of an entirely different nature than had his physical death.[2]

The example of Stalin's death points to dual processes: on the one hand, the loss of a person and the loss of an ideal; on the other hand, individual and collective reactions, psychological and social dimensions. In this essay I examine the concept of collective memory and inquire into the extent to which belonging and adherence to a highly structured group affect the manner in which individuals imagine their past. To clarify my perspective at the outset, I do not intend to apply psychoanalysis to a political phenomenon, assuming that psychoanalysis accounts for or exhausts the meaning of political processes or gives us better tools than those disciplines whose specific object is politics. Nor do I wish to use psychoanalysis in an analogical or metaphorical manner when speaking of "collective mourning," in the way in which, for example, Henry Rousso has used the concept in his work on Vichy.[3]

Rather than making metaphorical use of psychoanalysis when discussing the losses occasioned by the two deaths of Stalin, and rather than applying an analytical scheme appropriate for individuals to a group, I consider the interaction between the individual and the group, where the object of attachment was collective, and grief was shared. And rather than trying to study "collective mourning" with regard to Stalin's physical death or with regard to the subsequent revelation of his crimes, I try to distinguish and then articulate the codified and ritualized practices used by the French Communist Party in the wake of Stalin's "two deaths," and I look at the diversity of individual reactions among party members in 1953 and 1956.

"UNCLE JOE'S" death in 1953 provoked a powerful emotional reaction in the Communist world, revealing the extent of the devotion to his person. If the archives are to be believed, there was a strong outpouring of grief in the Soviet Union itself. But the emotion was even greater in the Stalinized Communist parties of western Europe for whom the Stalinist myth had not been contaminated by reality and lived experience. Following Robert Hertz's "Contribution à une étude collective de la mort" (Contribution to a study on a collective representation of death), we can interpret this outpouring of emotion as a consequence of the identification of individuals not only with the group to which they belong but also with the person who symbolizes it.[4] The death of the leader threatens the foundations of the entire group as well as "the mutual ties among individuals," as Freud has pointed out.[5] The function of the social rituals that structure the mourning process after the death of a leader is to affirm the permanence of the group and its values beyond the leader's death. However, the revelation of Stalin's crimes in 1956 provoked a far more powerful shock than had his death alone: the identity of the group itself was suddenly threatened. The undermining of the group ideal of Communism itself was all the more violent given the magnitude of Stalin's crimes, including not only mass murder but also the murder of Communists, members of the ideal community, themselves. Suddenly the great figures of Soviet and eastern European Communism who had been treated as traitors under Stalin became victims and even martyrs. Mourning for the lost ideal extended to mourning for the victims.[6]

The French Communist Party turns out to be a particularly interesting subject of study in this regard, since it, along with the Italian Communist Party, was the most powerful Communist party in western Europe. More than all other European parties, it proudly proclaimed "the honor of being Stalinist" to such a degree that people spoke of "stalinisme à la française" (French-style Communism), and it was the most resistant to de-Stalinization.

My discussion of the French Communist Party is divided into three parts. First, I briefly discuss the concept of collective memory and the framework within which the interviews underlying this essay were gathered. This provides the methodological context for my analysis of the events of 1956 and the revelation of Stalin's crimes. Secondly, I describe the reactions to Stalin's death and show how political ritual avoided the breakup of the Communist Party by organizing the idealization of the dead leader. Thirdly, I examine the reactions to the Twentieth Congress of the Communist Party of the Soviet Union and highlight the resistance of the French Communist Party apparatus to de-Stalinization, a collective resistance that contrasted with the diversity of individual reactions to the revelations of the crimes of Stalin. In conclusion I attempt to interpret the political development of the French Communist Party in light of the inability of many activists from the Stalinist era to engage in the process of mourning for their lost ideal due to the lack of an appropriate process of collective mourning.

Collective Memory

The concept of "collective memory" that I developed in an earlier study of Communist memory was founded on Maurice Halbwach's work and was refined by Roger Bastide's study of African religions in Brazil. "Collective memory" is here defined as the homogenization of the representations of the past by the French Communist Party. To study collective memory from this point of view presupposes a combined study of the official history as written and disseminated by the French Communist Party, together with the individual memories of the activists. In order to observe to what extent belonging and adherence to this highly structured group affected the matter in which these individuals imagined their past, I therefore investigated the written partisan sources to get an idea of the norms produced by the organization, together with personal histories and individual reconstructions of the history of the party. Nondirective interviews, oral histories, and projective test interviews based on commentaries on photographic documents were conducted between 1982 and 1986 (prior to the great upheavals in 1989) with forty Communist activists of different age groups. In the first two types of interviews, the activists interviewed spoke little or not at all about Stalin—a telling indication in and of itself. However, in the projective test interviews, they were asked to comment on a photo of Stalin, a procedure that loosened tongues and revived emotional memories.

When trying to establish a link between a series of written sources (the press, history books, brochures, and autobiographies) and oral material gathered in interviews, we are dealing in part with a black box situation. Although we can weigh the convergences or divergences between official memory and living memory, nothing tells us with certainty that this or that official history or article has or has not been read by the interviewees. Moreover, there is no way provided by this method of inquiry to verify what these activists say and transmit about their lived experience and their past in their party cells or their living areas. Nonetheless, the nondirective character of the interview situations often allowed the expression of private feelings and thoughts, especially when activists of the Stalinist era spoke of Stalin himself.[7]

Reactions to the Announcement
of Stalin's Death

To get an idea of the strength and nature of French Communist activists' attachment to Stalin, we should briefly recall the scope of the homage to Stalin on his seventieth birthday in 1949. The attachment of party members to Stalin at this time was, of course, linked to their political beliefs and to the myth of true socialism. It had been reinforced after the war by continuous references to the battle of Stalingrad and was cemented by the mutual reinforcements provided by a largely closed group, which the Communists themselves described as "the family."

To prepare for Stalin's birthday, beginning in early November 1949, meetings were organized, gifts were sent, and articles appeared in the Communist press. Five hundred thousand leaflets, thirty thousand posters, and brochures entitled "Stalin, the man we love most" were printed and distributed. Ten decorated trucks criss-crossed France to collect presents and messages. Jean Chaintron, member of the Central Committee, former commissar of the International Brigades, and member of the French Resistance elected to the Senate in 1948, was entrusted with this campaign and its ceremonies, most notably the exhibition of the gifts that was held from 6 to 15 December 1949.

Forty thousand people saw the twenty-three murals illustrating themes of Stalin's life together with his huge, illuminated portrait and were able to drink to his health at the exhibition bar. Chaintron said of the campaign that it "directly or indirectly touched up to two million people." The exhibited gifts expressed not only gratitude, love, and confidence but Communist values as well. Among the exhibits—quoting Chaintron again—there was a "rosary embossed in silver which a 92 year old French woman had offered to Stalin, explaining that with it she had prayed for his victory; there were also the slippers of a baby girl who died during the war in the camps, the marriage ring of a woman's husband 'who was killed by the police of Jules Moch,' a racing bicycle which Stalin later gave to a young metalworker in Moscow, wool socks knitted for Stalin by an old Ardéchois mother, suspenders, and good old French wines."[8] This moving inventory, corroborated by the memories of Communist activists, testifies to the devotion to Stalin's person above and beyond political conviction.

French Stalinism was at its apogee when Stalin died three years later in March 1953. On 4 March, the front page of the party daily l'Humanité spread over eight columns the headline: "World-wide grief greets news of Stalin's serious illness." The leader died on the fifth, and for days l'Humanité was framed in black. Here again, multiple accounts testify to what Dominique Desanti called "the death of the father" and "the funeral ceremonies of a god."[9] Before a stunned Central Committee, Auguste Lecoeur could hardly bring himself to announce Stalin's death, "his voice was so filled with sobs." Roger Pannequin tells us that these tough men of the Central Committee who knew what is to "be imprisoned and to live in hiding and who had learned to look death straight in the eye" all lowered their heads.[10] "The minute of silence was spontaneous," he reports. As the historian Philippe Robrieux has aptly noted, this was a telling sign in a party where spontaneity rarely manifested itself.[11] More pertinent to our subject are Pannequin's remarks on the anxiety that gripped the members of the Central Committee: "We were so entirely convinced of the political and military

genius of Stalin that his disappearance seemed to us a defeat of the
socialist world, a step back which threatened the flanks of the
socialist fatherland, exposing them to the terrible blows of the
enemy." Interpreting the "anxiety of the Central Committee and
of the whole Party," one Central Committee member somberly
predicted that "it was possible to replace Lenin but not Stalin."

The Communist Party nonetheless stayed its course. On 10
March, during a mass meeting, the Communists of Paris paid their
solemn respects to the fallen leader, remaining faithful to their
image of Stalin. The affair surrounding Picasso's portrait of Stalin
testifies to this: because his portrait of the young Stalin was far
from the social realism of the tutelary images of official portrai-
ture, the artist was violently attacked. The leadership of the party
remained stable up to and beyond 1956. Whatever tensions irrupt-
ed within during these years of uncertainty and reshufflement in
the Soviet Union, they were never made public. It seems—and
this is an important point—that political ritual combined with
prescribed and controlled party activities succeeded in channeling
the anxiety of party activists, as it did after the death of Maurice
Thorez ten years later.[12] The praises sung to the dead leader and
the affirmation that Stalin "remained at the helm" beyond death
were part of a very codified political practice.

However, while the Communist press relayed expressions of
grief in response to Stalin's death, other accounts, gathered in the
working-class area of Longwy, demonstrate that the homage to
Stalin in fact was a mostly formal affair. It was organized by party
activists on orders from on high, in contrast to the spontaneous
and highly emotional nature of the "minutes of silence" observed
by workers on hearing of the death of the Italian bicycle champion
Fausto Coppi or the death of Humphrey Bogart.[13]

A final remark: In the interviews I conducted with Communist
activists, Stalin's death was associated only with the memory of
his birthday or with the year 1956. This makes clear that the meaning of his death in the memory of activists was structured around
a "before," when "things were clear and healthy"—in the words
of one interviewee—and an "after," marked by the eruption of
reality into a world of myth. One can thus suggest that the over
idealization of Stalin in 1953 gave stability to the party, allowing
it to maintain its values and projects and to secure the future
above and beyond the death of the leader. Portraits at home and his
embalmed corpse abroad kept the dead leader in the world of the

living. This made the political price of the revelation of Stalin's crimes in 1956 all the greater.

Reactions to the Twentieth Congress of the Communist Party of the Soviet Union

The Twentieth Congress and Krushchev's revelation of Stalin's crimes provoked an enduring rupture, generating splits, disillusionment, and resignations from the Communist Party. Quite a few Communist intellectuals from the 1950s broke with the party and left accounts of the shock and the trauma provoked by the Twentieth Congress. The congress cast a shadow on a past that once had appeared glorious, and irrevocably fractured the political convictions of even those who decided to stay in the party.

However, the French Communist Party itself, far from Moscow, remained basically unshaken. In contrast to what happened in 1953 at the time of Stalin's death, the shock in France was greater around the periphery of the party than among the Communist activists, especially those from the working class. The leadership of the party simply refused to question Stalin and even went so far as to deny the existence of Krushchev's secret report—the French delegates to the Congress would for a long time claim that they never heard of it. The French Communist Party chose a strategy of denial, or "repression," to borrow the expression of Georges Lavau.[14] To limit the impact of the event, the party apparatus—creator of official memory—condemned "Stalin's errors" and later admitted his "crimes and errors" and his "personality cult," calling the lack of democracy in the USSR a "tumor on an otherwise healthy body." But otherwise the party leadership was silent. In 1972, Politburo member Jacques Duclos published memoirs that contained neither any new information nor any new analyses of this period but that revealed some of the reasons for the French Communist Party's defiance concerning the revelations.[15]

Reporting on the first public meeting that made public the secret report, in the course of which Stalin's name was warmly applauded, Duclos writes: "When I made my speech at Wagram hall, I was still wondering whether the accusations had not been exaggerated. The business about the world map had made me jump." Duclos was referring to the accusation that Stalin had directed wartime operations off of a map, an accusation all the more unacceptable to the speaker because it cast doubt on Stalin's role and the role of the Soviet Union in the victory against Nazi Germany. The glorification of the Soviet role in defeating the Nazis had been, after all, at the core of the homage made to Stalin and continued to be well after 1956. Today we know that Duclos and Italian Communist Party leader Pietro Secchia had been informed by the Communist Party of the Soviet Union of the leader's "faults," his "deviations," and his "personality cult" a few months after his death. Duclos's active role in withholding information has been confirmed.[16] The French Communist Party's cover-up effort was also clearly revealed in Maurice Thorez's often-quoted answer to Jean Pronteau, who had just returned from Poland with a copy of the secret report: "You see, as far as I am concerned this report does not exist and soon will never have existed."[17] The leadership aside, the fact remains that the Communists present at the Wagram rally warmly acclaimed Stalin's name.

The cover-up strategy of the party apparatus fell on fertile ground—these were activists shaped during the Second World War. It was only in 1977 that the Politburo of the French Communist Party finally made an official rectification "on a point of history relative to the XXth Congress of the Communist Party of the Soviet Union" and revealed the conditions under which the French delegation learned of Khrushchev's secret report. The chronological development becomes clear: at first denial (or repression in the psychoanalytic sense), formulated as formal condemnations and interpretations emphasizing causes extrinsic to the Stalinist phenomena; then, cover-ups (1956–76); next, revelations and the subsequent disorganization of the structuring poles of Communist ideology, that is, relations with the Soviet Communist Party on the one hand and with the French Socialist Party on the other (1976–79); and lastly, historiographic revisions (1980–90).

How did Communist activists react to these turns of events, and what memories did they keep of the Twentieth Congress? Only a small minority of interviewees who lived through the Twentieth Congress spontaneously talked about it. The events of Budapest, the Second World War, and the triumphant phase of Stalinism, the Communist Party of the Soviet Union, and a mythified Soviet Union were themes most often raised in the interviews I held. The activists who were around during the Twentieth Congress and the few interviewees who did talk of the shock of the Twentieth Congress explained their continued fidelity to the Communist party by stressing their attachment to the working-class dimension of Communist policy and the role of the Soviet Union in the Second World War. Others stressed the anti-Communism provoked in France by the repression of the Hungarian revolt. Stalin himself was almost never mentioned. When asked in the course of the last interview to comment on a photo of Stalin, this second group was more talkative than the first. Touched and often relieved—as if the material reality of a photo lifted a taboo—they spoke at length of the times when "things were clear," emphasized Stalin's positive role, and regretted the forms taken by de-Stalinization as well as its abuses.

Their silence in the course of their first discussions betrayed their unease. Confronted with the condemnation of Stalin, most interviewees denounced the excesses of de-Stalinization but not its limited character. An unconditional defense of the Soviet Union was the only point on which their statements were in accord with their intimate convictions and their recollections. Stalin was indeed present in their minds, but they did not dare speak of him, probably because of their concern not to make their disagreements explicit, or their desire to avoid the hostility of recent party members. Their reactions to Stalin's photo, however, testified to the fact that they kept the memory of a triumphant Stalinism alive and discussed it among themselves. On hearing them, one is led to the conclusion that for most of these interviewees, de-Stalinization was just a question of words, of official declarations and interpretations, that is, of everything that in a party can be fixed in writing, whereas the Stalinist myth was also based on images and today is kept alive through speech.

When one considers the long-term consequences of the Twentieth Congress on the French Communist Party, one is struck by generational differences. This is probably a sign that the cover-up caused a lack of transmission and collective elaboration of meaning that would have been needed to deal with the loss of the ideal, or at least with the loss of the figure who embodied the ideal. It is true, as mentioned previously, that the party stayed the course and that the political strategy of its leaders—the protection of Stalin and the idealized memory of Stalinism—was undoubtedly in harmony with the desire of many activists shaped in the Stalinist school. However, the apparent unity of the party was grounded on silence and denial, on what René Kaès has called in his work on the Argentine case the "pact of denial," the agreement of silence for the sake of the survival of the community.

However, this silence did not interfere with the diversity of the individual ways of negotiating the loss of the ideal. Barring the case of those who left the French Communist Party in 1956 or immediately thereafter, three types of party members emerge. The first were activists who refused the dissociation of the ideal from its personification in Stalin, locking themselves in nostalgic renderings of the past. The second were those activists who held onto Stalin's image but also accepted the undermining of the ideal that had initially motivated their commitment. Today these people explain that the ideal had to accommodate itself with reality and that Stalinism in fact was a product of . . . anti-Communism. Lastly, there are those who chose the ideal over Stalin and who consider the question of Stalinism external to the issue of Communism, and thus a question that does not concern them. At various points, all found themselves in implicit or explicit disagreement with the party that they had joined and of which they continued to be part. The crises of French Communism, which began well before the collapse of the socialist block, can thus be understood as reflecting the incapacity of the organization to facilitate the process of mourning needed by activists who had an enormous emotional investment in the Communist micro-society.

To conclude, I quote Norbert Elias's *Studien über die Deutschen:* "It is well established today, much more so at any rate than in the past, that violent traumas provoke serious and lasting scars in individuals if the traumatic event is not made conscious through speech and discussion, in other words if the possibility for healing is not given. I have been convinced for quite some time that in the life of peoples and social groups there are collective traumatic experiences which become profoundly anchored and cause serious damage to the psyche of members of these peoples, if they are not allowed the release of catharsis."[18]

Notes

I thank Philip Golub and Celia Brickman for the English translation of this paper.

1. Sigmund Freud, *Métapsychologie*, trans. Marie Bonaparte and Anne Berman (Gallimard, 1940; reprint, 1978), 148.
2. Freud's "Mourning and Melancholia" provides no further insight into the process of mourning for lost ideals, nor on shared mourning linked to an object of collective attachment. However, Freud's "Group Psychology and the Analysis of the Ego" does provide some keys for exploring these issues.
3. Marie-Claire Lavabre, "Du Poids et du choix du passé: Lecture critique du syndrôme de Vichy," in *Histoire politique et sciences sociales,* ed. Peschanski, Pollak, and Rousso (Complexe, 1991).
4. Robert Hertz, "Contribution à une étude collective de la mort," in *Mélanges de sociologie religieuse et folklore* (Alcan, 1928).

5. Sigmund Freud, *"Deux foules artificielles: L'Eglise et l'armée"* ("Two artificial groups: The church and the army") in *Psychologie collective et analyse du moi* (Payot, 1962), 47.

6. For more, see Pierre-Yves Gaudard, "Mémoire et culpabilité en Allemagne: Contribution à l'étude du processus de deuil collectif allemand après le national-socialisme," Ph.D. diss., dept. of sociology, Université de Paris X–Nanterre, 1995.

7. See Marie-Claire Lavabre, *Le Fil rouge: Sociologie de la mémoire communiste* (Paris: Presses de la Fondation nationale des Science politiques, 1994).

8. See Sophie Jeannelle, in "Le PCF et le 70e anniversaire de Staline," *Communisme*, no. 3 (1983).

9. Dominique Desanti, *Les staliniens, une expérience politique, 1944–1956* (Paris: Fayard, 1975), 256.

10. Roger Pannequin, "Adieu, camarades," *Sagittaire* (1977): 305–14.

11. Philippe Robrieux, *Histoire intérieure du Parti communiste, 1945–1972* (Fayard, 1981), 341.

12. See Delphine Dulong, "Mourir en politique: Le discours politique des éloges funèbres," *Revue française de science politique*, no. 4 (1994): 629–42.

13. See Fabrice Montebello, "Joseph Staline et Humphrey Bogart: L'hommage des ouvriers. Essai sur la construction sociale de la figure du héros en milieu ouvrier", *Politix*, no. 24 (1993): 115–33.

14. Georges Lavau, "Les enfants de Barbe-bleue et le cabinet sanglant: Les Partis communistes français et italiens et le refoulement du stalinisme," in *Les interprétations du stalinisme*, ed. E. Pisier (Paris: PUF, 1980).

15. Jacques Duclos, *Mémoires*, vol. 5, *1952–1958, Dans la mêlée* (Paris: Fayard, 1992).

16. See Marc Lazar, "Les partis communistes italien et français et l'après-Staline," *XXe siècle*, no. 12 (1990).

17. Cited by Robrieux, *Histoire intérieure du Parti communiste*, 449.

18. Norbert Elias, *Studien über die Deutschen: Machtkämpfe und Habitusentwiklung im 19. and 20. Jahrhundert*, Suhrkamp Taschenbuch wissenschaft (Frankfurt, 1992), 549, quoted and translated by Gaudard, in "Mémoire et culpabilité en Allemagne," 17.

Further Reading

Gaudard, Pierre-Yves. *Le Fardeau de la mémoire: Le Deuil collectif allemand après le national-socialisme*. Paris: Plon, 1997.

Pierre-Yves Gaudard stresses the preeminence of the individual psyche in the dynamics of collective memory and, more particularly, of collective mourning. Basing himself on Freud's work, he takes up an analysis of the collective German mourning not only of the Führer and of the Third Reich but also of the victims. A reflection on the intergenerational transmission of guilt, this book interprets the German terrorist, feminist, and ecological movements as the effects of the work of mourning.

Halbwachs, Maurice. *Les Cadres sociaux de la mémoire* (The social framework of memory). Paris: PUF, 1952.

———. *La Mémoire collective* (On collective memory). 1950. Reprint, Paris: Albin Michel, 1997.

By suggesting that the isolated individual is a fiction and that memory should therefore not be considered as a purely individual function, Maurice Halbwachs, following the path indicated by Emile Durkheim, takes up the question of the influence of the social framework on the memories held by individuals. *Les Cadres sociaux de la mémoire* sets itself the task of demonstrating that memories, even intimate memories, become possible only through the frameworks provided by society and, in addition, attempts to describe how the collective familial, religious memories of the different social classes are maintained. These hypotheses are deepened in *La Mémoire collective,* a collection of texts published after Halbwachs's death. This collection places the accent on the manner in which individuals actualize collective memories, and thus it goes beyond the opposition between the individual and the group, introducing instead the idea of an interpenetration of individual consciousnesses.

Lavabre, Marie-Claire. *Le Fil rouge: Sociologie de la mémoire communiste.* Paris: Presses de la Fondation nationale des Science politiques, 1994.

This book expands on many of the themes on French Communist memory in this volume.

Rousso, Henri. *Le syndrome de Vichy: De 1944 à nos jours* (The Vichy syndrome: From 1944 to today). Paris: Editions du Seuil, 1987.

Le syndrome de Vichy is the first French work to reflect upon the national myths born out of the Second World War and at the same time upon the downplaying and covering up of Vichy. Based on the notion that this period of the past concerned events that do not disappear easily—to which the strength of the French political debate twenty years later testifies—the work is constructed around a psychoanalytic metaphor: because France "suffers from her past," because there was a "trauma" and a "neurosis," the memory of this troubled period retreats into an "unfinished work of mourning" and to "repressions" between 1944 and 1971.

Valensi, Lucette. *Les Fables de la mémoire: La Glorieuse Bataille des trois rois.* Paris: Editions du Seuil, 1992.

An extraordinary event is recounted at the beginning of this remarkable historical study of the phenomena of memory: a war and a battle that lasted several hours in 1578 ended with the death of three kings and the victory of Morocco over Portugal. From the first echoes of this memorable battle to today, this book retraces the history of memory among the victors and the vanquished. For the latter who were crushed, the mourning of the dead, and particularly of King Sebastian, was also the mourning of the grandeur of Portugal. This impossibility of this mourning is expressed as such by rumors denying the death of King Sebastian and in the hoaxes of several false Sebastians.

PETER HOMANS

LOSS AND MOURNING IN THE LIFE AND THOUGHT OF MAX WEBER

TOWARD A THEORY OF SYMBOLIC LOSS

THIS ESSAY argues that Max Weber's theory of disenchantment is an as yet unexplored theory of collective loss, and as such, it is an unexplored resource as well for contemporary discussions of collective loss, mourning, and memory. However, that an experience of disenchantment is basically an experience of loss is not readily apparent in many discussions of the term *disenchantment*, even in some of Weber's own writings. The best way to demonstrate that disenchantment is a form of loss is to examine the formation of the concept in the context of Weber's personal, inner life.

Early in his adult life, Weber underwent what was then called a "nervous breakdown," which lasted for several years. At the time, he had just begun a promising career in law and economics. But as his mental distress began to heal, he radically altered his career, turned to the lifelong study of religion and sociology, and wrote *The Protestant Ethic and the Spirit of Capitalism,* which contained his first discussion of his concept of disenchantment.

This study explores the life and thought of Max Weber, especially the interplay between them, as one important context in which Weber's thinking about disenchantment took place. It seeks to show that Weber's illness was a response to a double loss: loss of frustrating attachments in childhood and adolescence and the loss of the collective past of his family and his generation—the waning of Christianity. His breakdown was a form of mourning, and his writings a creative attempt to come to terms with his own past, in this twofold sense.

The following discussion builds upon three sources: Weber's

formal writings, his life course, and instances of his "fantasy thinking." The value of the first is taken for granted, as is the second,
given Marianne Weber's truly remarkable modern (for its psychological sensitivities) biography of her husband. Even now, it remains
the best source for the study of Weber's inner life. "Fantasy thinking" refers to passages in Weber's writings that indicate the presence of unusually strong emotion and, by implication, equally
strongly held convictions about life and the world.

Loss and Mourning: Background
and Life Course

Max Weber was born in Erfurt in 1864 into a prosperous, middle-
class German Protestant family. He was a highly successful university student and chose a university career in law and economics. As a young adult, he lived in his parents' home until the age of
twenty-nine, when he married. In the summer of 1897, at the age
of thirty-three, Weber was financially independent of his parents,
and he and his wife had moved to his own house in Heidelberg,
where he took up a promising academic position. As he stepped
forward into his adult life, Weber believed that he had relegated
whatever family conflicts he may have had to the past. But in a
single dramatic episode he brought those forces back, and his life
and work underwent a series of reversals that neither he nor anyone else could ever have imagined.

Two central conflicts made up the life of the Weber family, his
parents' relationship with each other and Max's relation to each.
Max Weber Sr. had long since taken up an amiable, comfortable,
and servile place in his city's bureaucracy. At home, however, like
most men of his position at that time, he played the role of *pater-
familias*, arrogating to himself the right to control most of his
family's activities, especially his wife's. In turn, Helene Weber
antagonized her husband in three ways: she was unable to enjoy
sexual pleasure freely; she was deeply religious and devoted herself to encouraging similar sentiments in her children, especially
eldest son Max; and she had, the year before, inherited a substantial sum of money, the income from which easily surpassed her
husband's salary. He could do little about his sexual frustrations,
but he openly disparaged her religious activities and insisted upon
detailed explanations of her every financial need, including even
daily expenditures. Helene accepted all this but turned from him

to her children and their religious nurture as the sole source of satisfaction in her life.

Max's relationship with his parents was equally impoverished. He bitterly resented his long financial dependence on his family, but he also despised his father's easy compliance with the values of the "power state," and he resented his father's disrespect for his mother's autonomy. She shared her misery with her son, and he listened attentively. But he also distanced himself unequivocally from her religious solicitations, thereby reluctantly taking up his father's attitude toward his mother in this respect. So the basic "family dynamics" consisted of a set of personal relationships characterized by suppressed, bitter resentments and an overall sense of desperation and sadness.

Weber's relationship with his mother was especially important. The key to Helene Weber's personality was her religious faith. Marianne ascribed to her a "rich and difficult emotionality," adding that she mastered life through "religious resources, ethical passion and selfless kindness."[1] She had an "iron will." Her sense of the divine was experienced as the inner voice of conscience urging her to transform her "selfishness" into devoted love for others. Her faith performed several psychological functions for her. It provided her with a capacity to become introspective. At times it left her prey to periods of shame, guilt, yearning, and sadness; and she was unable to become empathic to anyone who did not share her religious view of the world. As a Protestant woman of her time, issues of autonomy and their opposites, attachment and dependence, were, along with sexual pleasures, central for her.

Because his father was rather emotionally distant and his mother so religiously solicitous, Weber's confirmation at the age of fifteen was an important and revealing event. He was bookish, with history and classics his main interests at the time. An intellectually precocious and introverted boy, he also absorbed with pleasure the liberal German politics of his nonreligious father's home. His mother tried to evoke in him "her own religious excitement . . . the world in which she was at home."[2] She even enlisted the services of one of her son's older friends to influence him to adopt her religious feelings. Weber could not accept these solicitations, which centered upon the question of an afterlife, but he could not openly reject them, either. Instead, he chose a path of mournful and empty-hearted compliance. As he explained to an old friend in tones of undisguised sadness, "I really believe that a man who could honestly say he had absolutely no conviction or hope of a hereafter must be an extremely unhappy creature. To wander into life without any hope and in the belief that every step only brings one closer to utter disintegration, a dissolution that ends existence, must truly be a terrible feeling, and deprive a man of all hope of life."

Then he softened his thoughts out of respect for his friend and especially for his mother, by taking upon himself some of her disapproval: "I believe it is in my nature that I seldom share my feelings with others. . . . I am a bad companion too."[3] In the face of these objections, his mother "had to realize painfully that the fifteen-year-old boy did not experience any deeper religious excitement and, above all, that he resisted her maternal influence."[4] Indeed, Helene Weber's piety was, like her sexuality, inseparable from her maternity.

At the time of her marriage to Max, Marianne had been living virtually as an adopted daughter in the Weber household. Like Helene, whom she revered, Marianne was religious, community-minded, maternal, nurturant, and devoted to others—she was "selfless." But she was less religious, her sense of self was more separate and bounded, and she was consequently far more autonomous and independent. And she wanted a career for herself, an unprecedented aspiration for a young woman at this time. Most important of all, she was deeply concerned with her husband's individuality, especially his independence from his parents and the future success of his work and career. This is seen with special clarity in his recovery from his illness, as it gave shape not only to his adult life but also to much of his originative intellectual achievement.

Such were the central figures and their principal features in Weber's life, before his so-called breakdown.

Breakdown and Recovery

Helene Weber needed to maintain periodic contact with her children, and in the early summer she planned a visit to Max and Marianne, without her husband. He exercised his prerogatives and insisted on accompanying her. Weber and his wife objected in angry letters, but to no avail. The two parents arrived together. Then, in an uncharacteristic display of filial indignation, Max Jr. made his views on the matter known to his father and insisted that the older man accept them. "We demand that Mama should have the right to visit us alone quietly for four or five weeks each year at a time that is convenient for her. As long as this is not done, any family relationship with Papa is meaningless to us and its outward maintenance has no value for us."[5] Max Sr. did not accept this. Weber ordered his father out of his house, and so the father left. Helene retreated into religiously inspired guilt, remorse, and hope, while her husband simply washed his hands of the affair and went on a trip with a friend. Although in good health at the time, he died suddenly, still in the midst of his journey. The funeral was held in August. Weber did not mourn his father's death, either at the time or later in life.

Toward the end of the summer the breakdown began. Marianne described its onset: "irritable and annoyed at minor things—noises are a torment—nervous exhaustion—feverish and apprehensive— strong feeling of tension—weeping—sits paralysed for hours." But the upshot was relatively simple: "Everything was too much for him; he could not read, write, talk, walk, or sleep without torment."[6] Weber gradually withdrew from the social world into the constant, dedicated, and supportive presence of his wife, where he was to remain for several years.

The worst time was 1898–99. In the summer of 1898 Weber entered a sanitorium for a few weeks, the only time he was separated from Marianne. There he came to realize that his illness would be "a long siege." But that period forced upon him a greater intensity of introspection and self-definition than he had ever known before. So he could write to his wife: "Such an illness has reopened (for me) the purely human side of living, which Mama always somewhat missed in me. . . . I could say, 'An icy hand has let go of me.' . . . I want, above all, to live a full and personal life with my *Kindele* [baby] . . . earlier I did not even know how to live as close together with someone as I have lived with you these past years."[7]

At first, Marianne wondered whether what she called her husband's "sovereign self-sufficiency" had rendered her superfluous, but she soon realized that he "needed her constant care and presence." His mother could not understand his "weak will" and recommended "some act of self-transcendence." But the psychologically astute Marian understood this theological gesture: "Her own heroic will, constantly and mercilessly exerted, had mastered all psychological and physical exertions. Surely her son could do the same."[8]

For some time, we are told, Max and Marianne lived in complete solitude. Then, gradually and bit by bit, there were improvements, and Max was able to travel, but only with Marianne. In 1901, the couple made several visits to Rome. There, healing finally began. Weber began "to do a little reading." His mother visited for several weeks. One volume followed another. The two women "secretly nudged each other: 'Look, he's reading.' And a bit later: 'He even dared to talk.'" The couple left Rome at Easter 1902. This long visit to Rome "really marked the beginning" of his recovery, "after three and a half years of illness."[9] Max Weber had become Max Weber once again. And so the question is, How?

In attempting to explain her husband's recovery, Marianne emphasized the confluence of several factors. She spoke of art, Rome, and land: "Weber wanted to submerge his illness and his earthbound self in a sea of powerful impressions. He owed to the sun and to the magnificence of the Eternal City hours impregnated with the past. . . . He parted from the south as from a second homeland." Of this stay in Rome, Weber himself said, "A historical imagination is the main thing."[10]

It is not possible to know to what extent the illness remitted spontaneously. But a constant and devoted maternal presence was surely important. And then there is the illness itself, which, when viewed psychodynamically, was an attempt at self-cure. In sum: the supportive, soothing, and unconscious influence of natural, artistic, and maternal objects over a long period of time, that duration determined entirely by "the patient" (sufferer) himself. D. W. Winnicott, a founding figure in the development of object-relations psychology, observed that some patients, especially those whose central pathology is an excessively built-up ego that has become oversocialized into a too-pervasive sense of "false self," need a period of total dependence toward the end of treatment in order that the "true self," masked but also protected by the false self, can dare to come into existence.[11]

Loss and Mourning: Work

We now turn to the work of Max Weber and explore it in relation to what has been said about his life. The principal point here is that Weber's life, especially his breakdown and recovery, posed the question: how to describe and understand a world in which spontaneous emotions, especially feelings of warmth and affection between people, have been lost? Weber's work was his reply: the world has become disenchanted. The following discusses the meaning of disenchantment and its central organizing function for Weber's work as a whole and then presents examples drawn from those works that display feelings of loss, sadness, and bitterness—that is, works that in their form as well as in their content suggest feelings of loss and mourning.

DISENCHANTMENT AND PROTESTANTISM

The writing of the book on Protestantism coincided with the beginning of Weber's recovery in 1903. It was closely followed by the crucial methodological essay on the ideal-type in 1904. This connection between life and work did not escape Marianne Weber. She noted an intimate relation between *The Protestant Ethic and the Spirit of Capitalism* and her husband's inner life. His book was, she said, "connected with the deepest roots of his personality and in an undefinable way bears its stamp."[12] But she could not fathom exactly how her husband's personality had stamped itself upon his book, and vice versa. Earlier in this essay I noted that Marianne's devotion to her husband took the form of a lifelong desire to nurture his individuality, a process also known as individuation.[13] As Weber began to separate and differentiate himself (that is, to individuate) from the conflict-laden attachment to his mother, he also began to mourn that ambivalent relationship and as a result built up a stronger sense of his own self-definition.

Without saying why, and probably without knowing why, Weber turned away from the study and teaching of law and economics and to the study of Protestantism, the religious tradition or common culture that had so decisively shaped his mother's personality. She in turn had mediated that culture to him, decisively shaping his personality as well. There, in that Protestantism, in that sociohistorical process that he later called an "ideal-type," he "saw" a cluster of past events that he chose to call "disenchantment" (*Entzauberung*) and "rationalization"—a process whereby the spontaneity and immediacy of religious belonging, ritual, and belief (he called it "magic") undergoes waning and is replaced by a detached inner-worldly asceticism and its psychological substrate, inner loneliness. He always thought that he had acquired his driven, compulsive work habits (which we can also refer to as his false self) from her, and his illness had insisted that he "suddenly" give these up.

In no sense am I suggesting that Weber "transferred" his "unconscious" feelings and attitudes from his mother to the worlds of ethics and economic history. Rather, I am proposing that the so-called breakdown forced upon him an all-too-sudden and all-too-forceful imperative to individuate. At first, that task overwhelmed him, but as time passed he was gradually able to assimilate it. His wife's capacity to be benign and empathic was his principal source of assistance. Helene could be neither of these. She was unable to become interior to his or anyone else's nonreligious view of the world. Nor could she provide any of the unique forms of support that a brilliant intelligence such as that of her son simply had to have in his earliest years if he was later to dare to show how his thinking differed from everyone else's.

To put the matter in yet another way, by detaching himself somewhat from an intimate personal bond and from the traditional values mediated by that bond, Weber had become sufficiently differentiated to see some of the things that were "really there" in the customs and habits of his mother's heritage. In one sense, of course, he was himself in the grip of the forces he was describing (the "icy hand"). But as he separated, he was able to transform some of these forces into a piece of social and cognitive space in which he could give expression to his brilliance and genius and share it in ways the rest of the world could understand (the "icy hand has let go of me").

This view is born out further by the unusually intense emotional tone of parts of Weber's book. These are passages of "fantasy thinking," a construct first advanced by the historian Fred Weinstein.[14] They are drenched in bitterness, irony, and disappointment. Consider these references to the Protestant personality and his ethical ideas: "magnificent consistency . . . colorless deist . . . inner loneliness . . . a renunciation, a departure from an age of full and beautiful humanity . . . fate decreed, the cloak should become an iron cage . . . duty prowls about in our lives like the ghost of dead religious beliefs." And, of course: "Specialists without spirit, sensualists without heart, this nullity." These are not scholarly flourishes; Weber was no stylist. He said he was not "religiously musical," but he was not literarily musical, either. At the center of this melancholy vision was the Protestant's historically shaped subjective-psychological state of loneliness or inner-worldly asceticism. This state characterized not only the ideal-typical Protestant but also the great sociologist who described it, but with one crucial difference. Unlike the Protestant, Weber was free enough to "see through" the surface of ideas that embodied the religious ethic and glimpse the real historical trends or forces that had shaped it.

As one progresses through the works that followed the book on Protestantism, their author draws his reader back again and again into this, his central preoccupation. That is especially so in the case of Weber's sociology of culture and religion. They form the core of his system, insofar as he had one, and he did not really have one. In this sense, however, his studies of religion are elaborate compare-and-contrast exercises around the idea of inner-worldly asceticism and its Protestant and biblical prototypes. In Judaism we see parallels, especially in the lives of the prophets, whom Weber admired greatly. This is quite understandable, for they appeared to him as magnificent, monumental, and highly individualized figures with astounding renunciatory capabilities. In some sense, they, too, were disenchanted or disillusioned—with the idolatry and waywardness of Israel. On the other hand, India and China—and of course Catholicism as well—fascinated Weber precisely because these traditions lacked an inner-worldly ascetic and renunciatory ethic and emphasized instead the gratifications that communal and mystical beliefs and practices confer —they remained "enchanted."

Religion, Disenchantment, Science, and the Cultural Sciences

At the end of his life, at the age of fifty-five, one year before he was to die, Weber felt obliged to restate with even more grim clarity— and also with courage—the meaning and centrality of disenchantment by demonstrating its relation to religion and the cultural sciences in his lecture "Science as a Vocation." Science brought about disenchantment when it was placed next to religion—that is, the impact of science on religion was disenchanting. Weber built his argument by creating a series of contrasts between the three.

He began by driving a wedge between religion and science. Separating the two were the historical forces of disenchantment, rationalization, and intellectualization. He described science as the link and motive force to disenchantment: "There are no mysterious and incalculable forces that come into play" in the work of the sociologist, because the world is disenchanted, "and so one need no longer have recourse to magical means." The rules of logic and method and the "technical means and calculations perform the service." The cultural sciences shared the ethos of the physical sciences, and on the basis of this affinity their task was "to determine . . . the internal structure of cultural values."[15] But it was not their task either to advocate or to discredit the cultural values whose inner structure they discerned. It was in exactly this sense, and only in this sense, that social science is "value free." Weber was not a positivist, nor is "value free" a positivistic construct.

For his second contrast, Weber defined religion as an open and fervent embrace of value and meaning and a passionate commitment to "the cultural community" that shared and sacralized such value and meaning. He recognized that science, of course, did have its own presuppositions, values, and meanings, but these were minimal and in any case not religious. In his third contrast, religion was unconditional devotion "to revelation, faith, holy states, and possession by the sphere of the holy," whereas science eschewed the unconditional or extraordinary because it was conditional or ordinary. So he concluded that there was an "unbridgeable tension" between the two. The tension between religion and the cultural sciences that disenchantment guarded could be resolved only by what he called "yearning," "tarrying," and "return." In the face of this breach or break, it was best, he said, to go forward in "the dignity of purely human communal relations."[16]

As Weber once again worked through and set forth his key ideas for his audience, he chose not to suppress the scorn that he felt for those of his academic colleagues who continued to seek some sort of religious consolation in specific forms of intellectual work. He referred to his opponents in the academy as people "who cannot bear the fate of the times like a man" (which I think can be read to mean, "who cannot bear to become independent from a woman"). With mocking but inadvertent psychoanalytic precision, he called them "big children," the "football masters in the vital problems of life." He noted further that for them "the arms of the old churches are opened widely and compassionately. . . . After all, they do not make it hard." But then, in the final moments of this address, he completely reversed his field, mastered his contempt, set aside his scorn, and quietly stated his own view with courage and dignity. He at least would not make "an intellectual sacrifice in favor of unconditional religious devotion." Instead, he would obey the "plain duty of intellectual integrity" that required "the courage to clarify one's own ultimate standpoint." In so doing he resisted the temptation to "return" to a religious view, so characteristic of "the many who today tarry for new prophets and saviours." He concluded that "nothing is gained by yearning and tarrying, and we shall act differently."[17]

Yearning, Tarrying, Returning—and Mourning

The emotional tone of both *The Protestant Ethic* and "Science as a Vocation" is one of conflict between the consolations of religion and a resoluteness and determination not to indulge in any of them. This conflict is brought about by the realization, inevitable among thoughtful persons, that the world is disenchanted. That disenchantment includes a struggle to mourn is convincingly evident in the emotional tone of these two works. To read these works is to sense and feel that a loss has taken place. There is grief in these sentences. But to read them is also to sense that the struggle to lay this loss to rest—to come to terms with the past—is still "in progress," at least in the case of this author, even as he writes, even as we read. This is borne out by the fact that both works are rich in scorn, derision, sarcasm, and mockery, as well as in a sense of loss and sadness. Scorn such as this is often present when the realization that a loss has occurred is accompanied by a reluctance or an inability to let go of what has been lost. This is the inability to mourn.

Conclusion: Mourning, Disenchantment, and Symbolic Loss

In what ways are symbolic loss, understood as a special kind of mourning, and disenchantment similar and different, given what has been said about the life and thought of Max Weber? The most important observation we can make is that the framework for thinking about both is attachment and loss. Within this frame, further distinctions can be made.

In both cases, the object that has been lost is in the past, both experiences are a coming to terms with the past, and the lost object in both cases is a symbolic system such as a creed, or an ideology, or a way of living. On the other hand, the inner struggle in symbolic loss is grieving and working-through, which can eventuate in some sort of healing, whereas disenchantment would appear to be more cognitive, more a working over or reworking, eventually in resignation.

However, mourning and disenchantment cannot be distinguished in an absolute sense: there is some mourning in disenchantment, and some disenchantment in mourning.

Notes

1. Marianne Weber, *Max Weber: A Biography,* trans. and ed. Harry Zohn (New York: Transaction, 1988), 17.
2. Ibid., 57.
3. Ibid., 58.
4. Ibid., 57.
5. Ibid., 231.
6. Ibid., 234–39, 242.
7. Ibid., 236.
8. Ibid., 236, 240, 239.
9. Ibid., 251–52, 251.
10. Ibid., 255.
11. D. W. Winnicott, "Ego Distortion in Terms of True and False Self," in *The Maturational Processes and the Facilitating Environment: Studies in the Theory of Emotional Development* (New York: International Universities Press, 1965).
12. Marianne Weber, *Max Weber: A Biography,* 335.
13. This use of the concept of individuation is drawn from the work of both M. Mahler and C. G. Jung. See M. Mahler, *The Psychological Birth of the Human Infant* (London: Hutchinson, 1975) and the entry on individuation in Andrew Samuels, Bani Shorter, and Fred Plaut, *A Critical Dictionary of Jungian Analysis* (New York: Routledge and Kegan Paul, 1986). The two views are far more alike than otherwise.
14. Weinstein has written extensively on the relationship between the individual and society in modern social and psychological theory. See, most recently, Fred Weinstein, *History and Theory after the Fall: An Essay on Interpretation* (Chicago: University of Chicago Press, 1990), especially the section entitled "The Social Significance of Fantasy Thinking," pp. 93–111, where Weinstein devotes particular attention to the discussion of fantasy thinking in the writings of Karl Marx.
15. Max Weber, "Science as a Vocation," in *From Max Weber: Essays in Sociology,* trans. and ed. H. H. Gerth and C. W. Mills (New York: Oxford University Press, 1958), 139, 146.
16. Ibid., 155.
17. Ibid., 155, 150, 155, 156.

Further Reading

Ariès, Phillipe. *The Hour of Our Death.* New York: Oxford University Press, 1981.
    A sweeping chronicle of attitudes toward death in the West from the early European Middle Ages to the present by a distinguished historian in the *Annales* tradition. Ariès identifies five different understandings of death and mourning. Elegantly written and masterfully executed.

Counts, David R., and Dorothy A. Counts. *Coping with the Final Tragedy: Cultural Variation in Dying and Grieving.* Amityville NY: Baywood, 1991.

Contains fourteen essays on a wide variety of important topics, all written clearly by well-informed investigators. See especially Ann Zeller's essay on grieving in nonhuman primates and Ellen Badone's study of death and grief in rural Brittany, which also addresses the death of a society and of memory itself.

Erikson, Kai T. *A New Species of Trouble: The Human Experience of Modern Disasters.* New York: W. W. Norton, 1994.
    A careful study of several communities that have undergone severe damage. Especially valuable for its clear and precise reporting of interview data and its convincing exposition of the differences between individual and collective trauma.

Foster, Kurt W., ed. "Monument/Memory" [special issue]. *Oppositions: A Journal for Ideas and Criticism in Architecture* 25 (fall 1982).
    Many students of loss and mourning will be interested in monuments, and not only in those that are heavily politicized, such as the Vietnam Veterans Memorial. The monument and its long and varied history are controversial subjects in the fields of art and architecture. This entire issue is devoted to discussions of these topics.

Fussell, Paul. *The Great War and Modern Memory.* New York: Oxford University Press, 1975.
    A pioneering study of the ways in which historical events are remembered and conventionalized in the forms of literature and myth. Fussell's subject is the British experience on the Western Front during the Great War. This is one of the first studies to recognize the importance of memory as a major approach to the study of history.

Hutton, Patrick H. *History as an Art of Memory.* Hanover VT: University Press of New England, 1993.
    A thorough and informed discussion of the history-memory problem, with excellent chapters on Halbwachs, Ariès, Foucault, and Nora. Written with clarity by a historian with a broad knowledge of the field.

Jackson, Stanley W. *Melancholia and Depression: From Hippocratic Times to Modern Times.* New Haven: Yale University Press, 1986.
    A thorough, careful, and well-written survey of the ways melancholia and depression were experienced, described, and treated in Western medicine. It is sensitive to issues of grief and mourning and informed by contemporary clinical psychiatry.

Lepenies, Wolf. *Melancholy and Society.* Cambridge: Harvard University Press, 1992.
    A study of the ways in which entire social classes and groups have been cast aside by society and as a result become melancholic (but not depressed). Important for its use of the sequence attachment→loss→inability-to-mourn as a tool for the study of social groups in historical situations.

Metcalf, Peter, and Richard Huntington. *Celebrations of Death: The Anthropology of Mortuary Ritual.* New York: Cambridge University Press, 1991.
    A major study and point of view in the anthropology of mortuary ritual, carefully and precisely written, with discussions of leading figures and their work and with sections on ritual and emotion and on the American way of death. An indispensable tool for studies of loss and mourning.

"Monumentality and the City" [special issue]. *Harvard Architecture Review* 4 (spring 1994).
    This entire issue is devoted to discussions of monumentality and the city.

Parkes, Colin Murray, and Robert S. Weiss. *Recovery from Bereavement.*
    New York: Basic Books, 1983.
        Combines a comprehensive discussion of major issues in understanding
    grief with an empirical study of work with bereaved persons. The author is
    a leading figure among a large cluster of workers dedicated to developing
    both the theory and the practice of caring for the bereaved. Provides stu-
    dents of loss and mourning with an anchor in the empirical and clinical
    study of grief.
Pollock, George H. *The Mourning-Liberation Process,* 2 vols. Madison
    CT: International Universities Press, 1989.
        Essays on many different facets of mourning: psychodynamics and psy-
    chopathology, anniversary reactions, biography, aging. Combines classical
    and ego psychological perspectives.

CONTRIBUTORS

PAUL A. ANDERSON is a postdoctoral scholar in the Michigan Society of Fellows and Assistant Professor of History and American Culture at the University of Michigan. His book *Deep River: Music and Memory in Harlem Renaissance Thought* is forthcoming.

DORIS L. BERGEN is Professor of History at the University of Notre Dame. Her writings include *Twisted Cross: The German Christian Movement in the Third Reich*.

MITCHELL BREITWIESER is both Professor of English and Director of the Center for the Study of American Cultures at the University of California, Berkeley. His work includes *American Puritanism and the Defense of Mourning: Religion, Grief, and Ethnology in Mary White Rowlandson's Captivity Narrative*.

PETER HOMANS is Professor of Psychology and Religious Studies at the University of Chicago, where he is also a member of the Committees on Human Development and the History of Culture. His books include *The Ability to Mourn: Disillusionment and the Social Origins of Psychoanalysis*.

PATRICK H. HUTTON is Professor and Chair in the Department of History at the University of Vermont. His writings include *History as an Art of Memory*.

MARIE-CLAIRE LAVABRE is Research Associate at the National Institute for Scientific Research in Paris. Her work includes *The Red Thread: The Sociology of Communist Memory*.

PETER SHABAD is Assistant Professor of Clinical Psychology at Northwestern University Medical School and Senior Staff Psychologist at Columbia Michael Reese Hospital and Medical Center.

His writings include *The Problem of Loss and Mourning: Psycho-analytic Perspectives.*

LEVI SMITH is Adjunct Lecturer in the Department of Museum Education at the Art Institute of Chicago. His books include *Objects of Remembrance: The Vietnam Veterans Memorial and the Memory of Vietnam, 1979–1993.*

JULIA STERN is Associate Professor of English at Northwestern University. Her work includes *The Plight of Feeling: Sympathy and Dissent in the Early American Novel.*

JAMES E. YOUNG is Professor of English and Judaic Studies at the University of Massachusetts, Amherst. His books include *The Texture of Memory: Holocaust Memorials and Meaning.*

INDEX

ability to mourn: defined, 27
Abraham, Nicholas, and Maria Torok:
on the "phantom," 48–49, 61
"acting-out." *See* repetition
Action française, 147. *See also* Ariès,
Philippe
addiction: as repetition, 203. *See also*
remembering; repetition
Adorno, Theodor: on art after the
Holocaust, 127, 128, 141
affect, lack of: as defense mechanism,
176–78, 181
affirmation: and loss, 55–56
aggression: effect on children of
parents', 49. *See also* anger;
persecutory anxiety
alcoholism, 51, 59–60
anger: as inability to mourn, 14, 17.
See also aggression; persecutory
anxiety
anthropology: grief and mourning in,
1–3
Ariès, Philippe, 147–55, 169, 236; and
Action française, 147–48; and
Annales school, 4, 148; collective
memory in, 151–52, 161; "death
of the other" in, 153, 160; debate
with Vovelle, 159–65; destiny in,
161–62, 164–65; "forbidden
death" in, 153–54; historical
demography of, 150–51; historiography as mourning for, 148, 151,
152; history as substitute for
politics in, 148–49; history of
mentalities and, 148, 151–52,
160–61; history of traditional
family and, 151; "invisible death"
in, 5 n. 10, 10; "one's own death"

in, 153, 160; similar to Freud, 5;
"tame death" in, 3–5, 83, 153,
165; and World War II, 147–48,
149. Works: *Histoire des populations françaises*, 149, 150–51;
L'Homme devant la mort, 159; *Le
Temps de l'histoire*, 151–51;
Western Attitudes toward Death,
152. *See also* "invisible death";
mourning; "tame death"; Vovelle,
Michel
art: and aesthetics after the Holocaust,
127–28. *See also* countermonument; cultural symbols; films and
television; literature; monuments;
narrative; symbolic loss; uncanny
attachment, Freud's theory of, 8; in
Bowlby, 32–34; in Parkes, 33–34.
See also loss; symbolic loss
autobiography, 54; as act of meta-
mourning, 62–79; of African
American life under slavery, 62;
as cultural symbol, 15; and the
Holocaust, 62. *See also* bearing
witness; biography; cultural
symbols; films and television;
history; individuation; literature;
memory; monuments; narrative;
remembering; symptomatology;
working-through; writing

Baker, Houston A.: on commodifying
black expressiveness, 86–87
bearing witness: another, as protection
from trauma, 200–201; another
reifies and gives meaning to
experience by, 204, 206; self
re-creates original trauma as way

STUDIES IN RELIGION AND CULTURE

Frank Burch Brown, Gary L. Ebersole, and Edith Wyschogrod,
EDITORS

Edmund N. Santurri
Perplexity in the Moral Life: Philosophical and Theological Considerations

Robert P. Scharlemann
Inscriptions and Reflections: Essays in Philosophical Theology

James DiCenso
Hermeneutics and the Disclosure of Truth: A Study in the Work of Heidegger, Gadamer, and Ricoeur

David Lawton
Faith, Text, and History: The Bible in English

Robert P. Scharlemann, editor
Theology at the End of the Century: A Dialogue on the Postmodern

Robert P. Scharlemann, editor
Negation and Theology

Lynda Sexson
Ordinarily Sacred

David E. Klemm and William Schweiker, editors
Meanings in Texts and Actions: Questioning Paul Ricoeur

Guyton B. Hammond
Conscience and Its Recovery: From the Frankfurt School to Feminism

Roger Poole
Kierkegaard: The Indirect Communication

John D. Barbour
Versions of Deconversion: Autobiography and the Loss of Faith

Gary L. Ebersole
Captured by Texts: Puritan to Postmodern Images of Indian Captivity

David Chidester
Savage Systems: Colonialism and Comparative Religion in Southern Africa

Laurie L. Patton and Wendy Doniger, editors
Myth and Method

Orrin F. Summerell, editor
The Otherness of God

Langdon Gilkey
Creationism on Trial: Evolution and God at Little Rock

Michael L. Raposa
Boredom and the Religious Imagination

Peter Homans, editor
Symbolic Loss: The Ambiguity of Mourning and Memory at Century's End